SAP R/3 Financial Accounting

SAP R/3 Financial Accounting

Making it work for your business

Sandra Brinkmann and Axel Zeilinger

An imprint of **Pearson Education**

Harlow, England · London · New York · Reading, Massachusetts · San Francisco
Toronto · Don Mills, Ontario · Sydney · Tokyo · Singapore · Hong Kong · Seoul
Taipei · Cape Town · Madrid · Mexico City · Amsterdam · Munich · Paris · Milan

PEARSON EDUCATION LIMITED

Head Office:
Edinburgh Gate
Harlow CM20 2JE
Tel: +44 (0)1279 623623
Fax: +44 (0)1279 431059

London Office:
128 Long Acre
London WC2E 9AN
Tel: +44 (0)20 7447 2000
Fax: +44 (0)20 7240 5771

Websites: www.informit.uk.com
         www.aw.com/cseng/
_____

First published in Great Britain in 2001

© Galileo Press GmbH 2000

The rights of Sandra Brinkmann and Axel Zeilinger to be identified as authors of this work have been asserted by them in accordance with the Copyright, Designs and Patents Act 1988.

ISBN 0-201-67530-7

British Library Cataloguing in Publication Data
A CIP catalogue record for this book can be obtained from the British Library

Library of Congress Cataloging in Publication Data
Brinkmann, Sandra.
  [Finanzwesen mit SAP R/3. English]
  SAP R/3 financial accounting/Sandra Brinkmann and Axel Zeilinger.
    p. cm.
  Includes bibliographical references and index.
   1. SAP R/3. 2. Accounting--Computer programs. 3. Client/server computing. I.
Zeilinger, Axel. II. Title.

  HF5679 .B7513 2001
  657'.0285'53769--dc21   2001020276

10 9 8 7 6 5 4 3 2 1

Designed by Claire Brodmann Book Designs, Lichfield, Staffs
Translated by TransScript Alba Ltd
Typeset by Pantek Arts Ltd, Maidstone, Kent
Printed and bound in the United States of America

The publishers' policy is to use paper manufactured from sustainable forests.

Contents

14   SPECIAL-PURPOSE LEDGERS   223

15   TRAVEL MANAGEMENT   235

CHAPTER 1

Introduction

In today's world, workplaces and business processes are becoming integrated with each other to form company-wide data-processing, information and communications systems. This integration is being achieved by implementing flexible standard software that is modified to meet the needs of the user.

A few years ago, the situation was different. Then, software – the application programs that handle and update logistical processes, create financial statements, and perform financial control – was usually developed by in-house IT departments, and was used to support company business processes. This situation meant that companies set up large IT departments to develop and maintain their data processing systems and operate them from day to day. However, in many cases it was not possible to create an integrated global solution, including all of a business's functional areas; nor was it possible, therefore, to minimize data redundancy.

Companies now face ever-increasing pressure to reduce costs. In addition, more and more mainframe computers are being replaced by globally-networked, decentralized systems with uniform software solutions. As a result, standard software solutions, such as SAP R/3, are becoming increasingly widespread.

Information is another factor that is gaining ever greater significance, particularly in Western industrialized nations. Today, information is either the end product or the raw material even for manufacturing industries. Information already represents a considerable amount of most countries' gross national product. Nowadays, a company's prosperity is no longer indicated by its level of industrial development; the crucial factor is a company's ability to use training and know-how to acquire information resources. A company can then make the best possible use of these resources by means of the right communications media and infrastructures, so as to distribute them, and convert them into knowledge, new technologies, methods and procedures in the quickest, most effective way possible.

In a company, information resources can be seen as the fourth production factor because they not only determine the quality of decisions but also influence other production factors. Commercial actions and events are viewed in terms of the information they contain, and are therefore directed towards information structures and information processing. To achieve this, a thorough understanding of the business is required.

Because of modern developments in information technology, it is now possible to carry out more extensive computing tasks, and more data-intensive commercial processes, than ever before. This, in turn, allows business opportunities to expand, where the expansion is supported by each individual component used in information technology. For example, improvements in database technology make it possible for companies to collect and analyze ever-larger amounts of data.

The addition of new functions to business applications, such as the SAP R/3 System, means that more and more commercial knowledge is actually programmed into the software. This software can then be used by any number of companies. Logical process-control systems integrate the expanding database to the very latest commercial functions. This means that a system such as SAP R/3 can support a wide range of differing objectives; it is an administration system that can be used to process mass data effectively in one administration session. At the same time it can be used as a management information system to supply correctly-processed management data to every level. It also acts as a control system to monitor plan data, allowing decisions to be corrected early on in the planning process.

In addition to the purely technical developments that affect information, the development of communications technology and networks is of particular significance. In future, not only will company-wide networks continue to be extended and optimized but inter-company communications will also be improved in order to increase overall integration. Furthermore, the growing number of Internet users has led to changes in communication with end customers. This in turn has affected internal company processes: in financial accounting, payment transaction processes and dunning procedures are changing, as reflected in revised accounting regulations. And no one can see an end to current developments.

The new releases of the SAP R/3 System support the ongoing development of new commercial knowledge and can therefore adapt to new market requirements. This allows companies to carry out Continuous Business Engineering. The system's ability to change and develop also prevents the need for radical modifications to it.

1.1 STRUCTURE OF THIS BOOK

The implementation of complex software such as the SAP R/3 System has considerably increased the demands made on the users of that software. This book is designed for:

■ members of SAP implementation projects

■ SAP consultants

■ people who already use the SAP System and are interested in new developments

■ students

It can be used to increase your understanding of SAP's customizing functions and applications.

This book does not contain exercises to teach you how to use the system; it is designed to add to the knowledge you already have of the customizing functions and help you make management decisions about implementing the SAP System. It contains both the knowledge required by consultants, and the legal background required for the Financial Accounting (FI) module.

The individual chapters provide an overview of how to customize the FI module. These chapters do not cover all the settings but they use the most important ones as examples. This book shows you how to navigate through the Customizing function and it also illustrates the numerous default settings in the FI module. In many cases, these default settings are all you need to cover a company's business requirements. However, it is assumed that you are familiar with the business principles dealt with in each chapter, and that you can therefore use the standard software as effectively as possible.

Chapter 2 introduces SAP AG and its product, the SAP R/3 System. Chapter 3 covers technical aspects and organizational integration. This chapter is rounded off with information on FI component integration. This tells you what you need to know about the complex structure of SAP R/3's standard software.

Chapter 4 explains the basic principles of accounting, as an introduction to the FI module. This ensures that you fully understand the commercial expressions used in later chapters.

Chapter 5 introduces the fundamental legal aspects of financial accounting. These are the basic accounting principles that are also used in the SAP R/3 System. The first settings within the Customizing function are made here, in the framework of the legal information set out.

Chapter 6 explains the components of the Customizing function. It describes its structure and its most important aspects, especially those that affect project work.

Chapter 7 then explains SAP's organizational structures. These are used to represent a company in the SAP R/3 System. This chapter also takes a closer look at how these organizational structures can be customized for the FI module. The most important customizing settings related to these business processes are explained in this section, because this is the logical point for you to create a link to the individual business processes in financial accounting.

Each of the later chapters deals with one particular aspect of customizing the R/3 system; for example, Chapter 8 contains an explanation of the Customizing function paths and settings for tax on sales/purchases. Each of these chapters is supplemented by a section explaining the business background to the process described, which we strongly recommend you read in order to help your general understanding. This will help you navigate through the Customizing function and understand the settings, after you have read the points covered in the chapters. In this way you will gradually come to understand all aspects of the Customizing function for the FI module. If you do not already work with Customizing, these chapters will help you become familiar with the relevant specialized SAP terminology and also provide you with relevant background commercial knowledge.

In the same way, Chapter 9 describes how withholding tax is handled. Chapter 10 then shows how the SAP R/3 System deals with inflation.

Chapter 11 explains how you create a year-end individual financial statement. It also provides the legal background for the individual balance-sheet account items and profit and loss account items. This information will allow you to make strategic decisions for evaluating and reporting individual items throughout the year. The chapter also covers the accounting knowledge you require, as well as specific information about the SAP R/3 System. Chapter 12 then describes how you create consolidated financial statements and provides related information about Customizing.

After the activities relating to year-end accounts, Chapter 13 deals with asset accounting and the FI-AA module. In this chapter you will find descriptions of commonly used SAP terms, possible evaluation methods, and Customizing for this area. (Chapter 11 also contains a few additional legal points that are connected with individual financial statements.)

Chapter 14 is more technical, and explains the evaluation options in the special-purpose ledgers. These options can be used to replace the Controlling module to a certain degree.

Finally, Chapter 15 deals with travel management, a new Customizing function for Financial Accounting that was introduced in Release 4.0.

CHAPTER 2

SAP AG and its product SAP R/3

2.1 HOW SAP AG DEVELOPED

The company known as SAP (standing for Systemanalyse und Programmentwicklung – systems analysis and program development) was founded in Germany by five former-IBM employees in 1972. Their aim was to develop standard application software for real-time processing. The first milestone was the completion of the RF System (Financial Accounting module) in 1973. This system was the basis for the R/1 System, which consisted of several modules.

In 1976, the company officially changed its name to SAP GmbH Systeme, Anwendungen und Produkte in der Datenverarbeitung (Systems, Applications and Products in Data Processing). At the company's first trade-fair appearance in Munich, Germany, that year, the R/2 System already had the same high level of stability as the previous generation of programs. The increased performance of mainframe computers led to a growth in the company's customer base. By this time, as many as 200 companies were already using SAP software.

In 1987, the beginnings of standardization in the software industry motivated the company to start developing a new generation of software. This was the R/3 System.

In 1988, the company was quoted on the stock exchange for the first time. Its stock capital increased from DM5 million to DM60 million. In its first full year on the stock exchange, *Manager* magazine named SAP as 'Company of the Year'.

At the CeBIT trade fair in Hanover, Germany, in 1991, SAP presented the first applications created using the R/3 System; these were received with widespread acclaim. The R/3 System was based on a client–server concept, its graphical user interface was uniform in design, it made consistent use of relational databases, and it could run on computers supplied by different manufacturers. It enabled SAP to open up new markets in the sector covering branch offices and subsidiaries of large corporations and medium-sized companies. By the end of the year, SAP employed 2685 staff in 14 local branch offices in Germany, earning revenues of DM707.1 million.

The market launch of the R/3 System, in 1992, led to an increased demand for implementation consultants for this software. To deal with this situation, SAP developed a partnership strategy. As part of this strategy, independent consulting firms (known as 'logo partners') provided customers with support in implementing standard R/3 System software. SAP also worked together with Microsoft, one of the world's largest software manufacturers, to port the R/3 System to Windows NT. In 1994, the R/3 System on Windows NT was launched onto the market. In 1996, as a result of increased cooperation with Microsoft, SAP introduced its Internet strategy. Internet applications can now be linked to the R/3 System via open interfaces. IBM's AS/400 platform is also now available to customers as a new platform. In 1996, SAP was named 'Company of the Year' by the European Association of Financial Journalists.

On SAP's 25th anniversary, its annual turnover went into the billions for the first time, reaching DM1.6 billion. Release 4.0 of the R/3 System was completed. Since the CeBIT trade fair in 1999, the SAP R/3 System has also been compatible with Linux.

SAP AG, whose headquarters are in Walldorf-in-Baden, Germany, is regarded worldwide as the leading manufacturer of standard business software. The company currently employs over 17 000 people. It is represented in over 40 countries by local subsidiaries, branch offices and partner companies.

2.2 SAP AG'S SOFTWARE CONCEPT

SAP's software concept is designed to meet the information requirements of companies throughout the world. Customers include both international corporations and a large number of small and medium-sized enterprises (SMEs). SAP would like to see its software being used to an even greater extent among medium-sized firms. SAP AG provides this wide spectrum of customers with software products for two different system architectures. These are the R/2 System, for mainframe computers, and the R/3 System for client–server configurations. Both software systems have the following features: extensive business functions, a modular structure, high-level integration of the individual modules, a wide selection of business processes (both general and industry-specific), and an ability to operate on an international basis.

The R/3 System's great advantages are its wide-ranging scalability and its uniform, modular structure, which makes it very user-friendly. Each of the SAP modules can be used as a standalone system or be integrated with others. Another advantage is that R/3 works with applications made by other manufacturers (e.g. Microsoft). Currently, 500 000 workstations worldwide have been equipped with the SAP client–server system.

As the R/3 System is based on international standards, its high levels of openness and flexibility mean that it can link a variety of hardware systems and applications from different manufacturers to form a unified company-wide entity. This provides users with new means of collaborative information processing. The R/3 System links application systems that previously worked autonomously in different locations into a company-wide network that supports event-controlled communications.

2.2.1 The R/3 System

What is the R/3 System? 'R/3' stands for Real-time [system], version 3. The following principles were used to develop this system:

- a holistic view of all processes in a company to ensure the integration of all business data, regardless of the process levels or organizational units in which it is used
- consideration of customer requirements from various industry sectors and countries when developing business applications
- a clear, hierarchical system-architecture that separates application solutions from low-level functions. This architecture is then split into an application layer and a base layer

The R/3 System's architecture is based on a multilevel client–server concept. It uses implemented methods to control the server–client relationships between individual software components. Special servers can be used for specific tasks without putting at risk the integrity of data and processes of the system as a whole.

2.2.2 The R/3 System's modules

The applications (modules) of the R/3 System are based on a general business model, which permits a holistic overview of all the data and business processes used in a company. This general model covers the following application areas:

- Financial Accounting (FI)
- Controlling (CO)
- Executive Information System
- Procurement Logistics (integrated in the MM module)
- Materials Management (MM)
- Production Planning (PP)
- Sales and Distribution (SD)
- Quality Management (QM)

- Service Management (SM)
- Plant Maintenance (PM)
- Project Planning (PS)
- Human Resources Management (HR)
- Office and Workflow Functions

The business applications are supplemented by software development tools (including SAP's own programming language, ABAP/4). These can be used to create individual solutions and supplement the R/3 System's standard applications. There is also another range of tools (e.g. ASAP, Reference Model) that are used to implement the R/3 System at customer sites and to control and monitor the system in day-by-day operation.

2.2.3 The R/3 System's architecture

The R/3 System's software is based on a multi-level client–server architecture, which gives it a modular structure. The R/3 System is structured in layers in which the largely independent function levels are linked to one another by interfaces. The most important layers are the *base layer* and the *application layer*.

The application layer, which contains the R/3 System's business functions and processes, is built on the base layer. The base layer is written in the programming language C and the application level is written in SAP's 4GL (fourth-generation) programming language ABAP/4. The System's design is based on internationally accepted standards and open interfaces:

- TCP/IP (used as a transport protocol in communications networks) – *see* section 3.6.1
- RFC (Remote Function Call), used as an open high-level programming interface – where RFC can be used to start application functions from other systems
- CPI-C for program-to-program communications between systems
- SQL and ODBC for accessing business data stored in the system's relational databases
- OLE/DDE and RFC for integrating PC applications
- X.400/X.500, used as an open e-mail interface
- EDI (Electronic Data Interchange), used for business data interchange at application level – *see* section 3.6.2
- ALE (Application Link Enabling) for the online integration of decentralized applications by exchanging business objects
- open interfaces for special applications such as CAD (computer-assisted design), optical archiving and technical subsystems in areas related to manufacturing (e.g. business data recording)

The R/3 System's open architecture gives it virtually unlimited portability.

2.3	R/3 AND THE INTERNET

The Internet capabilities of the R/3 System will open up completely new areas of business in electronic commerce (*see* section 3.6.2). The R/3 Reference Model (*see* section 6.1) performs well in optimizing business processes, i.e. in the transition from a function-oriented organization to a process-oriented organization. The model contains approximately 800 business-process modules. These can be combined so that any company can create its own specific value-chain for individual customers on the basis of its own modules. The model also has over 60 sample profiles that represent the various divisions in a company.

SAP's standard software is designed to be non-industry-specific. This is why the system as a whole is made up of a number of business processes that are needed in all branches of industry. The system also has industry-specific processes, each of which may be required in several industries. In addition, SAP is able and willing to develop other software components that are crucial for certain business processes in specific industries. SAP works closely together with leading industry users (pilot customers), and with consulting partners, to integrate new knowledge from real-life applications into its industry concept on an ongoing basis.

CHAPTER 3

Integration

The end of the millennium has brought with it radical changes in our social and economic environment. Improvements in travel, and the rapid development of telecommunications, have meant that the location at which a service is performed has in many cases become an insignificant factor. In particular, services are now provided from very remote locations. An example of this is software development in countries such as India or Pakistan for European or American clients. For Internet services, location is also virtually irrelevant. The world has moved closer together, and the buzzword is 'integration'.

Increasingly, companies work on an international scale, and the growing complexity of their management tasks, which must be carried out within ever shorter periods, require different tools – tools that are more suited to the job. The idea of integration must therefore result in the use of modern, standard business software. For many years, research in the natural sciences has shown that problems cannot be solved in isolation, and that influences and effects from other areas, some of which might be very remote, must be taken into account.

However, the benefits of integration are usually very difficult to measure. In many industries, it is quite simply a basic requirement to be able to respond to complex market situations with integrated software that links all sections of a company together, in order to maintain its current position in rapidly changing markets. The technical knowledge in companies, especially in the IT departments, is usually already there, but its integration with business requirements has often been neglected. Enormous investments are made in information technology so that companies remain competitive in difficult market situations. In this context, it is usually the case that IT departments, rather than other departments, are the prime movers in the implementation of the SAP R/3 System. The business potential of SAP R/3 is ignored – in the implementation phase at least. It is generally accepted that, after implementation, Continuous System Engineering can be used to optimize business processes (*see* R. Thome and A. Hufgard, *Continuous System Engineering*, Würzburg, Vogel, 1996). Management teams can therefore make their decisions on the basis of the figures provided by a modern Enterprise Resource Planning (ERP) system. This is why SAP regularly provides new release versions that take into account the latest innovations in the field of business management.

The development of information processing began in the 1970s with individual, unintegrated applications; data exchange between individual applications was more or less unheard-of. This state of affairs often led to inconsistencies in the data in the individual applications. In contrast, the R/3 System covers the functions of the different areas in a company and integrates these applications with one another. The modules of a SAP system access the same basic data. As the functionally-oriented modules of this system are interlinked, it is possible to represent a wide range of business processes.

The sections below describe how the technical integration of the SAP System takes place and how the organizational requirements are put into practice in R/3.

3.1   THE MODULAR STRUCTURE OF THE R/3 SYSTEM

The SAP R/3 System is divided into a large number of modules, and all the modules are linked to one another via the basis system (Figure 3.1). The R/3 System follows the basic principle that each business transaction is only recorded once and then is available to all applications. This integration links together those areas of a company that, historically, were functionally separate, i.e. it leads to process orientation.

Data is stored in a central database. This ensures that the dataset is unified and free from redundancy. This data can be accessed by all the applications of the R/3 System. This unique set of data means that up-to-date analyses and evaluations such as internal reports or financial statements can be produced. External reporting, in particular, demands information from companies at certain set intervals in order to meet the requirements for being listed on a certain stock market.

Invoicing is carried out in the SAP SD (Sales and Distribution) module. This invoicing data is also available to the financial accounting department because the two modules, SD and FI, are integrated with each other (Figure 3.2).

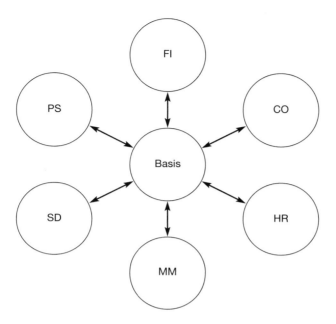

FIGURE 3.1   The Modular structure of the SAP R/3 System (© SAP AG)

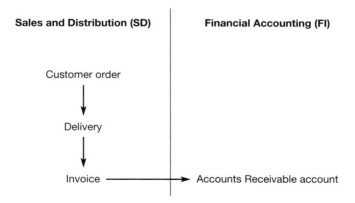

FIGURE 3.2   Integration of the Sales and Distribution and Financial Accounting modules (© SAP AG)

The invoice amounts from invoicing in the SD module are used by the accounts receivable department. Accessing the same dataset prevents data redundancy and ensures that the data is kept continuously up-to-date.

3.2 THE AIMS OF INTEGRATION

The most important aims of integration include:

- redundancy-free data storage
- keeping the data up-to-date
- providing the most detailed possible illustration of the links between all processes in a company
- recording data only once
- reducing the number of system interfaces to a minimum

3.3 THE CHALLENGE OF INTEGRATION

Integration is a challenge both for companies and their employees. For instance:

- Nowadays it is scarcely possible to process individual transactions manually, even if this were simpler and cheaper.
- Implementation and system tests are complex tasks that involve a large number of interactions.
- A good knowledge of IT is absolutely essential.
- A knowledge and understanding of processes are essential for all points of the company.

Above all, the risks that go hand-in-hand with integration place high demands on employee qualifications. This is why as many employees as possible should be involved in the system implementation process from the very beginning, and interim results should be passed on regularly in order to add continuously to employee know-how.

3.4 INTEGRATION IN THE FINANCIAL ACCOUNTING MODULE

The Financial Accounting module is divided into the following areas: the General Ledger; the subledgers for Accounts Receivable, Accounts Payable, Asset and Bank Accounting, Consolidation, Budget Management, Travel Management; and special-purpose ledgers (Figure 3.3). In earlier releases, budget management was included in the Treasury application component.

The business transactions are recorded in detail in the various subledgers. The General Ledger accounts only contain the balances – the related business transactions are not shown. The double-entry accounting technique ensures that the balances of

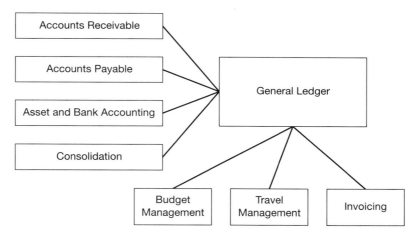

FIGURE 3.3   Integration in the Financial Accounting module (© SAP AG)

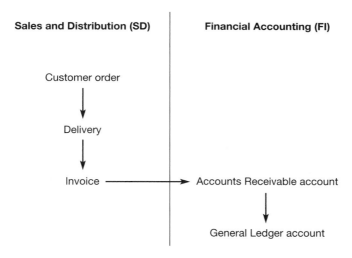

FIGURE 3.4   Integration in Financial Accounting using the double-entry accounting technique (© SAP AG)

the subledgers and the ledger accounts match (Figure 3.4). The customer accounts have an account as a reconciliation account in General Ledger accounting.

3.4.1 Integration of Financial Accounting with commercial banking

Bank statement data can be obtained electronically. This usually takes place using the Banking Communication Standard (BCS). Data is transferred from banks into the SAP

System via the MULTICASH transfer program. After the data has been imported, it is first converted and then analyzed. The R/3 System identifies each individual business transaction, such as fees for bank transfers, cashed checks or credit transfers, and filters out information such as document numbers or customer bank account details for posting. The system then automatically posts the corresponding transactions and, in doing so, clears some of the open items. The process is shown in Figure 3.5.

Occasionally, problems occur when incoming payments are posted to accounts receivable: it may happen that customer invoices can only be partially cleared, or bank transactions have been carried out with incorrect or incomplete data. In such cases, these items must be posted manually and corrected as needed.

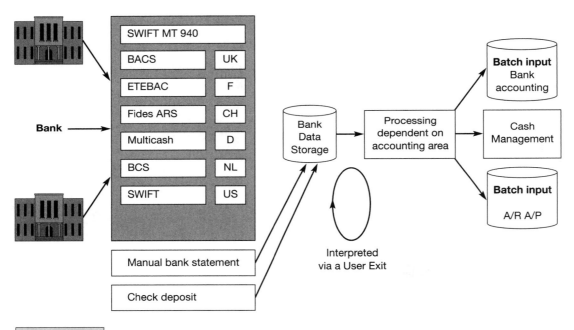

FIGURE 3.5 Process for electronic bank statements (© SAP AG)

The process used for electronic bank statements involves the following steps:

- The electronic bank statement is collected from the bank at regular intervals using EDI or another data-transfer medium.
- The bank statement is imported into the WINS bank data memory.
- The data is interpreted. This filters balance information out of the unstructured data.
- Finally, the batch-input sessions are created or the bank statements are posted directly.

In most cases, the statement files are received with software that conforms to BCS. BCS is used in virtually every country. Banks sell these programs and offer appropriate training courses. In Germany, for example, data is transferred using MultiCash software. Unfortunately, nearly every bank has its own data-exchange software.

The MultiCash format is generated from the SWIFT and MT940 formats using BCS software. SAP recommends that MultiCash, or another data-exchange program that uses the SWIFT format, is used to create electronic bank statements. This format is the standard format used by banks, and can be easily managed using a spreadsheet or word-processing program. There are two files with each of these formats.

The system usually carries out four steps to determine the balance information for accounts receivable:

- a bank-details check to establish who made the payment
- a search for the document number (DOCNO) or reference document number (XDONO) in the supplementary information field in a payment
- a comparison of the numbers it finds with the possible number ranges of the documents, which can be specified in the variant for processing a bank statement
- a check as to whether the documents it finds are open items

If no balance details are found, the system automatically checks whether a payment advice is stored for this customer in the Payment Advice database. If a payment advice is present, it is used for account clearing.

3.5   INTEGRATION WITH THE TREASURY MODULE

The way that the Financial Accounting module is integrated with the Treasury module is described below, using Cash Management as an example.

3.5.1 The term 'Cash Management'

The literature covering this topic contains various definitions of the term 'cash management'. At the beginning of the 1980s, 'real' definitions were still being used to describe cash management. These were closely related to familiar financial expressions. For example, the terms 'cash balancing' and 'financial management' were regarded as the same as cash management. This did not leave a lot of leeway for structuring the content of cash management.

In current literature, cash management is no longer viewed as an expression covering one area. It is more a broad range of tasks that different authors define in different ways. Eistert, for example, describes cash management as 'liquidity management', which covers the decisions for the targeted control of liquid funds in a company. He assumes typical ideal phases for each management process: planning, realization and control. Liquid funds include the balance in cash and the credit balance maintained as 'primary liquidity', as well as secondary liquidity in the form of overdraft limits granted, term deposits, securities and short-term bonds.

In general, cash management is viewed as a subdivision of asset management. It involves all the tasks that are designed to optimize coordination of the current payment processes. It includes the executive tasks of financial management i.e. controlling and monitoring, observing the criteria of solvency, costs, profitability, and risk minimization. It is hardly possible to differentiate between cash management and operative financial controlling and the treasury function without having areas that overlap. In the SAP R/3 System, this is why cash management is located in the Treasury module. Figure 3.6 shows the Customizing area for cash management in the Treasury application component.

In most of Europe, the introduction of the euro (*see* section 4.3) will reduce transactional and collateral costs, which contributes to achieving the aims of cash management. In eurozone countries, both the elimination of trade in the (foreign) currencies participating in European Monetary Union and the replacement of regional bank connections, used by bank subsidiary branches with main bank connections, follow the principles of cash management.

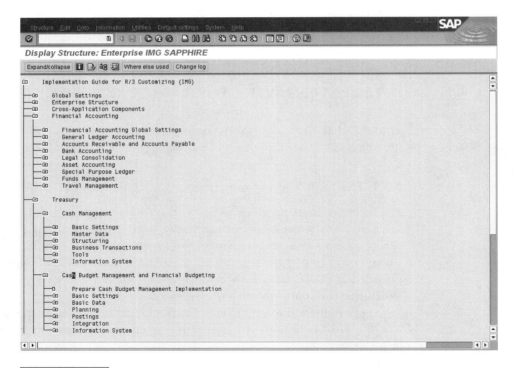

FIGURE 3.6	Customizing area for cash management in the Treasury module
	(© SAP AG)

3.5.2 The functions and tasks of cash management

Cash management can be subdivided into the following three areas:

1. money management
2. credit management
3. foreign-currency management

These subareas can be assigned specific tasks, as shown in Table 3.1.

The primary aims of efficient cash management are therefore to preserve liquidity at all times and to manage the liquid funds in order to maximize profitability for the company.

However, ensuring liquidity and trying to achieve maximum profitability are two different things, because liquid capital creates a very small return, if any. One of these two aims must be prioritized according to the situation of the company. If the company's solvency is at risk, liquidity assurance has priority, and vice versa. This is a crucial point because 40 per cent of all company bankruptcies are caused by a lack of liquid funds.

Generally, cash management systems are used to carry out effective cash management. Cash management systems are a computerized form of communication between banks and companies, or within companies, that exchange data to control short-term financial planning. The R/3 System provides full support for these tasks.

TABLE 3.1	Tasks of Cash Management
Subarea of cash management	**Tasks**
1. Money management	■ Daily management of money inflows, money outflows, maturity of bills of exchange, stock of payment funds and short-term investments
	■ Accounts payable turnover checking
	■ Dunning and billing for interest on delayed payments
	■ Arrangement of customers' down payments
	■ Management of factoring
	■ Utilization of cash discounts for vendor accounts
	■ Cashing checks
2. Credit management	■ Determining and checking capital requirements
	■ Monitoring punctual provision of capital
	■ Monitoring short-term credit limits (bills of exchange, overdraft, Eurocredit)
	■ Monitoring money and capital markets
3. Foreign-currency management	■ Ensuring payment transactions in international trade avoiding currency risks
	■ Foreign currency forward-exchange transactions
	■ Forfeiture and export factoring (exchange-rate fluctuation)

INTEGRATION WITH THE INTERNET

The commercial use of information and communications technologies allows companies to gain enormous competitive advantage over their rivals. The Internet capabilities of the R/3 System allow companies to open up completely new areas of business. The key phrase used here is *electronic commerce*, or *'e-commerce'*. This strengthens the market position of those companies that participate, with instant information transfer, even over large distances.

3.6.1 Origins and structure of the Internet

The name 'Internet' came from 'interconnected networks'. The Internet is a chain of networks that are linked to one another via network nodes (routers). In principle, any user can access all the resources of the network. Until the 1980s, the Internet was used exclusively by the US armed forces and for scientific applications. It was only at the end of the 1980s that it was opened up for commercial use. Since then, it has increasingly become the center of public attention. It is no longer subject to any political or geographical borders.

The Internet is characterized by a uniform, generally compatible language and uniform family of protocols: TCP/IP (Transmission Control Protocol/Internet Protocol). TCP divides the data to be transferred into data packets and numbers them, so that they can be recompiled in the correct sequence when they reach the recipient address; IP ensures that they are addressed correctly. This means that the individual parts of packets can reach the recipient address by different routes. This ensures that the data can be transmitted even when the system is overloaded or connections break down.

The technical and logical structure of the Internet is similar to the principle on which the R/3 System architecture is based, i.e. the client–server principle (*see* section 2.2.3). The data is provided by the server and used by the client. Here, the Web browser corresponds to the client software. This Web browser can receive, process, display and relay the multimedia documents of the World Wide Web (the Web), an Internet service.

The commercial use of the Internet has enhanced the central importance of the Web. Its popularity is due to the fact that it is easy to use. SAP also uses the Web for its Internet connections.

3.6.2 Electronic commerce

There are many definitions of the term 'electronic commerce' though none of them really covers the entire concept. One view, which goes beyond a simplistic approach but which has nonetheless established itself, is that the term comprises not only actual sales transactions over the Internet but also all the other economic uses of the Internet (for example, procurement).

An e-commerce solution optimizes and automates trade-related business processes. To guarantee that messages are transmitted without errors, data is exchanged between computer systems without manual input or output. This can potentially make savings for a company and reduce the number of error sources. The resources that a company can save in this respect can be used to concentrate on providing a better service for the company's customers.

The electronic commerce solutions currently commercially available deal with two principal scenarios: Business to Consumer (B2C) relationships and Business to Business (B2B) relationships.

Business to Consumer (B2C)

B2C supports the relationship between companies and consumers. It corresponds to electronic retailing ('e-tailing'). Here, the main emphasis is on information systems that are used to provide marketing and sales applications and various service functions for the consumer – for example, parcel services can trace the current location of shipped goods on the Internet. However, because security standards are still not stringent enough, most payment transactions are handled through conventional channels – although rapid technical developments and vested commercial interests will ensure that electronic payment solutions are available soon.

Examples of SAP B2C solutions include applications for job offers and applicant status that are integrated into the HR (Human Resources Management) module.

Business to Business (B2B)

B2B supports inter-company Internet applications. This market segment is becoming increasingly significant. Data exchanged in the B2B area frequently takes place on *extranets*. An extranet is a protected area of the Internet where sensitive data can be exchanged safely.

Until now, inter-company communication has been implemented (mostly in large corporations) by using *Electronic Data Interchange (EDI)*. EDI is a standardized method used to exchange structured business data electronically. The R/3 System also works with EDI interfaces (*see* section 2.2.3). Before they can use the EDI interface, business partners need a means of physical communications, in the form of a network connection, and also special software that can convert data.

Examples of B2B solutions for the R/3 System can be found in the following areas:

- consignment stock queries
- meter level recording
- quality certificates

- quality notifications
- KANBAN relationships (a system used for organizing production that aims to reduce stock levels in the warehouse, thus reducing production costs)
- bank balance queries

3.6.3 R/3 interfaces to the Internet

The R/3 System's Business Framework provides the base modules for the alternative Internet connection options and is therefore the technical basis for Internet integration.

The Business Framework consists of several modules, described below:

- business components
- business objects
- Business Application Programming Interfaces (BAPIs)

Business components

Business components are specific business-software components that have stable interfaces. Examples of business components are the availability check, the Human Resources Management module and the Internet components in the R/3 System.

Business objects

Business objects are core elements of the business framework. They are managed centrally in the Business Object Repository, an element of the ABAP/4 development environment.

SAP business objects consist of four layers that divide data and business processes into four different levels. The first level of business objects contains the central business logic, and therefore the actual data such as components and specializations. The second level consists of 'constraints', which are object-related, and also business rules, which apply to the environment. The third level, the interface level, contains methods (BAPIs – *see below*), attributes, the input event check, and output events. The fourth and final level enables external access to the object data by means of COM/DCOM (Component Object Model/Distributed Component Object Model), CORBA (Common Object Request Broker Architecture) or RFC (Remote Function Call).

Business Application Programming Interfaces

A Business Application Programming Interface (BAPI) is a business object's method. It is always assigned to one specific business object. A BAPI can be used to provide external access to business processes, business data and business objects. BAPIs are managed centrally in the same way as the business objects in the Business Object Repository. A total of approximately 200 BAPIs have now been developed for the R/3 System.

R/3 customers can use the BAPIs to create their own Internet applications with the programming languages Java and C++. This means that you no longer need a knowledge of ABAP/4 to develop an Internet connection.

Another way of connecting to the Internet is by using the Internet Transaction Server (ITS), which is supplied with the R/3 System. This simulates the SAP graphical user interface, helps to implement HTML, and is also the interface to the Web server.

3.6.4 Security measures for Internet connections

Connection to the Internet also involves the permanent risk of attacks on your own system. For this reason, protecting your own R/3 System must be given high priority when an Internet connection is being implemented. The security standards (user-authorizations concept and authentication) present in the R/3 System cannot guarantee full protection; you have to implement additional security mechanisms to protect data storage and transfer.

One way of protecting your system is to use the SAP Transaction Server. This installs firewalls between the individual elements. These have special protective mechanisms and specify who is allowed access to the system. This measure is designed to prevent hackers from gaining illegal access to the R/3 System used within a company.

CHAPTER 4

Basic principles of business accounting

4.1   TASKS AND STRUCTURE

4.1.1 Overview of business accounting

The term *business accounting* refers to all the procedures used to record and monitor the amounts and values of the flows of money and services that are primarily caused by business transactions. This is known also as the business accounting *documentation and control task*. It is achieved by the integration of SAP modules.

The finer points of this documentation-and-control task can include, for example, ascertaining a company's assets and liabilities on a specific date, or determining changes in assets – for example the increase or decrease in accounts receivable and accounts payable within a certain period. The more detailed tasks also include determining the profit at a certain point in time, e.g. the level of expenditures and earnings over a particular accounting period. These tasks can also be directed towards determining the prime costs of company output, i.e. those related not only to time but also to units of output.

Business accounting also plays a role in materials planning. By checks on a fixed date or by comparing asset and income variables over a particular period, the MP module can be used to control the efficiency and profitability of business processes. It also provides corporate management with informative documents for their planning procedures.

In addition to these tasks that are carried out within a company, the business accounting function must also perform external tasks. Because of statutory regulations, it must ensure accountability and provide information about the company's situation with regard to assets, finance and earnings, for the following:

- company owners (shareholders, owners of the private company, partners etc.)
- creditors (suppliers and lenders)
- employees
- taxation authorities
- the public (potential shareholders and creditors, government agencies, scientific institutes, the financial press and other interested parties)

As a consequence of the many different tasks that business accounting has to perform, it can be divided into four separate, but closely-linked areas. They use the same figures, to some extent, but have different objectives. These areas are:

1 Financial accounting and the preparation of financial statements (periodic accounting)

2 Prime cost accounting (job-order cost accounting)

3 Business statistics and comparative accounting

4 Cost budgeting

For practical reasons the first two areas, which involve accounting, have been split into financial accounting (business accounting), which generates the financial statements, and control (cost-based accounting), which calculates and distributes costs. Cost-based accounting is usually referred to as *prime cost accounting*. This leads to the following divisions:

1 Financial accounting and preparation of financial statements:

a) Accounting

b) Inventory

c) Annual accounts (annual balance sheet, profit and loss account and, where applicable, supplements and annual report)

d) Special-purpose accounts, interim accounts

2 Prime cost accounting:

a) Operational accounting (cost-based accounting)

 – Cost element accounting

 – Cost center accounting

 – Cost object controlling

 – Short-term profit and loss accounting

    b) Cost-of-goods-sold accounting

3 Business statistics and comparative accounting

    a) Business statistics

    b) Individual company comparison

        – Time comparison

        – Process comparison

        – Target-actual comparison

    c) Inter-company comparison

4 Cost budgeting

These various subdivisions all have a theoretical aspect and a practical aspect. It is not usually possible to determine exactly where one ends and another begins. One problem is that theoretical knowledge can often only be put into practice when it is made 'calculable'. Not everything that is recognized in the area of business accounting as acceptable can be calculated down to the last penny. So far, it has not been possible to implement a solution that is seen in theory to be correct for all distribution and allocation problems. This is either because it is not possible to quantify all the variables required for exact calculation, or because the application of economically sound and calculable solutions is not permitted under commercial or tax laws. An example of this is the inventory-valuation methods useful for managerial reports, such as HIFO (highest in, first out), which are not allowed by most international accounting standards. Valuation methods are discussed in more detail in section 11.6.2.

Both the structure and organization of business accounting depend on a company's specific circumstances. This is influenced by factors such as the sector in which it operates, its legal and commercial form, the size of the company, its situation in the market, the manufacturing process(es) it uses, and the range of products it manufactures. The R/3 System contains an 'enterprise structure' that can be used to reflect this company organization. Figure 4.1 shows where this is implemented in R/3 Customizing; Chapter 7 describes the SAP organizational structures required to represent a company's organization.

A company's accounting function will emphasize different aspects, depending on the branch of industry or commerce in which the company is involved: an industrial company may emphasize recording and distribution costs in order to determine the precise primary costs of products and to control the economic efficiency of production, whereas a trading company is more likely to emphasize controlling turnover and the management of stocks.

The legal form of a company determines which classification and valuation regulations must be complied with for the Balance Sheet and Profit and Loss accounts (*see* Chapter 11).

The costing and pricing policy are affected by the company's commercial form (is it run as a profit-making or not-for-profit enterprise?), and its situation in the

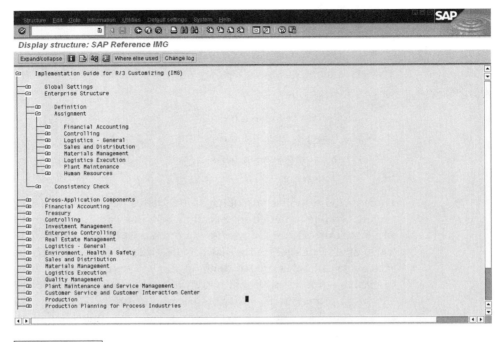

FIGURE 4.1 Defining the enterprise structure (© SAP AG)

market (is it a monopoly, an oligopoly or one of many companies in the market?).

The size of the company determines the extent to which business accounting can be refined and extended. For example, there is no point in using normal or budget cost accounting or making use of the entire scope of business statistics in every single company.

The manufacturing program (i.e. the number of different products, and the options for creating product variants) and the manufacturing process (e.g. linked production) influence the choice of costing methods from among process cost accounting, bulk accounting or job-order cost accounting for series manufacturing.

The introduction of standard SAP software brings with it not only significant reductions in wage costs in the accounting department (which are far from compensated for by the depreciation costs of IT hardware systems) but also leads to a considerable increase in the value of information in all areas of business accounting. However, even in this age of information technology, anyone who wants to understand software as well as use it must also have a thorough knowledge of the principles of double-entry bookkeeping and the legal regulations governing financial reporting. Such a person must also be familiar with the leeway that these regulations offer when compiling sets of annual accounts (*see* Chapter 11) and calculating taxable profit. This book aims to clarify these relationships for the reader.

4.1.2 Financial accounting and the preparation of financial statements

Financial accounting has the task of recording in chronological order all the business transactions (transactions that are of economic significance, and that are in figures) taking place in a company. This involves all the transactions that lead to a change in the amount and/or composition of the assets of the company. Accounting starts when a company is founded and continues until the company is liquidated.

All the asset and movement data that is recorded in accounting and in the financial statements is expressed in monetary units. A physical inventory means that the quantity of assets is recorded. This is performed before the financial statements are prepared or when a trading company starts up in business. This process results in a list of assets, called the inventory. In addition to the assets ascertained by the physical inventory, the inventory also contains the company's current assets and liabilities; these can be determined by means of the book inventory. Here, all the assets and liabilities must be listed according to type, quantity and value.

In the area of logistics, the R/3 System supports the following physical inventory procedures:

- For a *Periodic inventory, e.g. annual*, all the company's assets are physically recorded on the date set in the Balance Sheet. In this case, all the materials/items must be counted, measured and weighed. During the count, the entire warehouse must be blocked for all material movements.

- For a *perpetual physical inventory*, assets are recorded continuously throughout the entire fiscal year. Each item must be physically recorded at least once a year.

- *Cycle counting* is a physical inventory method in which stocktaking is carried out for the materials at regular intervals within a fiscal year. The intervals, or cycles, depend on the cycle-counting requirements of the material involved – for example, cycle counting may mean that frequently used materials are inventoried more often than less frequently used materials.

- In *an inventory sampling procedure*, random samples of the company's inventory are physically recorded on the specified date. If there is only a small difference between the result of this random sampling and the book inventory, it is concluded that the book quantities of the inventory not physically counted are correct.

In the R/3 System, the following three steps are usually carried out to create the physical inventory:

- create inventory document
- record inventory count
- write off inventory difference

The screenshot in Figure 4.2 shows the menu path for creating a physical inventory in the R/3 System.

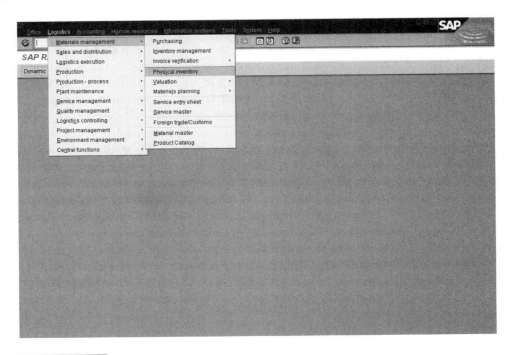

FIGURE 4.2 Creating a physical inventory in the R/3 System (© SAP AG)

The Balance Sheet uses a different form of accounts from the one used to manage inventory. Unlike in the inventory, only values are recorded in a Balance Sheet. A Balance Sheet also groups similar assets, such as buildings, into so-called **balance sheet items** (*see* Figure 4.3). Section 11.7 describes the individual balance sheet items that are likely to occur.

This is how the accounting procedures reflect periodic accounting, which can be either financial accounting (business accounting) or cost accounting. Financial accounting records the total appreciation or depreciation as well as changes to the capital and asset structure over a period of time (for instance, month or a year). The total costs in an accounting period are the **expenditures**. The total increase in an accounting period is the **revenue**. The expenditures and revenues of an accounting period are compared in the Profit and Loss account. The amounts of assets/liabilities and capital recorded by accounting on a certain fixed date (generally the Balance Sheet date) are set against one another in the Balance Sheet.

Accounting prepares all the figures required to prepare financial statements (annual reports, as well as commercial and tax reports and special-purpose reports such as those needed on conversion, consolidated, and liquidity accounts). It also provides the figures required for liquidity and financial control. And accounting uses the following types of accounts to record business transactions:

- *Balance Sheet accounts*. These show the initial inventory of an accounting period for each type of asset and capital. They also record acquisitions and retirements; that is, the inventory changes during the period. This means that the closing inventory can be determined by comparing the opening capital balance and the acquisitions, on the one hand, with the recorded retirements on the other.

- *Profit and Loss accounts*. These are split up according to the types of expenditure and profit. They record the expenditures and revenues that occurred in an accounting period. The difference between all the expenditures and revenues equals the profit or loss for the period. This profit/loss is included in the equity capital account, i.e., a profit increases the equity capital and a loss reduces the equity capital.

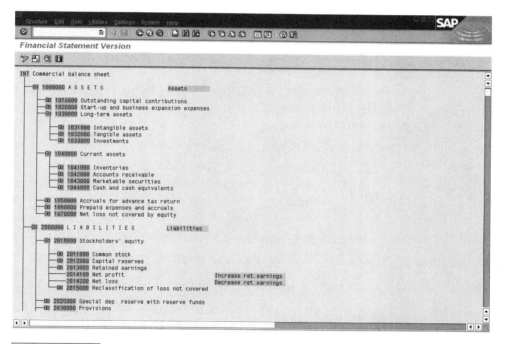

FIGURE 4.3   Balance Sheet and Profit and Loss account structure in R/3 Customizing (© SAP AG)

In the R/3 System, you can set up accounts in two ways:

1 *Create a General Ledger account in Customizing.* You can set up these accounts directly in Customizing. When an account is created in the SAP R/3 System, no distinction is made between Balance Sheet and Profit and Loss accounts; the accounts are all referred to as General Ledger accounts. The information that

shows whether an account is a Balance Sheet account or a Profit and Loss account is stored in the General Ledger account master record (*see* section 7.8.1) when the account is set up. The General Ledger account master records consist of *general information* that is derived from the Chart of Accounts (section 7.1.8) and *company code-specific information* in the general ledger account. The general information consists of the General Ledger account number, the designation and a feature that distinguishes it as a Profit and Loss account or a Balance Sheet account. The currency, the tax category and the administration of open items are assigned at the company code level. Figure 4.4 shows the Customizing path for creating General Ledger accounts.

2 *Create a General Ledger account in the General Ledger Accounting application menu.* Here, you can decide whether to record the chart of accounts and company code data at one time or separately for the General Ledger account, depending on how your company is organized. We recommend that you create General Ledger accounts in two steps if you want to assign values for company code-specific areas from a central location. Figure 4.5 shows a possible pathway.

You can determine the income received in an accounting period by structuring the accounting procedures in two ways: by comparing assets or by comparing expenditure and earnings.

- Comparing assets:

  INCOME = ASSETS AT THE END OF THE PERIOD
  - ASSETS AT THE START OF THE PERIOD
  + WITHDRAWALS
  - DEPOSITS

- Comparing expenditure and earnings:

  INCOME = EARNINGS − EXPENDITURE

You can use four separate types of postings for business transactions:

1 *Asset exchange*. This changes the asset structure on the asset side of the balance sheet, although the total assets retain their original value. A reduction on an asset account corresponds to an equal and opposite increase on another asset account – for example, purchasing a machine by bank credit transfer gives a gain of the machine's value in one account and a reduction by the purchase price of the cash in the bank.

2 *Liability exchange*. This leads to a change in the capital structure on the liability side of the balance sheet, although once more the total assets retain their original value. A decrease on one capital account corresponds to an increase on another capital account. Example: conversion of a vendor credit memo into a bank loan (reduction of the accounts payable; increase in bank liabilities by the same amount).

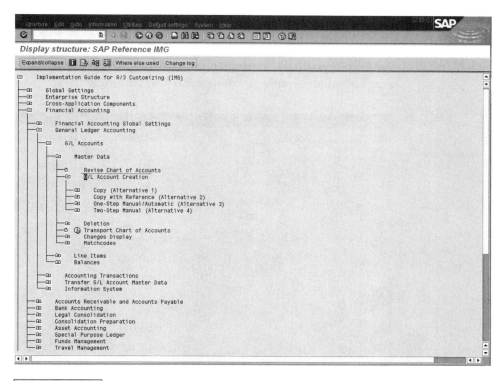

FIGURE 4.4   Creating a General Ledger account in Customizing (© SAP AG)

3 *Increase to the Balance Sheet*. This increases the assets and liabilities sides by the same amount. The acquisition on a capital account corresponds to the acquisition on an asset account, by the same amount, or vice versa. This increases the total assets. Example: financing the purchase of an asset by means of a bank loan (increase in assets; increase in bank liabilities).

4 *Decrease to the Balance Sheet*. This reduces the assets and liabilities sides by the same amount. A reduction on an asset account corresponds to an increase on a capital account by the same amount, or vice versa. This reduces the total assets, e.g. if a vendor account payable is settled by bank credit transfer (reduction in the supplier accounts payable; reduction of cash in the bank).

Business transactions that affect the Profit and Loss account change the amount of the equity capital and lead to either an increase or decrease in the Balance Sheet.

Accounting is based on *generally accepted accounting principles (GAAP)*. The integration of the individual modules in the R/3 System means that accounting data already created in workflows outside the FI module flows directly into the FI module's financial accounting system. For example, data from the SD module is recorded when a delivery is made (Inventory Change entry) or when the customer is invoiced. This integration process therefore has a documentary function, which is then also subject to the relevant accounting principles. As adherence to legislation in the SAP R/3 System is a popular auditing item, Chapter 5 provides more details of the generally accepted principles used in computerized accounting systems.

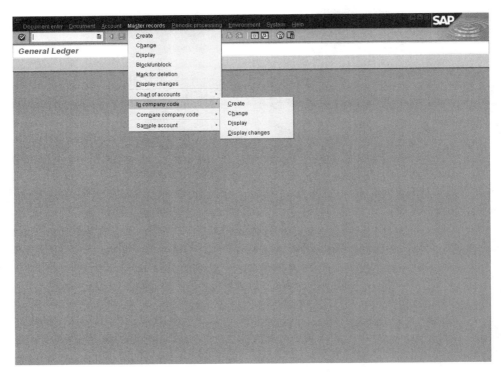

| FIGURE 4.5 | Creating a General Ledger account in the General Ledger Accounting application menu (© SAP AG) |

4.1.3 Prime cost accounting

Cost-based accounting (operational accounting), along with cost-of-goods-sold accounting (costing), which together make up prime cost accounting (see section 4.1.1), has the task of recording, distributing and allocating costs that result from a company's production. In particular:

▪ It compares the costs with production levels to determine the income (short-term profit and loss account), and therefore it makes it possible to control the economic efficiency of the company's production processes and to provide the basis for the company's materials planning.

■ It also uses the prime costs of production to make it possible to cost the unit selling price and/or set the lowest profitable price.

Cost accounting only records that part of depreciation and appreciation resulting from the company carrying out its specific tasks (production and sale of goods and services). Non-operating expenditures and revenues, which are recorded in financial accounting in addition to operating expenditures and revenues within the company, are not part of cost accounting. *Cost* equals the decrease in value that takes place in the course of producing the company's goods or services. The appreciation this brings with it is called *production*. Whereas financial accounting only records the drop in value caused by expenses (expenditure), cost accounting also includes the drop in value that does not arise from expenses but is instead caused by producing the company's output. As it includes statistical methods for recording and distributing costs, the expression 'cost accounting' is not comprehensive enough, which is why the term *operational accounting* is frequently used.

Operational accounting is periodical accounting that, like cost accounting, determines which costs (wage costs, material costs, depreciation, interest, taxes, etc.) have been incurred in the company. Like cost-center accounting, it also distributes the types of cost determined to the individual cost centers (materials, manufacturing, administration and sales/distribution) to ensure that the costs are assigned precisely to the output of the period (cost-unit period accounting). By comparing the cost-center costs with other variables, operational accounting makes it possible, for example, to check the economic efficiency of individual cost centers. Using cost type and cost center accounting as a basis, prime cost accounting, like cost-unit accounting, determines the costs of the individual goods/services. It therefore creates the basis for an effective pricing policy.

Financial accounting and Balance Sheet preparation are closely interrelated with cost accounting. The stocks of semi-finished and finished goods and capitalized internal output (machines and tools made by the company for its own use) are valued in the balance sheet along with the manufacturing costs (*see* section 11.5.2) that were calculated in cost accounting. Although financial accounting records the types of expenditure (wages, salaries, material, etc.) consumed in an accounting period, it does not allocate them to the output produced (the *cost units*); this is the task of operational accounting.

A decisive difference between financial accounting for external reporting and control (cost accounting) is that the financial statements prepared represent periodical evidence of accountability that the enterprise (entrepreneur, managing director, or management bodies of joint stock companies) must present to the providers of equity capital (partners, or stockholders of joint stock companies), external providers of capital (creditors) as well as the local tax authorities. These requirements vary from country to country but exist in one form or another. The scope, form and content are also regulated by various laws and regulations. The structure and organization of control, on the other hand, is an internal company matter. Control does not have to meet external requirements, but is primarily for internal information purposes.

4.1.4 Business statistics and comparative accounting

This section of business accounting evaluates not only external documents (industry comparisons etc.) but also the figures from the accounting process, from the Balance Sheet, and frobv m cost accounting. This ensures that economic efficiency can be checked. It also produces useful documentation for general planning and materials planning. Business statistics are used to analyze company figures (e.g. inventory movements, turnover in different months, etc.) or investigate relationships between operational variables (e.g. the relationship between equity capital and profit, between wage costs and overall costs, between material used and scrap, etc.).

As a purely formal method, business statistics are also applied in the other sections of business accounting and either replace or supplement other accounting methods.

Like periodic accounting, comparative accounting (corporate comparison) can record the development of certain company variables over time (e.g. sales revenue, calculation of profit, etc.). Alternatively, in an inter-company comparison (benchmarking), it can be used to compare companies that operate in the same or different branches of industry with one another, or check figures from the company itself against average figures for its particular industry. Furthermore, as a comparison of processes, it can determine the economic efficiency of different processes (e.g. manufacturing processes) or perform a target-with-actual comparison.

4.1.5 Cost budgeting

Cost budgeting is used to estimate the quantity and value of the expected development of the company. Its task is to provide actual figures in the form of estimates of future expenses and revenues for corporate planning. On the one hand, it makes use of the figures processed and provided by the accounting process, as well as the financial statement, cost accounting and business statistics. On the other hand, because every plan tries to predict the future, expectations must also be taken into consideration.

Planning tasks become increasingly complex and require increasingly sophisticated calculation methods, according to the size of the company and the number of variants in its manufacturing program or product range. The overall corporate plan consists of several partial plans, which must be compiled by the individual company divisions and coordinated by the management because general planning is carried out by central management. Each partial plan – for example the sales plan, or the production plan or budget – also consists in turn of several partial plans.

Various scientific methods and processes have been developed to manage planning and coordination problems. These methods and processes are known collectively as 'operational research'. Operational research uses mathematical decision models that draw on special mathematical methods to solve problems. The development of operational research and the handling of its complex calculations using the SAP R/3 System have led to considerable refinements and extensions in business cost budgeting.

4.2   BASIC TERMS IN BUSINESS ACCOUNTING

The 'science' of business administration uses its own terminology to describe the processes of payment and the providing of services in business accounting. These terms include the following five pairs:

1   Income – Outgoings

2   Revenues – Expenses

3   Earnings – Expenditure

4   Income – Costs

5   Operating Revenues – Operating Expenses

The business variables listed above are called *flow variables*. They refer to payment and income transactions that take place within a certain period and lead to a change in the amount of assets. Positive flow variables (incoming payments, revenues, earnings and income) lead to an increase in assets, whereas negative flow variables (outgoing payments, expenses, expenditures and costs) cause a reduction in assets. Note that each of the pairs of terms causes a change to a differently defined set of assets (refer to sections 4.2.1 to 4.2.6).

4.2.1 Definitions: income, revenues, outgoings and expenses

The stock of liquid funds (cash in hand, cash in bank) is called *liquid assets*. If a business transaction leads to an increase in its liquid assets, this is called income. Examples of this are cash deposits, a cash loan, cash repayment of a financing loan granted by the company, or cash sales of finished goods or trading goods.

If the liquid assets are reduced, this is called *outgoings*. This is the case, for example, with cash withdrawals, cash repayment of financing loans granted to the company from a previous period, or cash purchase of production factors.

If the accounts receivable (i.e. those not yet included in the liquid assets) are added to the liquid assets and the sum of the accounts payable is subtracted, the result is the *monetary assets*. Every business transaction that leads to an increase in the monetary assets is called *revenue*. A business transaction that produces a reduction in the monetary assets is an *expense*.

This shows clearly that each pair of terms depends on the definition of the assets/liabilities involved. It also shows how these terms can overlap.

4.2.2 Definitions: earnings and expenditure

If the tangible assets (the value from financial accounting) are added to the monetary assets and the accounts payable are subtracted, the result is the **net worth** or **net assets**. Every business transaction that leads to an increase in the net assets is called **earnings**. Every operation that produces a reduction in the net assets is called **expenditure**. Here, too, the close link between the terms is clear.

4.2.3 Definitions: income and costs

The pairs of terms defined so far concern the figures from financial accounting. The following terms, **costs** and **income**, which are set against the terms **expenditure** and **earnings**, are used to describe business transactions that affect the figures in operational accounting.

'Expenditure' is a reduction in the net assets, i.e., a drop in the value recorded in financial accounting in an accounting period. This drop in value may consist of a restructuring of values (e.g. consumption of raw materials to produce finished goods, and/or the sale of finished goods and trading goods) where the drop in value is balanced by an offsetting value in the form of company output. Alternatively, it can occur without an offsetting value, for instance where a voluntary donation is made or where taxes are paid (compulsory). As described earlier, the part of the drop in value that is used for operational output is called the cost.

Expenditures and costs do not, therefore, occur at the same level. In the case of non-operating expenditures (e.g. a donation) or extraordinary expenditures (e.g. fire damage), they are more like neutral expenditures. There are also costs that are not posted at all in financial accounting, namely supplementary costs such as fictitious entrepreneur compensation) or only in varying amounts (e.g. third-party costs, imputed interest charges, imputed depreciation allowances). If the neutral expenditures are subtracted from the total expenditures, the result is the **appropriated expenditure**. This appropriated expenditure is transferred directly into cost accounting and therefore corresponds to the basic costs, namely, the costs without supplementary or third-party costs.

'Earnings' represent the money value appreciation in an accounting period in financial accounting terms. It is the business counterpoint to expenditure. The term **operating earnings** and/or **operating income** (sales revenues, increase in inventory of finished or unfinished goods) is used when the earnings result from the process of operational output. Otherwise, these are neutral earnings (increase in value of stocks, sale of assets above book value).

4.2.4 Definitions: operating revenues and operating expenses

The term **operating expenses** originates from tax law terminology and is used to determine the tax on profit. It represents the operating assets at the end of the previous fiscal year, increased by the value of withdrawals and reduced by the value of deposits.

The *operating revenues* increase the value of the company and are reduced by the operating expenses, which can be defined as operating expenses, that is, as 'expenditures incurred by the business'. However, this definition does not state that they correspond to expenditures in the sense of the previous chapter, as tax law also acknowledges expenditures that do not correspond to a drop in value in a period. This means that operating expenses correspond more to the term expenses, which nevertheless must be extended to include 'non-deductible' operating expenses, i.e. the operating expenses that, in contrast to the expenditure, are not permitted to reduce the (taxable) income of the accounting period (for example, expenditures for gifts).

4.2.5 Definitions: operating receipts and earnings

Operating receipts and *earnings* not only include receipts that affect profit but also receipts that do not affect profit, such as money obtained by a company through the taking of loans. In the same way as the operating expenses, not all operating receipts affect profit.

4.2.6 Definition: net income

Bearing in mind the terms defined so far, the ***net income*** of an accounting period is calculated from the following relationships:

- From the point of view of the commercial accounts:

  OPERATING EARNINGS − APPROPRIATED EXPENDITURE = OPERATING INCOME
  NEUTRAL EARNINGS − NEUTRAL EXPENDITURE = NEUTRAL INCOME
  TOTAL EARNINGS − TOTAL EXPENDITURE = TOTAL INCOME
  = BALANCE SHEET PROFIT (WHEN TOTAL EARNINGS > TOTAL EXPENDITURE)
  = BALANCE SHEET LOSS (WHEN TOTAL EARNINGS < TOTAL EXPENDITURE)

- From the point of view of the tax accounts:

  INCOME-CREATING OPERATING REVENUES − DEDUCTIBLE OPERATING EXPENSES = TAXABLE INCOME
  = TAXABLE PROFIT (WHEN INCOME-CREATING OPERATING REVENUES > DEDUCTIBLE OPERATING EXPENSES)
  = TAX LOSS (WHEN INCOME-CREATING OPERATING REVENUES < DEDUCTIBLE OPERATING EXPENSES)

- From the point of view of cost accounting:

  COSTS − INCOME = OPERATING INCOME

As a rule, an accounting period's operating income and operating result are not identical. This is because differences may exist between operating earnings and operating income, and also between appropriated expenditure and costs in the same accounting period. Furthermore, the total income and the taxable income do not match, because there may be differences both between the total earnings and the income-creating operating revenues and between the total expenditure and the deductible operating expenses.

4.3 ACCOUNTING IN EUROS

This section is primarily intended for readers interested in accounting for companies in the eurozone.

Accounting was confronted at a very early stage with the problems relating to the change to the euro, because it had to be able to process business transactions in both a local currency and the euro from 1 January 1999. This was because some business partners had already switched to the euro, while others continued to use their local currency. The SAP R/3 System permits this for all countries participating in the euro during the transition period (1 January 1999 to 31 December 2001), in which the euro can be set as a foreign currency.

Following this so-called *dual-currency phase*, the local currency (the currency in which amounts are listed in the system) of the SAP System must be set to euros (for companies operating in the eurozone). The local currency is handled in Company Code's global parameters (described in section 7.1.2): *see* Figures 4.6 and 4.7.

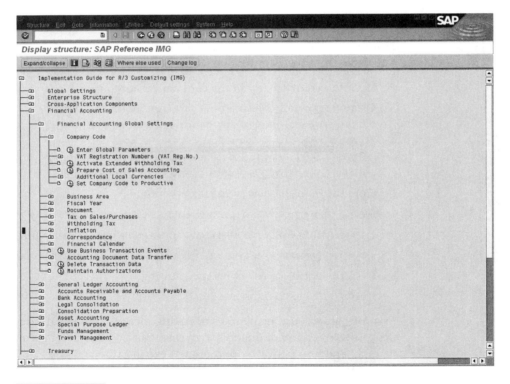

FIGURE 4.6   Global parameter handling for the company code (© SAP AG)

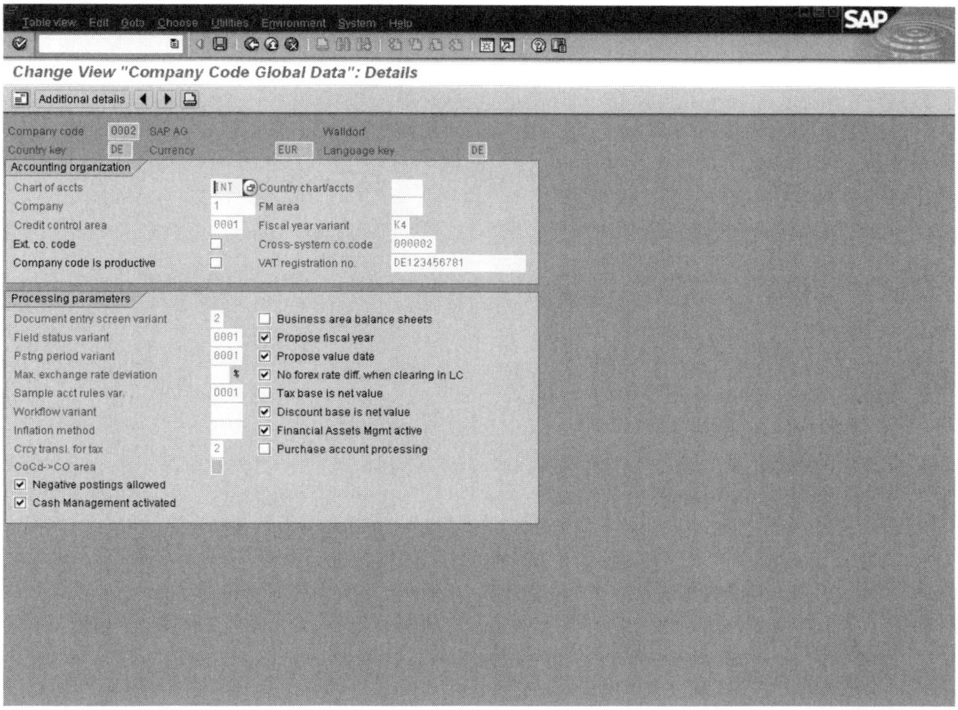

FIGURE 4.7   Setting the local currency in Company Code Global Data (© SAP AG)

CHAPTER 5

Complying in SAP R/3 with accepted accounting principles

5.1 GENERAL

Various local laws stipulate that company records or books and the other required records are to be stored for a set length of time for various purposes, such as for an audit. Such laws may require the information to be stored in written form but may also allow for storage via other media, such as electronic data storage. There are guidelines for computerized accounting that comply with the generally accepted accounting principles (GAAP) that have been laid down by international standard.

The accepted principles of computerized accounting systems are not intended to replace the GAAP. However, they do set out precise principles with regard to computerized accounting and describe the measures that must be taken by anyone who is required to keep accounts, to ensure that the postings and other required records are complete, correct, and in chronological order. Everyone who is required to keep accounts is also obliged to comply with the GAAP as they relate to computerized accounting.

Standard software within the SAP R/3 System, and in particular the FI module, is a computerized accounting system as defined by the accepted principles. Audits require that, while stored in IT systems, the books, documents and records otherwise required must be made available in a readable form at any time within a reasonable period of notice. In addition, any processes that lie outside the actual area of accounting (the FI module) but that record, create, process and/or communicate data relevant to accounting (through integration with other modules) must also be taken into consideration.

The application of these principles in the R/3 System is based on the results of discussions with various tax authorities in Europe.

Figure 5.1 contains an overview of the generally accepted accounting principles.

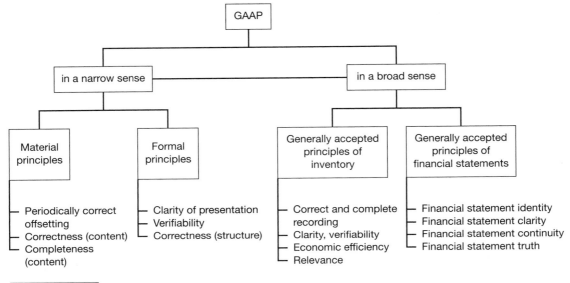

FIGURE 5.1   Generally accepted accounting principles (GAAP) in overview (© SAP AG)

As with any other type of accounting, a variety of legislation and the locally-accepted accounting principles must be complied with in the case of computerized accounting in the R/3 System. These requirements include the following points:

- The accountable business transactions must be correct, complete and recorded in chronological sequence. It must be possible to trace when they were created and how they were handled (Document and Journal function).

- Business transactions are to be processed in such a way that they can be shown in a structured manner and provide an accurate overview of the assets and earnings situation (Account function).

- Postings must be shown individually and allocated to accounts. These accounts must be updated according to account totals or balances and closing items. The accounts must also be made available in a readable form at any time.

- A third party with the relevant accounting knowledge must be able to understand each accounting method within a reasonable time and also be able to gain an overview of the business transactions and the situation of the company.

■ Computerized accounting must include process documentation that evidences the current and historical process content in a way that is comprehensible.

■ The process described in the documentation must fully correspond to the program (program identity) that is actually in use (release version).

5.2

THE DOCUMENT, JOURNAL AND ACCOUNT FUNCTIONS IN R/3

Computerized accounting must follow the principle of content-related and temporal verifiability for all business transactions subject to accounting control. In the SAP R/3 System, a Document, Journal and Account function is used to ensure that individual business transactions can be verified at any time.

The relationship between an original business transaction and its posting or processing in the R/3 System must be shown in process documentation that provides sufficiently detailed information, and it must be supplemented by proof that it is being used correctly (*see* section 5.6).

5.2.1 The Document function

The Document function forms the basis for providing evidence in accounting. It is an easily understandable means of checking the relationship between the operating and non-operating accounting operations. This is the relationship between the actual operation and the result of that operation that is entered in the company books.

In the SAP R/3 System, the Document function is performed in various ways. This is because computerized postings can be triggered not only by the existence of conventional paper documents but also increasingly by the automatic entry of data (e.g. operating data input, imports of old data), by routines that run within a program (automatic posting of documents in two or more modules) and by the exchange of data media or remote data interchange (e.g. EDI, electronic account statements). These processes are all supported by the SAP R/3 System.

No matter how the document function is implemented, the following content must be stored in addition to the posting:

■ a sufficiently-detailed description of the operation

■ the amount or quantity and value to be stored or entered, from which the amount to be entered can be calculated

■ time of the operation (to determine the posting period)

■ a unique assignment of document numbers

In Sections 7.5 and 7.8.2, the organization structures in the R/3 System are used to describe the Document function in greater detail.

5.2.2 The Journal function

Reports are usually created at various stages during the accounting process (when data is entered/imported, during processing, at the end of processing) to provide evidence that business transactions were recorded in a complete, formal manner at the correct time. If a report is not created when the data is entered or transferred, but is created at a later stage in processing, control measures must ensure that the business transactions were complete from the time at which they were created until they were logged. The business transactions can either be logged on paper, on an image medium, or on other data media.

It must be possible to provide complete and formally correct verification, in chronological order, (via the Journal function) that a business transaction was recorded, processed and output. This verification must be produced within a reasonable period in accordance with the legally prescribed periods of data storage (*see* section 5.8).

The business transactions must be shown in chronological order as well as in a clearly laid-out form, both fully and as extracts.

5.2.3 The Account function

To fulfil the account function, business transactions must be shown separately in General Ledger and personal accounts. The SAP R/3 System uses both ledgers (the General Ledger accounts) and subledgers (Accounts Receivable, Accounts Payable and Assets accounts) to do this. You will find more detailed information in sections 7.8 and 7.9.

To ensure that compound figures are posted correctly to the General Ledger and personal accounts, it must be possible to verify the individual items in the summarized figures. In the R/3 System you can do this at any time by branching to a line item report. You can also display accounts on screen and print them at any time.

5.3 POSTING IN THE R/3 SYSTEM

Business transactions in computerized accounting are judged to have been entered correctly when they have been recorded and stored in accordance with a principle of orderliness that ensures they are complete, formally correct, refer to the correct time, and can be processed. Within this:

- The requirement for the *principle of orderliness* in computerized accounting systems is that both the Document function and the Account function have to be implemented. The business transactions do not have to be stored according to any particular criteria of order. The requirement of a principle of order has been met if stored business transactions and/or parts of them can be accessed on demand, as is the case in the R/3 System.

- It must be ensured that the postings can be processed from the time they are entered (either automatically or manually) through to other processing stages. This requires that not only data relating to the business transaction itself is stored, but also the table data and programs needed for processing.

- Checks must be carried out to ensure that all business transactions are recorded in their entirety (in the SAP R/3 System, by using Field Status groups) and that, after a business transaction has been posted, no unauthorized changes are made. *Unauthorized changes* are those that do not comply with access-protection procedures (a special user-authorization concept that is set up in R/3 for this purpose), i.e. the previous status is not verified. In the SAP R/3 System, change documents are created when changes are made. These change documents record both the change and the person making the change. If recorded data is corrected before it is posted, e.g. because it is obviously incorrect, there is no need to determine its original contents. Furthermore, if a document has already been entered in the R/3 System, the amounts can no longer be changed. If an incorrect amount has been entered in the books, you must create a reversal document.

- The recording control measures must ensure that the postings are formally correct. This guarantees that the features required to process a posting either immediately or later are present and will work correctly. In the R/3 System, this control is carried out by means of the Field Status groups and a check that debit and credit amounts in the accounting document balance.

- The requirement for posting at the correct time refers to the fact that business transactions must be recorded to keep them up-to-date and in a manner appropriate to the accounting period. In the SAP R/3 System, this is implemented by means of a *period shifter* which blocks a posting period for further postings when it is closed. The posting periods are opened and closed in customizing and/or in the General Ledger accounting menu. Figure 5.2 shows the Customizing path required.

In the example shown in Figure 5.3, only Posting Period 3 (March) is open for postings to all accounts. Depending on what best suits company policy, a distinction can be made between accounts receivable postings, accounts payable postings, and General Ledger account postings. The opened posting periods are always dependent on the company code.

Further information on this topic can be found in Sections 7.5, 7.6 and 7.7.

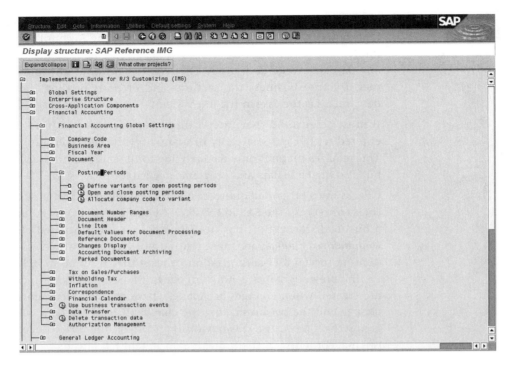

FIGURE 5.2   Opening and closing posting periods in Customizing (© SAP AG)

5.4   THE INTERNAL CONTROL SYSTEM (ICS) IN R/3

Essentially, the R/3 System's ICS involves all the coordinated and linked checks, measures and rules that have the following tasks:

- to secure and protect existing assets and information against loss of any kind

- to provide complete, precise, meaningful and up-to-date records

- to increase operational efficiency by analyzing and controlling records

- to support compliance with prescribed corporate policy

The aim of the R/3 ICS in the context of computerized accounting must be to support those people who are required to keep accounts. It does this by ensuring that accounting (*see* Chapter 4) and the annual accounts (*see* Chapter 11) conform with both the law and with the company's articles of association, as well as providing an overview of the economic situation of the company.

To be able to comply with the GAAP, one essential requirement must be met, which is the provision of complete, precise, detailed and timely records. The R/3 System is a powerful and practical tool because it integrates and maps the flows of documents in all the relevant modules.

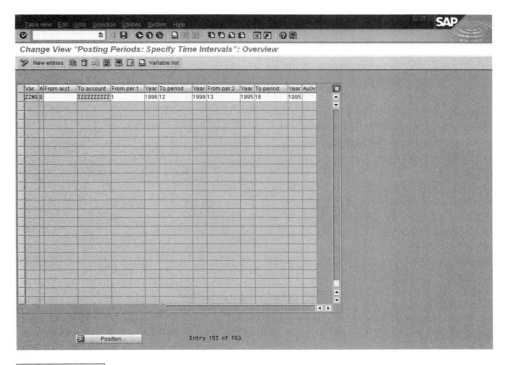

FIGURE 5.3   Open posting periods in Customizing (© SAP AG)

In addition, the R/3 System's internal control system covers the following aspects:

■ It uses a clear role and user-authorization concept to regulate authority and responsibility for operational functions.

■ The workflows that are relevant to accounting are clearly defined and their sequence is specified.

■ Manual and machine checks to be performed can be documented in Customizing (e.g. tolerance groups) and implemented by means of approval procedures (e.g. in the case of previously recorded documents).

One important aspect of control measures is that manual checks can be circumvented or performed without due care and attention. They therefore need monitoring at a later stage. Automatic checks can be defined as checking conditions that are integrated into program routines. They are designed to prevent processing of implausible and incomplete data.

One of the tasks of the ICS in the SAP R/3 System is to assure program identity, i.e. there must be period-related checks to find out whether the Customizing settings and/or add-ons (supplementary programming) are also included in the system documentation. A particularly important requirement for assuring program identity is to ensure that the existence and coordinated interaction of current company-specific features are taken into consideration.

This is why there are guidelines for defining the following:

- programming
- program tests
- program releases
- program changes
- changes to master records and table data
- access procedures
- deployment of test datasets/systems
- program deployment checks

The description of the ICS – insofar as this is relevant to an understanding of the SAP accounting system – is part of the process documentation (*see* Section 5.6).

5.5 DATA SECURITY

Considering how much companies depend on their stored information, it is obvious that a clearly defined data-security concept is absolutely essential before the requirements of the GAAP can be met. The vital point to remember here is that data security can only be achieved and ensured on a long-term basis when those responsible know what is to be secured and protected, what it is to be secured and protected against, the length of time for which security and protection are required, and the method to be used to achieve it.

In addition to the information relevant to accounting that is stored on data media, any other information that must be secured and protected in the interests of the company itself or because of legal obligation must be secured and protected at the same time. In this context, 'information' is regarded as the software (operating system, SAP standard software), table data, master records, transaction data (e.g. data relating to a business transaction), and other records. Any documents and other records, which are stored by accounting clerks in conventional form (paper), must also be secured and protected.

Information that is relevant to accounting must be secured and protected for the duration of the legally prescribed period of preservation (*see* Section 5.8). The company can also specify which information should be preserved for longer periods for its own purposes.

SAP provides special archiving concepts (e.g. from iXOS) that meet the requirement that information relevant to accounting must be readable at any time during the period that it is preserved. It also guarantees that the hardware is available along with the data and software. These concepts also use effective access checks to protect information against unauthorized changes.

Comprehensive data-backup procedures must be initiated to prevent data loss. It is a good idea to plan procedures for periodic data backup and, as an additional measure, to create ad-hoc backups if programs and/or data are changed or processed more often than usual in the period between two standard backups. Besides creating backup copies of the data that must be kept for legal reasons, you should also create backup copies of other sensitive data or programs. These backups should be stored in another location off-site (preferably at another secured site).

The backed-up data must also be secured against loss and disappearance, destruction and theft. To meet the first criterion, you should keep systematic records of the backed-up programs/data stocks. These records should tell you about the individual data media used, their location, content, date of backup and earliest date of deletion of their contents.

To minimize the risk of data media for this information being destroyed, the storage locations must provide an environment that protects the backed-up information from being destroyed or damaged by fire, heat, humidity, magnetic fields, etc. to the greatest extent possible. You can reduce the risk of theft by storing the data media in locked premises that are adequately secured against burglary and/or in safes.

You should also specify intervals at which the data media are to be checked, to ensure that the information that needs to be stored for long periods, because it is subject to data-preservation regulations, can still be read. The length of these intervals depends on the data storage techniques used.

You must also document the data security/backup method and procedures used in your company.

5.6   DOCUMENTATION AND AUDITING

Like every other form of accounting, that in the SAP R/3 System must be auditable by a suitably qualified third party within reasonable periods to ensure that it is formally and factually correct. The auditability refers both to the individual business transactions (individual audit) and the accounting method (methodology or system audit). The documentation must also clearly state whether the method has been applied in accordance with its description.

The content, structure and sequence of the accounting method must be fully explained in the method's documentation. The implementation of the requirements for a correct method described in the previous chapters must also be derived from the method's documentation.

The formal structure and techniques to be used for this documentation are generally not prescribed by law; they can be designed on an individual basis by those people who are obliged to keep accounts. However, it is essential that the documentation of the methodology must be comprehensible to a qualified third party in each case.

The scope of the required documentation on accounting methodology is based on the number of modules used, interfaces to other systems, or number of versions of the modifications in the system. Even if the documentation has been created by an external consulting firm as part of a SAP implementation, those people who are obliged to keep accounts are responsible for the completeness and information content of the process documentation.

CONTENTS OF THE PROCESS DOCUMENTATION

Process documentation must cover the following particular points:

- a description of the solution in logical terms
- a description of the solution from a technical programming viewpoint
- a description of how the program identity is preserved
- a description of how data integrity is preserved
- instructions for the user

In addition, the description of each of the above areas must illustrate the scope and method of operation of the internal control system.

5.7.1 Description of the solution in logical terms

A description of the solution in logical (and factual) terms contains the definition of the specialized tasks from the point of view of the user. In particular, this includes the following aspects:

- general definition of task(s)
- description of the user interfaces for input and output, including any manual tasks
- description of the data inventories
- description of data interchange (data medium exchange/data transfer)
- description of the machine checks and manual checks
- description of the error messages and the measures resulting from errors
- description of the interfaces to external systems

5.7.2 Description of the solution in technical terms

A description of the solution in technical programming terms shows how and where the logical and factual requirements have been implemented in programs within the system. It also specifies tables that can be used to change the way the programs' functions operate.

Program changes must also be listed in the process documentation. If program changes have not been documented automatically, additional organizational measures must ensure that both the old and new status of a changed program are verifiable. If changes have been made to tables with program functions, the documentation must be such that the contents of each table can be determined for the duration of the period of preservation.

5.7.3 Description of the program identity

To preserve program identity, those people who are required to keep accounts must prove that the factual and logical requirements will be met or have been met by means of specific programs used in the system. These include an accurate description of the approval procedures, with rules defining who has approval authority, the test sequences to be run and the data to be used for them, as well as instructions for program-deployment checks.

In particular, the certificate of approval along with existing test data inventories (e.g. integration test data) are ways of verifying a program's identity. The certificate of approval must clearly indicate which program version is planned for productive deployment and at what point in time.

5.7.4 Description of data integrity

The documentation of data integrity includes descriptions of all precautions to ensure that data and programs cannot be altered by unauthorized persons. This includes not only the user-authorizations concept, which is generated in the SAP R/3 System by means of the Profile Generator, but also evidence of the correct *assignment* of access authorizations.

5.7.5 Description of user instructions

The instructions that must be documented for the users so that they can carry out their tasks correctly are also part of the process documentation and must be set out in writing. The description of the checks and reconciliations to be included in the method are of particular importance here. The interfaces with the 'upstream' and 'downstream' system must also be taken into consideration.

5.8   PERIODS OF PRESERVATION

Data that documents information must be preserved for a legally determined period of time. The length of time depends on the country and the type of data.

In the example shown in Figure 5.4, the documentation procedure in the SAP R/3 System stores instructional and other organizational documents for 10 years. Parts of the documentation (e.g. correspondence or detailed postings, such as the documentation for the SD module calculation scheme, from which the accounts receivable postings are derived) are set up to be preserved for 6 years. The documentation can also be stored on image media.

The start of a period of preservation for the process documentation is the end of the calendar year in which the data relevant to accounting was recorded using the method, came into existence, or was processed.

Periods of preservation	
Documents required 1. Commercial accounts, inventory, balance sheets, P&L accounts, work documents, organization documents	10 years
2. Correspondence received	
3. Copies of commercial correspondence sent	6 years
4. Posting documents	

FIGURE 5.4   Example of information stored for various lengths of time (© SAP AG)

5.9   MAKING DATA AVAILABLE FOR INSPECTION

The people responsible for keeping accounts must ensure that the stored business transactions (postings), as well as the instructions and other organizational documents required to understand them, can be made available for reading at any time and within a reasonable interval throughout the period of presentation. They must also provide the data, programs and other facilities this requires (e.g. staff, monitors, scanners). If an authorized third party (e.g. a local tax authority or an auditor) asks to see the data, company staff must make the postings readable or, if asked to do so, provide a reproduction that can be read without additional facilities. The SAP archiving methods, e.g. from iXOS, ensure that the contents of the reproduction match the documents kept on machine-readable data media. This can be verified at any time.

The people who are required to keep accounts create written instructions that set out the method used to reproduce documents that are kept on image media and other data media. These can be printing instructions, COM (computer output on microfilm/fiche) instructions or instructions for dialogs used to select and display stored documents on viewing devices (e.g. optical storage systems). The instructions must describe the principles used to structure the reproduction, and the method of establishing the completeness and correctness of the reproduction. In addition, any reproductions of the financial reporting by those obliged to keep those accounts must be clearly assigned to the corresponding business transactions.

CHAPTER 6

Customizing in the R/3 System

Customizing involves all the activities that are needed to modify standard software so that it meets to company-specific requirements when it is implemented. This means that customizing is the process that is applied to implement SAP modules separately from each other and adapt them to the requirements of a business. The process is quick, effective and cost-efficient.

Customizing is designed to meet actual customer requirements, not to modify SAP standard software. You can use ABAP/4 programs to make these modifications. When you do this, you adapt the technical structures of the SAP System, i.e. its tables and the Data Dictionary.

The structures of the Customizing function within the R/3 System are oriented towards the business functions of the individual modules and guide the user through various system settings. Customizing consists of the R/3 Reference Model and the Implementation Guide, the functions of which are discussed in more detail in the sections that follow.

6.1 THE R/3 REFERENCE MODEL

The R/3 Reference Model describes the commercial scope of the areas covered by the R/3 System and the relationships between these areas. It uses event-controlled process chains (EPCs) to represent a comprehensive, integrated and cross-functional collection of commercial business processes in graphical form. The Reference Model is divided into functional areas, such as Sales and Distribution or Financial Management. This makes it easier for users to understand the model because they can view it from a familiar specialist area.

The Reference Model shows the most important processes that can be implemented in SAP R/3. The Reference Model's processes show the related tasks of an accounting specialist and are graphically represented in the EPCs by icons. The link between the processes shows the interdepartmental networking of business processes and the interplay of various functional areas. The terms used in the models also form a common and uniform terminology for all those involved in the project. This group includes consultants, company decision-makers, organizers and accounts staff. To allow all members of a project to access the Reference Model quickly and easily, it has a small number of icons and a standardized navigation system.

Possible starting points have to be decided when you start analyzing a process. Essentially, data is transferred automatically within the R/3 System. Nevertheless, it is a good idea to analyze the interfaces in the system at this point in time, so that a customer-specific value-exploitation chain can be set up later on. The model is a component of every R/3 installation. It contains the views set out next.

6.1.1 Function Model

The Function Model describes the main commercial functions of a company in a clearly laid-out, fixed form. The main functions, e.g. financial accounting, sales and distribution, or materials management, can be structured to various levels.

The tree structure of the Sales and Distribution function (SD module), for example, can be classified at four levels:

- Level 0 contains the description of the SD application.
- Level 1 contains the functional areas, e.g. Sales.
- Level 2 contains the main functions within a functional area, e.g. Order Processing.
- Level 3 contains the subfunctions of a main function, e.g. Scheduled Order Processing.

To keep things simple, the sub-functions below this level are not shown in a function tree.

6.1.2 Process Model

In contrast to the Function, Information, Communication, Organization, Distribution and Data models, the Process Model provides a dynamic view of a company's information system. The aim of the Process Model is to show the time line and logical relationships between functions and events. The mechanism that triggers functions in the process logic of an event-controlled process chain is called an *event*. Extended event-controlled process chains link together data, functions and organizational units. These chains also link input and output functions, as well as the settings to be made for the organizational units.

6.1.3 Information Model

Any process that consists of a sequence of individual functions requires information in order to function correctly. At the start of a project, there is usually not enough information available, and its quality may not be good enough. This is why the Reference Model contains the Information Model. The Information Model shows the information relationship between the sender and recipient in a flow chart. Temporal–logical dependencies are never taken into consideration here.

6.1.4 Communication Model

In contrast to the Information Model, which is oriented towards technical IT solutions, the Communication Model describes the communications relationships between existing organizational units. The aim is to represent communications between company units, e.g. between Sales and Cost Accounting.

6.1.5 Organization Model

The Organization Model shows the structure of a company in its organization charts. The organizational units are assigned business tasks. As a result, it is clear which unit will perform particular functions in the future and which transactions it will use to do so.

The possible Organization Models in SAP R/3 support the trend towards process-oriented structuring and therefore towards reducing the number of interfaces used in a process. However, functional base structures such as Sales and Distribution, or Production, in which most of the process takes place, are retained. The R/3 System is divided into the following three task areas expressed in commercial terms Accounting, Logistics and Human Resources Management.

The Financial Accounting module is that part of the Accounting task area that covers the areas of Company Code (see Section 7.1.2) and Business Area (see Section 7.1.3) to meet the requirements of accounting legislation. The company code shows legally separate units for which financial statements are created in accordance with the requirements of accounting legislation. The internal financial statements are created using the business area. This means a business area contains the non-autonomous economic units of a company.

The organizational units in the Controlling module are Controlling Area and Operating Concern. A complete, closed cost-accounting system can be shown within the Control area. This accounting process can be carried out not only across several cost centers but also across several company codes and business areas. The control area and company code use the same chart of accounts and the same currency. The profitability analysis can be structured according to products, sales territories or other criteria, depending on market requirements.

In the task area of Logistics, the plant is the central structural criterion (*see* Section 7.2.1). The plant can be either the physical warehousing or a production location, or a logical grouping of several locations. Planning and control activities can take place across several plants. The plant is closely linked to the structures of the Purchasing and Sales organization.

The areas of Accounting and Logistics are structured primarily according to business criteria. The Human Resources Management area is organized in accordance with criteria relevant to salary management. There, the central organizational unit is the 'job'. The structure of the organization that is based on human resources management criteria primarily takes into consideration the authority to issue instructions. The tasks of human resources management are divided into activities that are relevant to personnel administration, time management and payroll accounting.

You can use the R/3 Organization Model to create relationships between the task areas described above in order to represent a customer-specific organizational structure. In Chapter 7, these SAP terms are explained in more detail. Chapter 7 also explains how the Customizing links for the organizational units should be set up.

6.1.6 Distribution Model

The Distribution Model can be used to plan and implement applications within the framework of business integration. It shows which distribution scenarios are supported by the R/3 System.

6.1.7 Data Model

The Data Model shows information objects in the form of an Entity Relationship Model. The aim is to represent required data relating to multiple functions. Entities represent objects in the real world that are of commercial significance.

The R/3 Data Model shows the business objects of the applications in the R/3 System that are displayed in the form of Entity Relationship Models based on Chen's work. The R/3 System contains approximately 3000 interlinked objects. Of these 3000 objects, around 180 are objects that are highly significant for businesses. These are called 'business objects'. Business objects include, for example: the customer, the sales plan, the plant, or the control area.

6.2 IMPLEMENTATION MANAGEMENT GUIDE

While the Reference Model simply illustrates the processes, the Implementation Management Guide (IMG), in contrast, is used to modify the system to meet customer-specific requirements. Modifying the standard system with non-company-specific functions to meet specific customer requirements is also called 'customizing' or 'parameterization' of the SAP R/3 standard software.

Customizing is therefore not a method of modifying the standard program content in the R/3 System. Instead, it is a way of making settings in tables, to create the framework for R/3 users. In customizing, it is a general rule that you will not require all the standard functions of the R/3 System. The IMG is therefore restricted and modified to meet the needs of each specific customer.

From Release 4.5 onwards, you can also use the SAP tool ASAP (Accelerated SAP) to change the settings in the IMG directly.

There are the following types of Implementation Management Guide:

▨ **SAP Reference Guide (Reference IMG)**. Customizing in the SAP System starts with the SAP Reference Guide. This contains the complete range of functions and all the settings for all SAP application components in the R/3 System.

▨ **Company Guide**. The IMG components that are not used to implement the system in a company are removed from the company IMG.

▨ **Project Guide**. The Project Guides are individual sections of the company IMG and subprojects of the implementation in the company. A Project Guide can be generated for individual project teams or project groups.

▨ **Release-specific Implementation Management Guides (including Release Change Guides)**. In addition to release-specific Implementation Management Guides, other guides can be created that describe differences and innovations between two releases.

6.3 COMPONENTS OF THE IMG

No matter which view you select from those set out in section 6.2, each IMG lists the activities required to implement the standard SAP R/3 software (*see* Figure 6.1). It also supports the user when they use the system documentation. The Notes function also makes it possible to integrate project documentation into the IMG.

6.3.1 Information section

The IMG contains the actual work steps involved in customizing activities. Once again, no matter which view you select, each IMG's Information section contains an index, concept information, examples and a summary to provide you with an overview. All the information is linked and cross-referenced. To call this information, press the F1 key on your terminal keyboard at the relevant place in the IMG. (The F1 key is a 'help' key that provides additional information on any SAP field or for any Customizing setting.)

The concept information is extremely important because it provides users with some initial information about the business concepts on which the Customizing function is based. It also contains the requirements that explain which preparatory activities have to have been performed to complete a work step. In many cases, users can use cross-references to branch directly to these work steps. The concept information also contains descriptions of the default settings, SAP recommendations for organizational settings, and supplementary information.

Any examples set out in the IMG should use a practical case study to describe a real concept.

6.3.2 Project Steering section

The Project Steering section provides project support mechanisms to staff who are implementing the SAP R/3 System. The section is based on the status of the individual customizing points, and gives an indication of the progress of individual work steps.

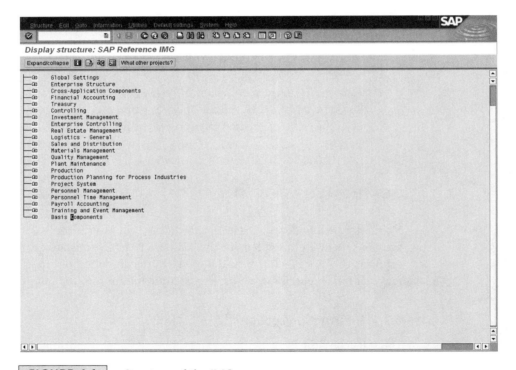

FIGURE 6.1   Structure of the IMG (© SAP AG)

The Schedule Administration function records the planned and actual deadlines for the beginning and end of each work step. The Personnel Administration function allows you to update project team information. The Project Assessment function enables you to assess the information in the Project Steering section according to various criteria.

In addition to the settings that affect all application components (global settings, enterprise structure, cross-application components), a range of settings is configured for each individual SAP component. Figure 6.2 shows the Financial Accounting section of the Implementation Management Guide, with the actual range of settings used in Financial Accounting.

The IMG will be used throughout this book to illustrate the Customizing functions in the R/3 System's Financial Accounting (FI) application components. It provides the reader with the background business knowledge required to understand the individual steps.

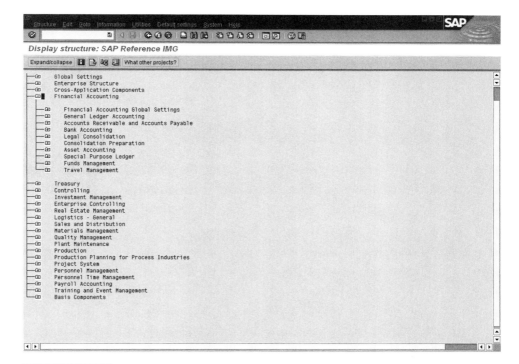

FIGURE 6.2 The Financial Accounting module split down within IMG (© SAP AG)

CHAPTER 7

Organizational structures and business transactions in SAP R/3

As mentioned in Chapter 6, SAP R/3 System covers the following commercial areas: Accounting, Human Resources Management, and Logistics (*see* Figure 7.1). To help users understand the system as a whole, the sections that follow, about the structures in Financial Accounting, also contain brief descriptions of the structures in Controlling and Logistics.

The Financial Accounting (FI), Controlling (CO) and Asset Accounting (FI AA) application component cover all aspects of the Accounting area. Human Resources Management is handled by its own specific application component, HR. The Logistics area includes the following application components: Production Planning (PP), Materials Management (MM), Sales and Distribution (SD), Quality Management (QM), Service Management (SM) and Plant Maintenance (PM).

You must represent both the legal and the organizational structure of a company in the application components. You can use a range of organizational elements to define the structure. These elements can be observed from different points of view. For example, by using a different point of view, you can define a structure for the Sales and Distribution application component that is fundamentally different from a Materials Management structure. For more information about this, please refer to the description of the 'Organization Model' in section 6.1.5.

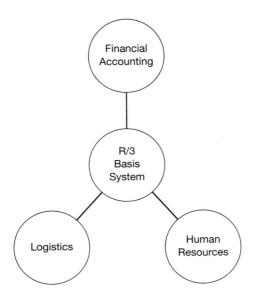

FIGURE 7.1   Structure of the SAP R/3 System in commercial terms (© SAP AG)

To set up the organizational structures, you must use the Implementation Management Guide's Enterprise Structure function. The way that you customize your company structure depends on the application components you want to use. Before you can make any settings, you must enter your own company's structure and organizational procedures. The next step is to match them to SAP's structures. In the standard version of the system, a number of organizational elements have already been defined as examples. However, in real life these elements will not cover all your requirements.

After you have defined the organizational units, use the Assignment function in Customizing to assign these elements to each other. This ensures that they can be integrated smoothly into the SAP R/3 System. After the SAP System has been implemented, only a limited number of people should be authorized to maintain the organizational elements. You can use the user-authorizations concept to define who these people are.

It is important to keep the number of organizational units to a minimum. If not, more time and effort is required to maintain the data and there is a greater risk of errors. It is much harder to change an organizational structure at a later date. Figure 7.2 shows the most important organizational structures used in the SAP R/3 System.

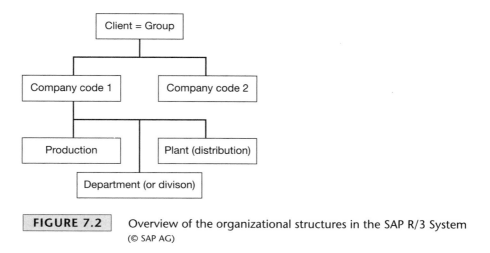

FIGURE 7.2   Overview of the organizational structures in the SAP R/3 System

---

7.1   ORGANIZATIONAL UNITS IN THE FINANCIAL ACCOUNTING MODULE

The following organizational units are used in the Financial Accounting module: Client, Company Code, Business Area, Company, Credit Control Area, Funds Management Area, Dunning Area, Chart of Accounts, and Controlling Area. Each of these is described further below.

7.1.1 Client

The Client is the central organizational element, not only in Financial Accounting, but also in all other application components. The Client is the top-level structural element of a company (*see* Figure 7.3). In organizational terms, it can often be regarded as being the same as the company group.

Each client is a separate unit that has its own separate master records and a complete group of tables. The system automatically uses a Client code in every master record. This code ensures that the data is stored for that specific client in the SAP System. Every user must enter a Client Code when he or she logs into the R/3 System, to specify the client in which they want to work. Data processing and analysis are also carried out on a client-specific basis.

Access authorizations are also assigned on a client-specific basis. A user master record must be created for each user, in the client in which they want to work.

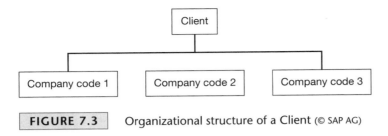

FIGURE 7.3 Organizational structure of a Client (© SAP AG)

7.1.2 Company Code

A client is subdivided into one or more Company Codes (*see* Figure 7.3 again). The company codes represent legally independent companies in the sense that, they are separate entities that create their own financial information.

The legal regulations governing balance sheets and profit and loss accounts are met at Company Code level. You can set up several Company Codes in each Client. This allows you to manage accounting data for different independent companies at the same time.

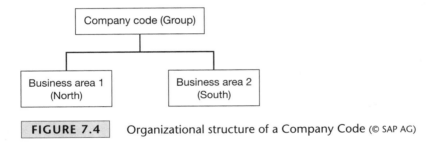

FIGURE 7.4 Organizational structure of a Company Code (© SAP AG)

7.1.3 Business Area

One company code can be divided into several business areas (*see* Figure 7.4). However, one business area may also be used in multiple company codes. In the SAP R/3 System, Business Area is only used to provide in-house information, and therefore does not meet the requirements of external reporting purposes. When you post a document, you must also specify a business area in the document items to ensure that the information is posted to the correct business area.

7.1.4 Company

Company is the smallest organizational unit for which legal individual financial statements can be prepared. A Company can include one or more Company Codes. Each one of a Company's Company Codes must use the same Chart of Accounts (*see* Figure 7.5).

A company's annual accounts form the basis of its consolidated accounts. The relationships are explained in more detail in Chapters 11 and 12.

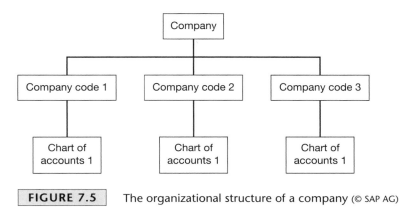

FIGURE 7.5   The organizational structure of a company (© SAP AG)

7.1.5 Credit Control Area

In the SAP R/3 System, Credit Control Area is the organizational unit in which all the accounts receivable from a customer are totaled. You can define a credit control area in such a way that it can be used in several Company Codes (*see* Figure 7.6). You can then use the Company Code to trace customer credit that has been granted elsewhere, i.e. outside the legally independent unit. If the level of total accounts payable reaches a certain limit, all the Company Codes in the Credit Control Area are automatically informed of this fact.

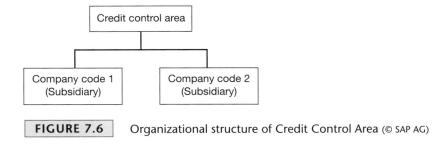

FIGURE 7.6   Organizational structure of Credit Control Area (© SAP AG)

In Customizing, you must first define the organization elements you want to use in accounting (Company Code, Business Area, Company, and Credit Control Area). You then assign them to each other (*see* Figure 7.7). When you define these elements, you simply give each one a unique name. No other details are required at this point. When you assign the elements, the system links the individual organization elements with one another.

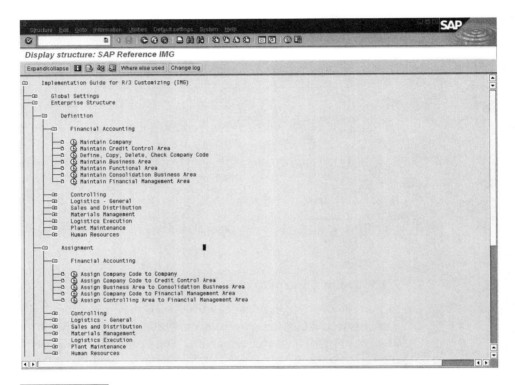

| **FIGURE 7.7** | How to define and assign accounting elements in the Enterprise Structure in Customizing (© SAP AG) |

After you have defined and assigned the organization elements, you can add contents to them. You do this in the Customizing area of the Financial Accounting application component. To add contents, use the Financial Accounting Global Settings function (*see* Figure 7.8).

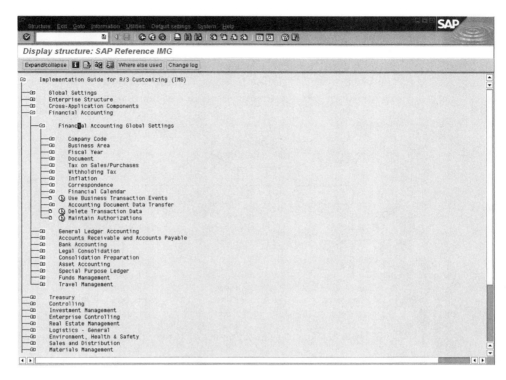

FIGURE 7.8   Adding detailed information to the organization elements in Financial Accounting (© SAP AG)

7.1.6 Funds Management (FM) Area

You use FM Area to plan the deployment of funds. In broad terms, the FM Area is identical to the Company Code and therefore controls budget management in an independent unit that draws up its own accounts. However, you can also assign several Company Codes to one FM Area, i.e. to organize funds planning beyond the limits of a legally independent unit. *See* Figure 7.9 for these two alternatives.

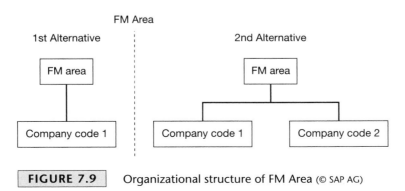

FIGURE 7.9   Organizational structure of FM Area (© SAP AG)

7.1.7 Dunning Area

Dunning procedures are usually managed in the accounts receivable and accounts payable departments, or one of their related departments. However, you must create Dunning Areas if dunning is managed independently by several organizational units, e.g. divisions or sales organizations in one company code (*see* Figure 7.10).

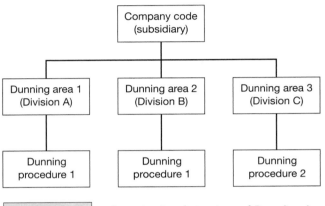

FIGURE 7.10   Organizational structure of Dunning Area (© SAP AG)

The accounts payable department of a company sends dunning letters about credit memos that are outstanding or have not been credited. The individual Dunning Areas can use the same or different dunning procedures, as required. Figure 7.11 shows where you make the settings for Dunning Areas.

7.1.8 Chart of Accounts

In accounting terms, the chart of accounts is a directory that contains all of a company's General Ledger accounts. All increases and decreases are shown accordingly in the accounts. Various charts of accounts have been predefined in the R/3 System to meet the requirements of various countries and industries, such as the international uniform system of accounts (INT), or country-specific charts such as CAUS (for the United States).

Chart of Accounts is used by both the Financial Accounting (section 4.1.2) and the Controlling modules. This means that there must be a one-to-one relationship between Chart of Accounts and Company Code or Controlling Area (*see* Figure 7.12). If a Controlling Area includes more than one Company Code, the Company Codes within a Controlling Area must use the same Chart of Accounts.

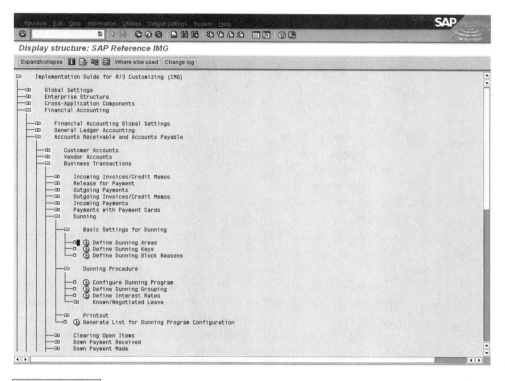

FIGURE 7.11   Customizing settings in a Dunning Area (© SAP AG)

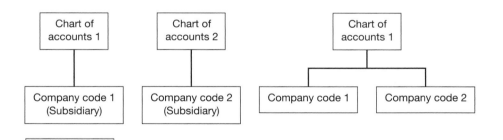

FIGURE 7.12   Organizational structure of Chart of Accounts (© SAP AG)

Although these relationships are less important if you use an IT-supported accounting system such as SAP R/3, you still need to understand the basic differences. You can structure the organization's internal and external accounting in two different ways. The first method is used if the Financial Accounting and Controlling modules are integrated with each other in one unit and access the same uniform accounting system. The second method is used when the modules are separate and use two independent accounting systems.

If internal and external accounting procedures form one unit, accounting procedures are not separated. This method is called the *single-code system.* Operational accounting is carried out in an account system. Accounting in account classes is carried out in one closed settlement area. In a single-code system, all the postings are accountable, no matter whether they are internal or external events. In this case you can only calculate a company's net income after determining the neutral expenditure and the neutral income.

In a *dual-code system*, financial accounting and operating accounting are carried out in two separate settlement areas. Each settlement area is a closed unit. In the Profit and Loss account, financial accounting balances incur expenditure against the proceeds earned. The income is determined by the Profit and Loss account, including changes to assets. Profit is calculated without internal accounting. Internal accounting takes place in a second settlement area in which the costs and revenues are compared. The operating result is determined after taking the changes in assets into consideration. The comparison between financial accounting and internal accounting takes place via mirror accounts, or by means of a transition system.

In some countries, financial accounting and controlling remain quite separate. These countries thus have charts of accounts that enable organizational separation between financial accounting and controlling, which is frequently no longer in account form but in tables. Such a chart of accounts is classified in the same way as the annual financial statements and forms settlement area 1 (*see* Tables 7.1 and 7.2).

The way in which internal cost accounting (cost and income accounting) is structured is based on the value-exploitation process (the process structure principle). It forms a separate settlement area 2 (*see* Table 7.3).

| TABLE 7.1 | Chart of Accounts analysis (1) |

Debit	801 closing balance account (CBA)		Credit
Account class	Assets	Liabilities	Account class
0	Tangible assets, Intangible assets	Equity capital, valuation adjustments, provisions	3
1	Investments	Accounts payable, prepaid amounts and deferred income	
2	Stocks, accounts receivable, prepaid amounts and deferred income		

TABLE 7.2	Chart of Accounts analysis (2)		
Debit	**801 closing balance account (CBA)**		**Credit**
Account class	**Assets**	**Earnings**	**Account class**
6	Material costs, wage costs, depreciation	Sales revenues, stock movements, other earnings	5
7	Interest, taxes, other expenditures		

TABLE 7.3	Chart of Accounts analysis (3): cost accounting
Account class	**Internal cost accounting (Accounting Code 2)**
9	Cost and income accounting – deferrals and accruals accounting

In Customizing, you use the General Ledger Accounting function to maintain the chart of accounts (*see* Figure 7.13).

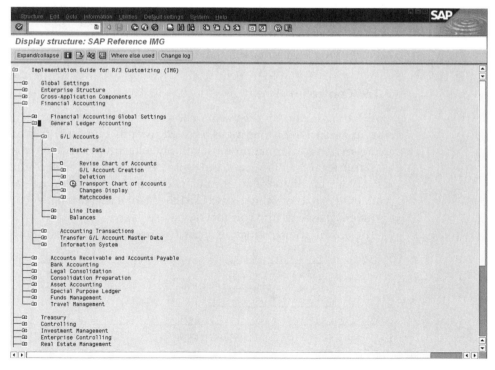

| FIGURE 7.13 | Customizing settings for a Chart of Accounts (© SAP AG) |

The General Ledger account master records in a chart of accounts contain a Chart of Accounts area and a Company Code-specific area. Every Chart of Accounts you set up can be used for several Company Codes. Each Chart contains information that applies to the master data records in the Company Codes (Account Number and Account Designation) that use that particular Chart of Accounts. The Company Code-specific part contains information that can differ from one company code to the next, depending on requirements (e.g. the currency).

The information in a Chart of Accounts controls how master records are created in the Company Codes. This is why you must first create the master record in the Chart of Accounts, before you can set up the account in the Company Code. In the SAP System there are two ways of doing this:

- In the first step, you set up a Chart of Accounts area. You then create the Company Code-specific part.
- You create a General Ledger account in the Chart of Accounts and in the Company Code in a single work step.

We recommend that you set up the general ledger account in two work steps if you want to specify certain values from a central location for use by the company codes individually.

The standard version of the SAP R/3 System already contains some charts of accounts (INT = International Chart of Accounts, CAUS = Chart of Account set up for the United States). Before you create a new General Ledger account, you should decide what information you want to define in the master data records.

7.1.9 Controlling Area

Controlling Area is an organizational unit in the Controlling module. The information in Financial Accounting is directed towards interested parties from outside the company. This information must comply with the regulations that govern commercial and legal accounting. Controlling does not have to comply with the legal regulations for financial accounting (*see* section 4.1.3). Although a great deal of data from external accounting is also used in internal accounting, you can also take other commercial aspects into consideration.

The organizational structure of the Controlling Area unit is shown in Figure 7.14.

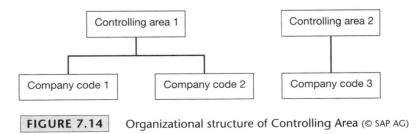

FIGURE 7.14 Organizational structure of Controlling Area (© SAP AG)

ORGANIZATIONAL UNITS IN THE LOGISTICS MODULES

As the descriptions in this book deal primarily with the FI application component, this section only contains a brief description of the Controlling Area and the organizational units in the Logistics modules within R/3.

You cannot view a company's organizational units alone, for the way in which SAP organizational units are linked together represents the structural organization of the entire company. Although Client is the top organizational unit, the legal character of Company Code makes it the central organizational element in the SAP System.

The Plant and Sales Organizations organizational elements within the Logistics modules are assigned to specific Company Codes (*see* Figure 7.15). This means that a sales organization can sell goods from different plants and one plant can sell its products and services across several sales organizations.

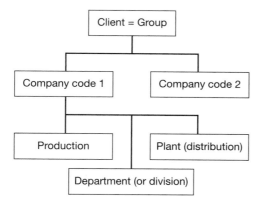

FIGURE 7.15   Overview of the organizational structures of Logistics elements (© SAP AG)

7.2.1 Plant and Storage Location

In the SAP System, a company's production locations and branch offices are represented by Plants. Each Plant is assigned to one specific Company Code. However, one Company Code may contain several Plants. You can also assign one Plant to several Sales Organizations. From the point of view of Materials Management (MM), materials planning and procurement take place at the plant. The master records required by these functions are therefore updated at plant level.

In production, the plant is the location at which goods are manufactured or a service is performed. The Sales and Distribution division of a company uses the plant to sell goods or services. Plant maintenance also takes place at the plant.

A Plant may actually consist of several physical Storage Locations (warehouses). These storage locations are places that are close together, where material inventories are kept. *See* Figure 7.16 for the logical structure that applies within the SAP R/3 System.

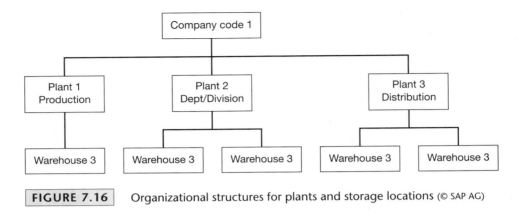

FIGURE 7.16   Organizational structures for plants and storage locations (© SAP AG)

7.2.2 Sales Organization, Distribution Channel and Line

In the Sales and Distribution module, the top organizational unit is Sales Organization. This is usually structured according to regional criteria. It is also the organizational unit against which customers can assert their rights of recourse and which is responsible for product liability.

You can assign one or more Distribution Channels to the same Sales Organization (*see* Figure 7.17). Typical distribution channels are wholesale and retail trading or direct sales. A customer can be served through several distribution channels. In the distribution channels, you can define prices or minimum quantities in different ways.

You can also assign several Lines to the same Distribution Channel. Lines represent various product groups. You use these product groups to make individual customer agreements. For example, you can make settings for partial deliveries or different terms of payment.

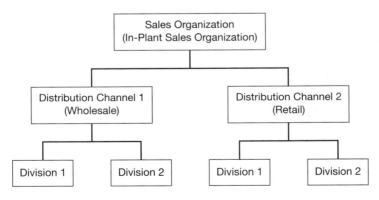

FIGURE 7.17   Organizational structures for Sales Organization, Distribution Channel and Line (© SAP AG)

7.3   THE STRUCTURE OF THE FINANCIAL ACCOUNTING MODULE

The task of a financial accounting department is to record all business transactions systematically and comprehensively (*see* Section 4.1.2). It must also enter all these transactions in the system, and document them. This makes it possible to comply with statutory regulations, such as creating a basis for taxation or protecting company owners and creditors. This data is also used as the basis for managing and controlling a company.

Financial accounting makes a distinction between General Ledger accounting and subsidiary ledger accounting. The SAP Financial Accounting module is subdivided into the following components based on this distinction:

- General ledger
- Extended ledger
- Accounts payable
- Accounts receivable
- Asset accounting
- Consolidation
- Financial controlling
- Investment
- Funds monitoring
- Travel management

These components are shown in diagrammatic form in Figure 7.18.

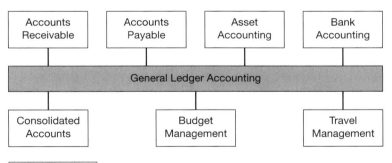

FIGURE 7.18   Components of the Financial Accounting module (© SAP AG)

7.4 CONNECTING TO OTHER SAP MODULES

The Financial Accounting module is linked to almost all the others in SAP. This is because it represents a large proportion of the commercial logistics processes in monetary terms.

In the SAP R/3 System, business transactions are recorded as they occur in the form of documents, and stored in a shared database. When a Logistics transaction is recorded, the system takes into consideration any information that is later required in Financial Accounting and in other modules. This is why each business transaction only has to be recorded once. All the applications can access this database. The system creates a flow of values simultaneously with the flow of output.

7.5 THE DOCUMENT PRINCIPLE

SAP R/3 uses the Document principle. This means that all postings are always stored in the form of Documents. Each Document must be complete before it is posted. The balance on the debit side must match the balance on the credit side. Each Document must also contain specific minimum information, e.g. document date, document type, posting key, account numbers and amounts. The system automatically checks whether all the necessary information is present and that it is consistent. Incomplete or inconsistent Documents cannot be posted (*see* Section 5.3).

7.6 REAL-TIME POSTING

When you confirm the posting of a Document, the system automatically changes the balances, the Balance Sheet and the Profit and Loss statement all at the same time. Real-time posting ensures that all employees at different levels have continuous access to a current and uniform dataset.

The SAP R/3 System supports real-time processing by using a combination of batch processing and dialogue processing. Database entries are updated separately from the actual dialogue. This improves system performance. Postings that place a greater burden on the database are controlled by another program. Even with this asynchronous processing, several hundred users can use the system without creating inconsistent database stocks. Asynchronous posting takes place so quickly that users do not notice that the data is being buffered. Once the posting process is complete and the data has been released, the next user can access the data.

| 7.7 | ## DOUBLE-ENTRY ACCOUNTING |

The double-entry accounting technique ensures that all the business transactions recorded in subledgers, such as Accounts Receivable or Accounts payable, are also posted to the relevant reconciliation account in General Ledger accounting. The double-entry accounting technique also means you can post data in the Controlling application component at the same time.

| 7.8 | ## GENERAL LEDGER ACCOUNTING |

The most important task of General Ledger accounting is to provide a comprehensive picture of the external accounting process and the accounts involved in it. The FI General Ledger accounting application component provides the following functions:

- automatic and simultaneous posting of all subledger items to the corresponding ledger accounts (reconciliation accounts, i.e. Accounts Receivable, Accounts Payable, Asset)

- simultaneous updating of the general ledger and controlling data (i.e. cost centers, internal orders, etc.)

- real-time evaluation and reporting of current posting data in the form of account displays and closing accounts with different financial statement versions, as well as additional analyses

General Ledger accounting is used to create a general overview of external accounting (Section 4.1.2) and the annual statements (Chapter 11). The subledgers show the details of individual business transactions.

General Ledger accounting contains the history data that is relevant for an account group. Accounts Receivable accounting shows the balances of the individual Accounts Receivable. In contrast, General Ledger accounting only contains the reconciliation accounts. The overall balance of all Accounts Receivable is shown in the General Ledger. For this reason, the General Ledger is the central component that is used in accounting (see Section 5.2.3).

7.8.1 General Ledger accounts

General Ledger accounts contain the increases and decreases that correspond to the flows of goods and services used in the Logistics modules.

General Ledger account master records

The General Ledger account contains master records that control how business transactions are recorded and posted to the account. These master records are also used to process posting data. This is why each account has its own master data record. In the General Ledger account master records, a basic distinction is made between information contained in the Chart of Accounts (Section 7.1.8) and Company Code-specific information.

The Chart of Accounts contains the General Ledger account number, its name, and a marker that identifies it as a Profit and Loss account or a Balance Sheet account. Each master data record is also assigned to an account group in the chart of accounts. When you set up an account, the SAP R/3 System ensures that all account numbers are unique. You can set up General Ledger accounting either in Customizing or directly in the General Ledger Accounting application menu. These two procedures have already been explained in detail in Section 4.1.2 (Figure 4.4 and Figure 4.5).

The currency, tax category and open item management are assigned at the Company Code level. The master data record also identifies whether an account is a reconciliation account. **_Reconciliation accounts_** group together the value items from the accounts of the individual subledgers in General Ledger accounting. For example, accounts from Accounts Receivable are aggregated in the 'Accounts Receivable' General Ledger reconciliation account. The double-entry technique ensures that the General Ledger account is balanced at all times and that individual balances correspond to the relevant subledgers. Postings to reconciliation accounts are made exclusively by the R/3 System. The balances must balance before the Profit and Loss statement or the Balance Sheet can be created.

To manage a General Ledger account, you use the system screens for account balance display, the open-item management functions and the individual items. The account balance shows both the transaction figures (postings to an account) and the overall balance. If you use the open-item administration functions, you can clearly see whether a reversal transaction has already been made as an adjustment. It is a good idea to use the open-item administration functions, e.g. for bank clearing accounts or payroll accounts. All document items are displayed separately in the individual item display.

7.8.2 Documents in Financial Accounting

Documents within FI are divided into a header area and a line item area (_see_ Figure 7.19), just like the other Documents used in the SAP System. The Document header contains information that applies to the entire document – for example, document date, document number or document type.

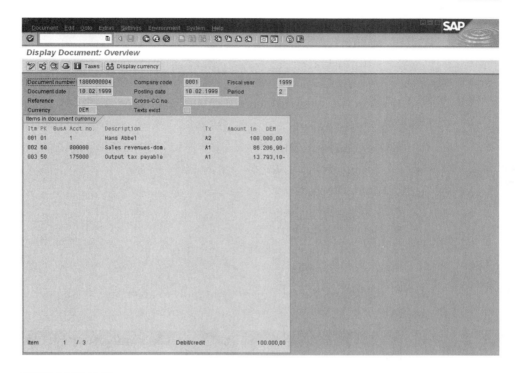

FIGURE 7.19   Displaying a Financial Accounting Document (© SAP AG)

Document type

In the SAP R/3 System, Document Type is an important control element. You use Document Type to identify different business transactions, for document type shows what type of business transaction is involved. You use the document type to control how account types (Accounts Receivable, Accounts Payable or the General Ledger account) are posted. It therefore controls access to the accounts.

The most important document types are already present in the standard version of the SAP R/3 System. The standard Document Types cover the following areas (*see* Figure 7.20):

- Financial Accounting
  - General ledger accounting
  - Accounts Receivable
  - Accounts Payable
  - Asset accounting
- Materials Management/Sales and Distribution
  - Receipt of goods/Goods dispatch

- Incoming invoices/Outgoing invoices
- Physical inventory
- Invoicing
- Consolidation

The standard system contains the following Document Types:

- Customer Invoice
- Customer Payment
- Customer Credit Memo
- Vendor Document
- Vendor Credit Memo
- General Document
- General Ledger Account Document
- Cash Document

The settings for Document Type apply to an entire Client.

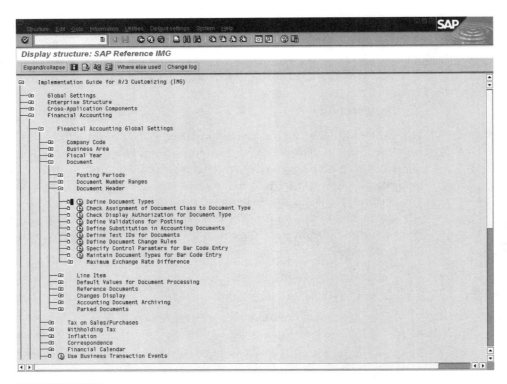

FIGURE 7.20   Document types in Customizing (© SAP AG)

Document Number

You use Document Type to assign Document Numbers. In the R/3 System, each Document Type is assigned to a number range, from which the System automatically assigns numbers (internal number assignment) or from which the user specifies certain values (external number assignment).

Posting 'gross' or 'net'

Document Type determines whether a 'gross' or 'net' posting is involved.

Document Currency

The following fields are important if you enter the amount in a foreign currency (*see* Figure 7.21):

- Currency Code
- Exchange Rate
- Translation Date

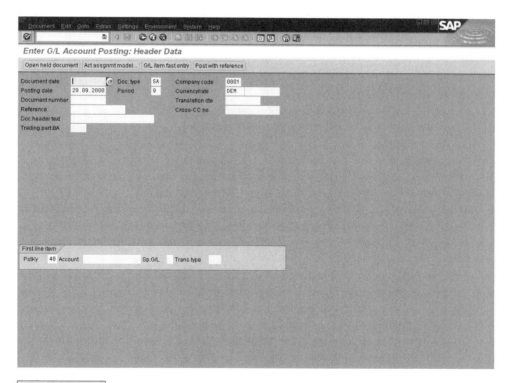

FIGURE 7.21   Entering the Document Currency (© SAP AG)

If you only enter the currency code, the R/3 System automatically uses the currency exchange rate that applies on the posting date. This is why the exchange rate must be stored in the system in the currency table. As a rule, the currency table is updated automatically by importing data requested from the company bank.

If you enter a conversion date as well as the currency code, the system uses the exchange rate valid on this date as the transaction exchange rate. If you enter a currency code and the conversion rate, the system uses this conversion rate. If you do this, the system does not use an exchange rate from the currency table.

Posting Key

Unlike entries in the Document Header that apply to the entire Document, the information in the Document's item lines only applies to the respective items. An item usually contains a Posting Key, an Account Number and an Amount. Other details depend on which business transaction is used in each case, for example, the flag for a special-purpose ledger transaction.

In the same way as the Document Type has a control function in the Document Header level, the Posting Key controls how document items are recorded. The Posting Key defines the recording input format and controls debit and credit postings.

The most important Posting Keys are already defined in the standard version of the SAP R/3 System, and in most cases you do not need to add any more. Figure 7.22 shows where you enter the settings for Posting Keys.

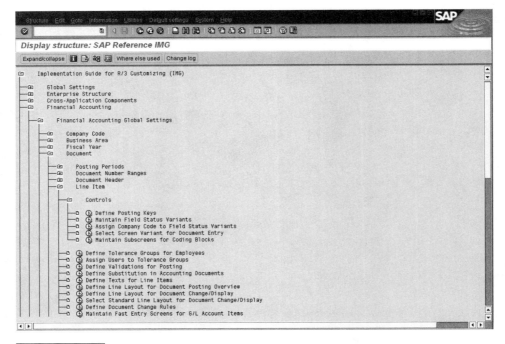

FIGURE 7.22   Customizing the settings for Posting Key (© SAP AG)

The standard version of the SAP R/3 System contains the posting keys shown in Table 7.4.

TABLE 7.4	Standard Posting Keys in the SAP R/3 System		
Posting key	**Debit / Credit**	**Account type**	**Description**
00			Account assignment model
01	Debit	Customer	Invoice
02	Debit	Customer	Credit memo reversal
03	Debit	Customer	Bank costs
04	Debit	Customer	Other accounts receivable
05	Debit	Customer	Outgoing payment
06	Debit	Customer	Payment difference
07	Debit	Customer	Other adjustment
08	Debit	Customer	Payment adjustment
09	Debit	Customer	Debit to special purpose ledger
11	Credit	Customer	Credit
12	Credit	Customer	Invoice reversal
13	Credit	Customer	Charge reversal
14	Credit	Customer	Other accounts payable
15	Credit	Customer	Incoming payment
16	Credit	Customer	Payment difference
17	Credit	Customer	Other adjustment
18	Credit	Customer	Payment adjustment
19	Credit	Customer	Special purpose ledger credit
21	Debit	Vendor	Credit
22	Debit	Vendor	Invoice reversal
24	Debit	Vendor	Other accounts receivable
25	Debit	Vendor	Outgoing payment
26	Debit	Vendor	Payment difference
27	Debit	Vendor	Adjustment
28	Debit	Vendor	Payment adjustment
29	Debit	Vendor	Debit to special purpose ledger
31	Credit	Vendor	Invoice
32	Credit	Vendor	Credit reversal
34	Credit	Vendor	Other accounts payable
35	Credit	Vendor	Incoming payment
36	Credit	Vendor	Payment difference
37	Credit	Vendor	Other adjustment

TABLE 7.4			*continued*
Posting key	**Debit / Credit**	**Account type**	**Description**
38	Credit	Vendor	Payment adjustment
39	Credit	Vendor	Special purpose ledger credit
40	Debit	G/L	Debit entry
50	Credit	G/L	Credit entry
70	Debit	Asset	Debit asset
75	Credit	Asset	Credit asset
80	Debit	G/L	Physical inventory
81	Debit	G/L	Costs
82	Debit	G/L	Stock variance
83	Debit	G/L	Price difference
84	Debit	G/L	Usage
85	Debit	G/L	Stock movement
86	Debit	G/L	GR/IR (goods receipt/invoice receipt) debit
89	Debit	Mat.	Incoming stock movement
90	Credit	G/L	Physical inventory
91	Credit	G/L	Costs
92	Credit	G/L	Stock variance
93	Credit	G/L	Price difference
94	Credit	G/L	Usage
95	Credit	G/L	Stock movement
96	Credit	G/L	GR/IR Credit
99	Credit	Mat.	Outgoing stock movement

7.8.3 Posting Documents

When a document is posted, the SAP R/3 System carries out a plausibility check on the data entered (see section 5.2.1) before storing it in the document file and updating the transaction figures of the accounts. The system checks whether all the (mandatory) input fields contain plausible entries, whether the balance of debits and credits equals zero and whether tax on sales/purchases amounts that were entered manually are correct in comparison with the tax rates stored in the system.

Users can also carry out additional checks. For example, you can authorize or lock postings to accounts, company codes or cost centers for individual users or user groups. You can also define a limit that an accounting clerk may not exceed. If a user breaks any of these rules, the system does not allow them to post the document. To prevent the data they have entered from being lost, a user can note the document in the system and have it handled by a third party, or process it themselves, later on.

7.8.4 Financial statements

Financial statements are divided by time into daily, monthly and annual financial statements (*see* Chapters 11 and 12). Legal regulations require that expenditures and earnings are compared at periodic intervals. The regulations also require that Accounts Receivable and Accounts Payable are evaluated, that a Balance Sheet and Profit and Loss (P&L) statement are created, and that posting data is documented.

Daily financial statement

You can create daily financial statements immediately, without the need for any extra steps. After you complete the last posting, the system automatically generates a financial account statement for that specific day and displays the balances of the accounts. This statement is sorted chronologically, or according to individually specified criteria, in a posting journal.

Monthly financial statement

To create a monthly financial statement (or the end of the posting period) you must carry out a number of closing tasks. When a posting period is closed, the system blocks postings for this period and other previous periods, but it allows postings for the next posting periods.

The SAP R/3 System already provides a range of evaluation tools. You can add your own evaluations to these as required. The evaluations used as part of the monthly financial statement can also be used for researching annual data. This has the advantage that both users and management are given a uniform display structure.

Annual statement

The tasks you carry out to create an annual statement are similar to those for the monthly financial statement. The annual account is designed to provide information for internal and external recipients.

Some of the reports required by law, depending on the country, include:

- Balance Sheet, Profit and Loss statement
- tax on sales/purchases advance return
- summary report
- report in accordance with export trade legislation
- statement of cash flows

Business transactions need to be entered in chronological order (*see* section 5.2.2). This is why, in SAP R/3, the posting material is kept in a book of original entry that shows the chronological order of the postings.

Information must be given to the local tax authorities and also to other external recipients such as shareholders and banks. In particular, lenders frequently request a variety of additional information (*see* section4.1.1).

Structure of the Balance Sheet and the P&L account

The Balance Sheet and P&L account have different forms (*see* Figure 7.23 for their generation). Various degrees of detail might be required in the same company group, depending on the organization, e.g. the number of Company Codes or Business Areas. Furthermore, in the SAP R/3 System, you can create Balance Sheets and P&L statements in various languages and currencies to meet the requirements of companies that operate internationally. You can tailor the format to meet the requirements of the companies involved; for example, you can display summary information for management.

You can also select different classification schemes for commercial, tax and internal reports. Chapter 11 covers individual financial statements and deals with these points in more detail.

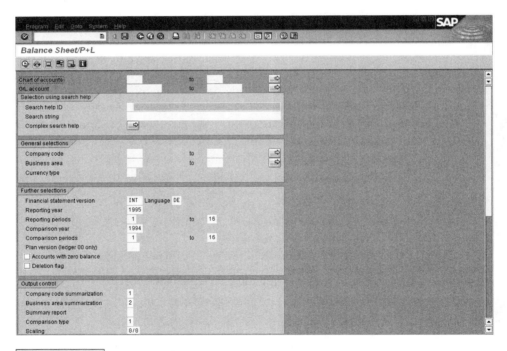

FIGURE 7.23   Balance Sheet/P&L generation (© SAP AG)

Closing tasks for the Balance Sheet and P&L account

The SAP R/3 System is an integrated system. This means that you must carry out some tasks in other modules such as Asset Accounting, Materials Management, Sales and Distribution, and Human Resources Management before you can prepare the Balance Sheet and P&L statement. In particular:

- You must enter all the relevant depreciation for this fiscal year in the Asset Accounting application component.
- In Materials Management, you must create a physical inventory to establish the inventory and carry out a valuation of materials.
- In Sales and Distribution, you must enter a goods issue for all delivery notes. The invoice linked to these delivery notes must also be available.
- All the wage and salary postings of the previous posting period must have been entered in the Human Resources Management.

The following tasks must have been carried out in the Financial Accounting application:

- foreign currency evaluation
- valuation of foreign currency stock accounts and open items that are listed in a foreign currency
- value adjustments
- correction for Accounts Receivable that are potentially or definitely not collectible, by means of a flat-rate value or individual value adjustment
- adjustment postings for vendor accounts receivable and customer accounts payable
- Adjustment of the Incoming Goods/Incoming Invoices clearing account for goods deliveries for which an invoice has not yet been presented, and vice versa for invoices for goods that have not yet been delivered.

The following two steps must be carried out in Customizing:

- transfer and sorting of accounts receivable and accounts payable
- In Europe, the classification of Accounts Receivable and Accounts Payable based on residual period according to the EU Fourth Directive (*see* section 11.7.4)

7.9   SUBLEDGERS

In the General Ledger accounting functions of the R/3 System, posting data is managed in an aggregated form. The related subledgers contain this information in more detail.

The following subledgers are part of the R/3 System's ledger, and some of these are described further below:

- Accounts Receivable
- Accounts Payable
- Asset Accounting
- Inventory Accounting
- Personnel Accounting
- Bank Accounting

7.9.1 Accounts Receivable

In the FI module, Accounts Receivable contains the accounting data for all the accounts receivable that are present in the system. The integrated structure of the SAP System means that the data is also available to the Sales and Distribution module. For example, credit and payment information is of interest to both the Sales and Distribution and to Financial Accounting.

Customer master data record

The customer master record contains all the data that describes the commercial relationship with a specific customer. In the R/3 System, master records are used by the Financial Accounting application component and also by other application components. The system's unique central storage method prevents the same data from being entered more than once. This would lead to inconsistencies in the data stored.

The customer master data record is divided into:

- a general section
- a section for individual Company Codes
- a section for sales data

General data such as a customer's name, address, telephone number and bank details is kept in the General section. Company Code data includes the reconciliation account in ledger accounting, payment terms, or the dunning procedure. Data that concerns the various roles of a customer is stored in the Sales Data section. This includes, for example, data for a ship-to business partner or an invoice-to business partner.

There is also facility to handle a One-time Customer Account ('conto pro diverse', CPD). This means you do not have to update all this data for one-time customers. The master data records only contain essential information, such as the reconciliation account. These records therefore do not contain address data, for instance, and you enter address data in the individual document.

Outgoing invoices and credit memos

If you are using the SD (Sales and Distribution) module, the system automatically posts invoices and credit memos in the Financial Accounting module when you create an invoice or credit memo in SD. If you are not using the SD module, you must create invoices and credit memos manually in the Financial Accounting module.

Processing incoming payments

In Accounts Receivable, you can process incoming payments in two ways: by computerized direct debiting, or manually, by check or bank order.

If the receipt of payment is posted manually, you must post the Payment Document itself and clear the payment item to be settled with the corresponding invoice item. To ensure that the business payment and invoice are assigned correctly, you must enter the Account Number, the Amount and the Document Number of the invoice to be cleared in the Receipt-of-payment Document. When the system balances the item, it checks whether the amount matches the amount to be paid after any reductions in customer sales price, such as cash discount or rebate, have been made. The receipt-of-payment Document is not posted unless the check for payment is actually deposited. The system then marks the item with the number of the adjustment document and the date.

If the information in a Payment Document is incomplete, the SAP R/3 System has a range of search options that you can use to find the missing information.

Dunning letters

If you want to include a customer in the SAP R/3 System's automatic dunning procedure, you must first enter a predefined dunning procedure in the Customer master data record. The dunning procedure controls the dunning cycle, the various dunning stages and any 'cooling-off' periods.

Before you can use the computerized dunning procedures, you must define when the due date check is to take place and which customer accounts the program is to check. After these checks, the SAP R/3 System creates a list of all the customer accounts receivable that it finds. You can now process these dunning proposals or, if required, prevent a dunning letter from being sent.

Like all other documents, you can modify the layout of dunning notices (reminders) to suit your own requirements. You should first check to see whether one dunning procedure and one form would meet your company's specific requirements. This avoids the time and effort involved in defining several complicated dunning procedures and forms.

Customizing background for defining the dunning program

Figure 7.24 shows the Customizing settings for automatic dunning in the SAP R/3 System.

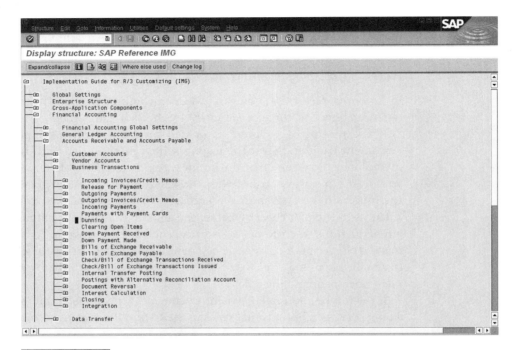

FIGURE 7.24   Customizing settings for dunning (© SAP AG)

In Customizing, you define:

- which company codes must always be included in dunning
- which dunning procedure is to be used
- which dunning costs are to be charged (you can either charge a fixed fee or a percentage of the unpaid invoice amount)
- the net due date on which a specific dunning stage is reached
- which dunning letter is to be sent to the customer

7.9.2 Accounts Payable

Accounts Payable manages all vendor accounting data.

Vendor master data record

You create the vendor master data record in exactly the same way as the customer master data record. It contains all the data required for handling the business relationship. It is subdivided into:

- General data
- Company Code data
- Purchase Organization data

Incoming invoices

If you are using the MM (Materials Management) module as well as Financial Accounting, you enter this data in the module's Invoice Check Procedure function. The Invoice Check Procedure checks the data of an incoming invoice against the data of the order and delivery. It prompts you to correct this data if any differences are found. If you do not use these functions, you must enter all invoice data manually.

Payments

In principle, the SAP R/3 System can use the payment program to handle cash transactions automatically. This is a two-stage process, similar to that used in the dunning procedure. First, the system uses the information in the documents and master records to create a payment proposal list. It uses the due dates of unpaid invoices, proposes appropriate payment methods, and selects bank information. As in all other areas of the SAP System, this automatic processing is only possible if the master records have been set up correctly and are updated continuously.

The terms of payment define an invoice's due date. Here, the R/3 System distinguishes between multilevel terms of payment with a maximum of two cash-discount dates and one net-payment date. The system selects the method of payment and the banks, based on the amount due, the currency, the liquid funds, the vendor's location and the location of the company bank.

You can edit the resulting list. You then use this revised proposal list as the basis for the posting documents and payment forms that you create next. You can then transfer this information directly to the company bank by remote data transfer, because the interfaces to the programs used by the banks have already been set up. Many banks use standard formats for data transfer, such as SWIFT.

You can also use the payment program to make down payments and to regulate payments with bills of exchange.

Customizing background for defining the payment program

Figure 7.25 shows the Customizing settings for automatic payments in the SAP R/3 System.

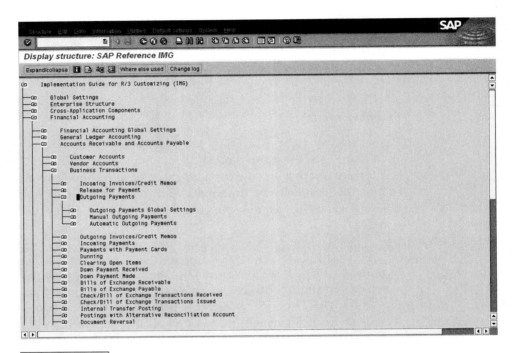

FIGURE 7.25   Customizing settings for the automatic payments program (© SAP AG)

In Customizing, you must define:

- which company codes always take part in cash transactions and which company codes are to handle payments
- which methods of payment are to be used in each case (a method of payment is the process used to make the payments, e.g. check, bank order or bill of exchange)
- from which bank account(s) the payment is to be made
- the form (document) to be used for payment

7.9.3 Asset Accounting

Asset accounting administers and monitors a company's fixed assets. The following functions are integrated in it:

▓ Asset accounting and valuation

▓ Leasing management

▓ Consolidation preparation

▓ Information system

In asset accounting, the entire history of a fixed asset, from its being ordered to its withdrawal from use, is shown in accounting form. Depreciation, interest or insurance is determined, posted and provided for analysis. This is why asset accounting is linked to a great many other modules of the SAP R/3 System. You can use the Materials Management modules to enter incoming goods directly into an Asset account. Leasing management is also part of the standard version of the System. You can use depreciation forecasts or simulations of the development of values in the assets to plan accounting measures.

7.10	**BILLS OF EXCHANGE**

A **bill of exchange** is a contractual security whereby the person issuing the bill places himself/herself or a third party under an obligation to pay a certain sum within a certain period. The recipient of the payment is called the **payee** and the person paying is the **drawee**. Bills of exchange are common in many European countries as a means of payment and thus feature in accounting processes. *See* Figure 7.26 for how they are catered for in the SAP R/3 System.

If the drawee of the bill of exchange is obliged to pay the sum of the bill himself, the bill of exchange is called a **promissory note** or **negotiable note**. If the drawee promises that a third party will pay, the bill of exchange is called a **drawn bill of exchange**. A drawn bill of exchange is more valuable because more than one person is liable for the sum, i.e. the drawee and the issuer (as 'regress' debtor – see later in section).

Generally speaking, anyone who signs a bill of exchange is liable for the sum. As long as the drawee has not signed the bill, there is no obligation to pay. This is called a **draft**. If the drawee signs, this is an **accepted** bill.

The laws regulating bills of exchange are generally based on articles, as they are of international origin. In accordance with the international law governing bills of exchange, many countries' legal systems have laws based on articles. This means that the chances of encountering bill-of-exchange laws that correspond to the local laws are relatively high. The formats mentioned below as an example are based on German legislation. Although the laws for bills of exchange are similar in other European countries, note that the formats are not always exactly the same.

▓ 'To B or its order': payment to B or someone named by B. This means that the payee can give an instruction that payment is not to be made to him but to a third party.

▓ 'to the order of . . .': payment to the person named.

A bill of exchange merely documents the legal aspects of payment claims. This makes a bill of exchange easier to use. This is why the owner function of the bill of exchange is also strictly defined. The person who is in possession of a bill of exchange and is formally legitimated by it is regarded as the creditor. The payee, of course, is also formally legitimated, as are any others who are to become new creditors if the bill is transferred by endorsement.

In the interests of preserving the bill of exchange as a means of payment, it is given priority in court cases. Very short summons periods apply here. Only official documents may be brought as evidence. The drawee of a bill of exchange can therefore only lodge objections that result directly from the document and not from the business transaction involved. Law dictates that a distinction must be made between the liability for acceptance and liability for payment. This is because the acceptance must already have been made, although the payment may be due later. This means that liability for the acceptance takes effect earlier.

7.10.1 Bill of exchange strictness

To create the required legal security, bills of exchange are subject to strict legal requirements. These requirements and the strict regulation of liability are referred to as *bill of exchange strictness*. This includes the greatly simplified and shortened court procedure in bill of exchange litigation.

A bill of exchange can be written on any sheet of paper, but only counts as a bill of exchange if it meets the legal requirements. In accordance with these legal requirements, the designation as a bill of exchange must appear in the text of the document, in the language in which it is issued. It must also consist of the following components:

- the unconditional instruction to remit a certain sum of money
- the name of the person who is to pay (the drawee)
- a specified expiry date
- a specified place of payment
- the name of the person to whom or to whose order the payment is to be made
- a specified day and place of issue
- the signature of the issuer

There are some exceptions to the above requirements:

- *Definition of a sight draft*: A bill of exchange without a specified expiry date is a *sight draft*.
- If the place of payment is not stated on the bill of exchange, the legal residence of the drawee is regarded as the place of payment.
- If the place where the bill of exchange was issued is missing, the legal residence of the issuer is assumed instead.

There are also ways in which the structure of a bill of exchange can vary. Although, normally, the issuer places the drawee under an obligation to make payment to the payee, and all three participants are different people, the following variations can apply:

- *The issuer can also be the drawee.* The issuer and the drawee can be the same person. Naturally this reduces the value of the bill of exchange. In this case, a certain person is only promising that they will pay.

- *The issuer can also be the payee.* The drawee can be under an obligation to make payment to the issuer.

- *The issuer places itself under obligation.* The issuer can place itself under obligation to pay to itself. At first glance, this does not appear to make any sense, but it is possible.

It does not matter who is the starting point of a bill of exchange. The decisive factor is that the statutory requirements for a bill of exchange have been met.

7.10.2 Accepting a bill of exchange

The drawee must sign a bill to confirm that the drawee is actually under obligation to pay. When the issuer issues a bill of exchange, the drawee is initially only empowered to pay to the payee. In this case, the payment is settled with the issuer and the sum is covered. The obligation of the bill only comes about with acceptance. This is also referred to as *crossing*.

However, acceptance is not a legal transaction. The core of the matter is that the drawee wishes to enter into an obligation (private autonomy). An obligation of this nature (towards another person) cannot happen from one side only. For this reason, at least two people are always required to create an obligation. There must be two matching declarations of intent. Here, the drawee is not under obligation to make this declaration of intent (at least not according to the laws governing bills of exchange in some countries).

In accordance with the theory of contract, a contract must be present. The declaration of acceptance from the drawee is addressed to the payee, not the issuer. The issuer, who later transfers the accepted bill of exchange to the payee, is merely the transferor of this declaration. When the payee receives the bill of exchange and in doing so accepts the declaration of acceptance of the drawee (second declaration of intent, the 'acceptance'), a mutual contractual obligation comes about between this person and the drawee. Here the drawee is now referred to as the acceptor. This mutual contractual obligation is completely removed from the original relationship and it consists of the formation of an independent exchange obligation.

If the drawee refuses the acceptance, the payee or the current holder of the bill of exchange has no legal claim to submission of the declaration of acceptance. In such cases, the relevant holder of the bill of exchange has a legal claim only against the previous holders in each case.

7.10.3 Transferring a bill of exchange

A bill of exchange is transferred by being handed over and endorsed. The transferor is the endorser and the recipient is the endorsee.

Although an effective endorsement can be made by someone who would not be entitled to do so from a material point of view, this person must fulfil the formal legal requirements for entitlement. The only person with formal legal authorization is the person defined in the bill of exchange as having this authorization. This person must be in possession of the bill of exchange. It must also be clear, from a corresponding chain of endorsers, that this person has formal legal entitlement.

When an issuer passes a bill of exchange to the payee, from the point of view of natural law they are showing intent not only to give the payee the actual paper but also the ownership involved. If the bill of exchange has already been accepted, the payee taking possession of the paper takes possession of the bill's claim towards the acceptor.

Further transfer of a bill of exchange

Frequently, a payee also wishes to pass on a bill of exchange, e.g. to a creditor, who takes the bill in lieu of payment, or to a bank, which purchases the bill (probably with some discounting). The payee agrees with the new owner that the ownership of the paper, and therefore all the rights from the paper, are transferred to the new owner. The bill of exchange itself is also surrendered. An endorsement is also required. This is placed on the reverse side of the bill and is different from the instruction on the face of the bill.

The possible forms of transfer depend entirely on the completely different time sequences that are possible. It may happen that the issuer might want to transfer the bill of exchange to the payee.

In spite of its abstract nature, a mutual transfer contract may have flaws, for instance because the previous owner had no entitlement (who may have, for example, stolen the bill of exchange from its previous holder and forged that holder's endorsement) or because the previous holder was not qualified to do business (bankrupt, a minor etc.) and the agreement with the next owner was null and void. In such cases, it is possible to purchase a bill of exchange in good faith, provided there is an unbroken chain of endorsers who apparently have legal authorization running from the payee to the purchaser.

Modified contract theory only protects the good faith if there is an obligation from the contract. Good faith in the existence of other facts, e.g. the existence of a legal document of entitlement, is not protected. The law governing bills of exchange states that only the immediately previous owner needs to have formal legitimization (demonstrated by the chain stretching back to the issuer).

7.10.4 Causal debt versus bill-of-exchange debt

A bill of exchange always produces an abstract claim in the same way as an abstract promise. The debt relationship is referred to as ***abstract*** because the bill of exchange does not imply its legal reason – as is the case, for example, with a purchase price liability. In contrast to the bill of exchange, the legal reason in the case of a claim, namely the conclusion of a contract of purchase, is already included. However, the bill of exchange also requires a reason.

7.10.5 Payment and fulfilment

When the drawee pays the rightful owner of a bill, all the causal relationships on which it is based and all the base legal transactions on which the surrender or transfer of a bill of exchange are based are terminated.

The owner of a bill of exchange can demand payment on the due date.

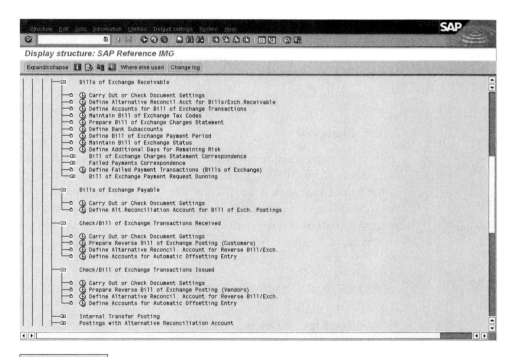

FIGURE 7.26   Customizing settings for a bill of exchange (© SAP AG)

When the owner who demands payment of a bill of exchange is not entitled to do so from a material law point of view, the drawee is unable to fulfil the demand. Only payment to the legally entitled person counts as fulfilment, although the law defines one exception. The payment that represents exceptional fulfilment as defined by law does not take place from the time of gross negligence. However, with a view to the circulation capability of the bill of exchange, gross negligence can only be assumed when the payer is in possession of 'liquid evidence'. Evidence of this kind will certainly be the same as what could be considered in bill of exchange litigation: this is practically non-existent.

When payment is made, the bill of exchange must be handed over. Otherwise there is a risk that, for formal reasons, a second payment must be made.

A **bill of exchange protest** is the formal documentation stating that a bill of exchange has not paid when due.

Regress

Regress, also known as **recourse**, can be used in two cases:

- when the drawee does not pay
- when the drawee does not accept liability to pay

The further back the regress is traced down the chain of those under obligation to a bill, the more expensive it becomes (due to legal fees). This is why the law provides a certain protection so that the issuer can ensure payment as quickly as possible before the costs build up.

7.10.6 Blank bill

Only deliberate omissions on a bill of exchange (excluding the signature) lead to the description **blank bill**. In law, this kind of bill of exchange is not yet a bill.

If a bill of exchange is incomplete, the owner is entitled to make additions to the bill so that it becomes a bill of exchange as defined by law. This legal act is referred to as **authorization**. It represents a separate legal institution. However, a blank bill is not involved when a key feature has been omitted on purpose.

7.11　REPORTING

An important task for users and management in Financial Accounting is the analysis of, and planning with, information from Financial Accounting. The extended ledger and financial-control functions are used here. You can also use the Report Writer to generate reports in a flexible manner.

Make a report selection is via a drop-down menu, as shown in Figure 7.27.

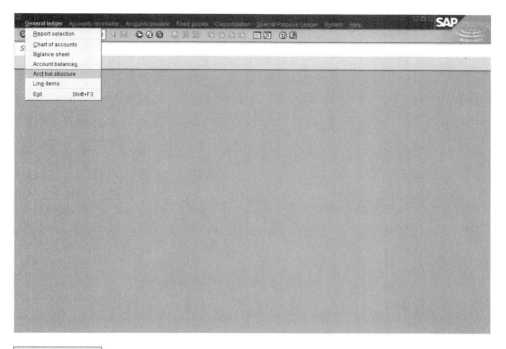

FIGURE 7.27   Initiating report selection (© SAP AG)

CHAPTER 8

Taxation of sales/purchases in the IMG

8.1 TRADING TAXES

Taxation of sales/purchases yields one of the **trading taxes**, i.e. it is linked to certain trading transactions but not to economic success or total assets. The tax is imposed when the income is used. The gross value (e.g. the price/fee paid) is usually used as the basis for assessment. The personal circumstances of the contracting partners have no influence on the obligation to pay tax and the amount of the tax debt. This means that the tax on sales/purchases is object-specific.

In most European countries, tax on sales/purchases is a significant source of government revenue. In general, it is determined in two ways:

- one-phase tax (where turnover is taxed only once)
- all-phase tax (where turnover is taxed at all levels)

These are illustrated in Figure 8.1.

With an all-phase system, the recipient of goods/services, insofar as that person is a trader and not a consumer, can always demand from the tax creditor with the price a rebate of the tax on sales/purchases invoiced, referred to as input tax. In this system, the added value of the company's goods/services being purchased is added to the previous turnover at every subsequent stage in the sales chain. The term **value-added tax**, or **VAT**, sometimes used (primarily in Europe) instead of **sales tax**, comes from the fact that the added value is recorded at every subsequent trading stage.

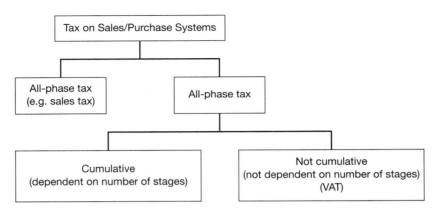

FIGURE 8.1   Systems used to determine tax on sales/purchases (© SAP AG)

The sales that a trader makes from its activities on the domestic market are subject to tax on sales/purchases. In its broadest sense, this means that all sales of economic goods and services are taxed. The point at which tax comes into the equation is in relation to economic trading transactions. Companies are intended only to be taxpayers, and final consumers are the *ultimate* taxpayers. Many countries have a fixed tax rate for all goods. However, there may be a reduced tax rate on food, magazines or goods related to culture. This is similar to sales tax plans, as in the United States. There, in some states, a flat rate applies to all purchases; in others, food is exempted; and in yet others, some states have no sales tax since revenue is generated from other sources.

The types of revenue listed below may be taxable, whereby these in turn must be checked to see whether they are exempt from tax:

- sales of goods/services
    - deliveries
    - other goods/services
- own consumption
    - withdrawal of objects
    - withdrawal of other goods/services
    - incurred non-deductible operating expenses
- owner consumption (deliveries without charge and the goods/services from sole traders, partnerships or joint stock companies to their owners)
- imports
- intra-community acquisitions

The following facts determine taxability and obligation to pay tax on a transaction:

- The revenue must have been generated by a trader (as defined by law).
- The deliveries and goods/services must have been provided within the framework of a company.

■ The revenue must have been achieved in the country of residence.

■ The transaction must involve goods/services provided for a charge.

8.2 HANDLING THE INPUT TAX DEDUCTION

The core of the net all-phase tax on sales/purchases system is the *input tax deduction*.

Taxation on sales/purchases only places a material burden on those who are unable to deduct the tax on sales/purchases paid as input tax, i.e. the final consumer. This means that input tax deduction is the right to deduct from the tax on sales/purchases debt those tax amounts that have been paid in purchasing goods/services from companies or traders (*see* Figure 8.2). In the case of imports, the relationship is with the import duty authorities.

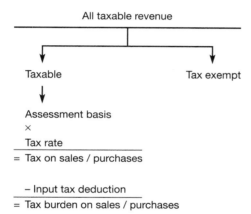

FIGURE 8.2 Determining the net tax burden (© SAP AG)

For the entitlement to deduct input tax, the following five requirements must be met:

1 There must be an invoice.

2 The tax on sales/purchases must be shown separately.

3 The provider of goods/services must be a trader.

4 The goods/services must be provided for the company of the recipient.

5 The goods/services must have been respectively delivered/performed.

Input tax amounts need to be differentiated into three categories for separate actions – *see* Table 8.1.

TABLE 8.1	Differentiating between the input tax amounts	
Deductible input tax amounts	**Non-deductible input tax amounts**	**Partly non-deductible input tax amounts**
Input tax amounts are only fully deductible if they can be apportioned to commercially deductible turnover.	Input tax amounts are not deductible if they are apportionable to secondary turnover.	Input tax amounts are partially non-deductible if they are (commercially) partial secondary turnover. The non-deductible portion is determined according to economic assignment.

8.3 HANDLING TAX-EXEMPT REVENUE

The aim of non-taxation is to relieve the burden on the consumer. For example, the following items are exempt from tax on sales/purchases:

- export sales
- money transactions
- sales in relation to social and cultural activities
- renting and leasing of real estate

Tax exemptions can be categorized according to their effects:

- tax-exempt sales with input tax deduction
- tax-exempt sales without option rights
- tax-exempt sales with option rights

Tax-exempt sales with input tax deduction lead to *full exemption from tax* on sales/purchases. If the input tax deduction remains, this implies that the sales are export sales.

Tax-exempt sales without option rights can lead to a tax reduction or a tax increase. The sales lead to a tax *increase* if tax exemption involves the prohibition of input tax deduction and the trader supplies to final consumer, *final-stage exemption* is permitted and this leads to a tax reduction. If tax exemption involves the prohibition of input tax deduction and the trader supplies to another trader, *intermediate-stage exemption* is permitted and this leads to a tax increase.

Examples of tax-exempt sales with option rights are:

- property ownership
- banking
- gold trading
- land leasing

Prohibition of input taxation deduction in the case of export of tax-exempt turnover can lead to disadvantages in companies. These disadvantages would violate the system and would therefore be undesirable. For this reason, companies are legally entitled to forgo certain exemptions if the revenue is exported to another trader for their company. The purpose of options of this kind is to be able to deduct the input tax paid in this case.

8.3.1 A worked example

The effects of tax exemptions are explained below on the basis of an example, where C1, C2 and C3 are companies at different points of the value-added chain. A tax on sales/purchases rate of 16% is used and invoice amounts in euros are assumed.

As can be seen from the example, because the tax-exempt goods/services serve as advance goods/services to the subsequent companies, they increase the basis for assessment of tax on sales/purchases. The cumulative effect that this creates is contrary to the concept of net tax on sales/purchases: i.e. it represents tax including sales/purchases including tax on sales/purchases!

Initial position

The initial situation in our example scenario is set out in Figure 8.3.

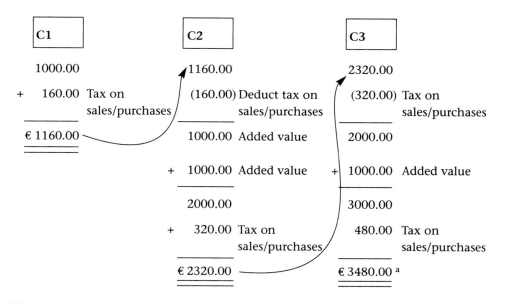

| **FIGURE 8.3** | Tax example: initial position (© SAP AG) |

Note: [a] €480 of the total for C3 is tax on sales/purchases.

Full exemption

On the one hand, the input tax can be deducted; on the other hand, no further tax on sales/purchases has to be charged. *See* Figure 8.4.

C3	
2320.00	
(320.00)	Tax on sales/purchases
2000.00	
+ 1000.00	Value added
3000.00	
(0.00)	Tax on sales/purchases
€3000.00	

FIGURE 8.4   Tax example: full exemption (© SAP AG)

Final-stage exemption

This kind of exemption occurs with doctors, for example. An example (using company C3) is shown in Figure 8.5; it results in a tax reduction (*see* C3 final price compared with the € initial position)

Intermediate-stage exemption

This situation is shown in Figure 8.6. This tax exemption has the effect of a tax increase, as shown in C3's end prices being greater than the initial position.

8.4   BASIS FOR ASSESSMENT OF TAX

The tax rate must be applied to a generally applicable assessment basis. The basis for assessment is a sum of money (in euros, for example, in the eurozone). All taxable revenue must therefore be expressed in a base amount.

The basis for assessment for deliveries and other activities is, in principle, the remuneration (as legally defined). **Remuneration** is defined as everything that the recipient of the goods/services uses in order to obtain the goods/services (but minus tax on

C3

2320.00

(0.00) [a]   Tax on sales/purchases
_____

2320.00

+ 1000.00   Value added
_____

3320.00

(0.00)   Tax on
sales/purchases
_____

€3320.00 [b]

FIGURE 8.5   Tax example: final-stage exemption (© SAP AG)
Notes: [a] No input tax can be deducted here and no further tax on sales/purchases can be charged to the purchaser.
[b] Instead of €3480.00 as in the initial position, the consumer now pays only €330.00.

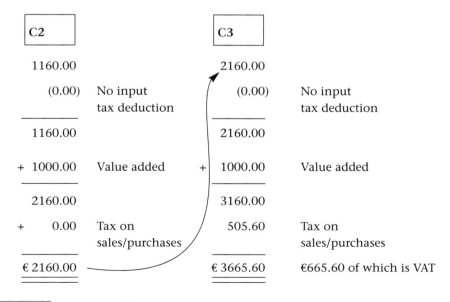

C2

1160.00

(0.00)   No input
tax deduction
_____

1160.00

+ 1000.00   Value added
_____

2160.00

+   0.00   Tax on
sales/purchases
_____

€ 2160.00

C3

2160.00

(0.00)   No input
tax deduction
_____

2160.00

+ 1000.00   Value added
_____

3160.00

505.60   Tax on
sales/purchases
_____

€ 3665.60   €665.60 of which is VAT

FIGURE 8.6   Tax example: intermediate-stage exemption (© SAP AG)

sales/purchases). Remuneration is reduced by price reductions (cash discounts and other discounts) and increased by incremental expenses (extra charges). The basis for assessment is always the agreed remuneration (nominal taxation, legally defined).

If the Customizing settings and/or the master records are correctly maintained in General Ledger accounting (using the Account Number of the tax account and a Posting Key) in the SAP R/3 System, the system automatically generates the tax items when a Document is posted.

8.5 CUSTOMIZING SETTINGS FOR TAX

In Customizing in the R/3 System, you must make general settings, as well as those used to calculate and post tax on sales/purchases. You must also enter data for input tax on sales/purchases returns and post-payment of tax on sales/purchases. Figure 8.7 shows these points, which must be processed at various places in the IMG.

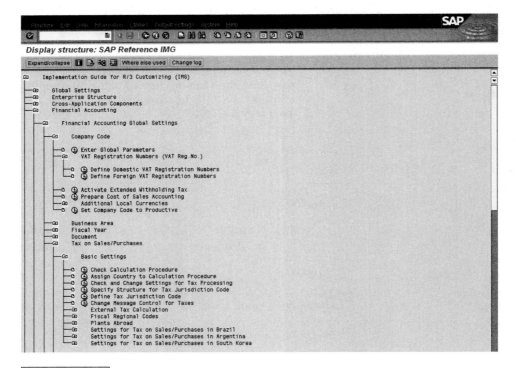

FIGURE 8.7   (a) Settings for tax on sales/purchases in the IMG (© SAP AG)

8.5.1 VAT Number settings

This entire section (8.5.1), and the rest of this chapter, describe the VAT functionality in the SAP System. Although it primarily applies to countries that are member states of the European Union, regardless of whether they have joined monetary union (***the eurozone***) or not, it can also be used by US companies or others in countries that have sales tax.

```
├─ ⊟   Calculation
│   ├─ ▢ ⊕ Define Tax Codes for Sales and Purchases
│   ├─ ▢ ⊕ Assign Company Code to Document Date for Tax Determination
│   ├─ ▢ ⊕ Specify Base Amount
│   ├─ ▢ ⊕ Change Foreign Currency Translation
│   ├─ ⊞    Settings for Tax Calculation in Brazil
│   └─ ⊞    Settings for Tax Calculation in Argentina
└─ ⊟   Posting
    ├─ ▢ ⊕ Define Tax Accounts
    ├─ ▢ ⊕ Define Account for Exchange Rate Difference Posting
    ├─ ▢ ⊕ Assign Tax Codes for Non-Taxable Transactions
    └─ ▢ ⊕ Transfer Posting of Tax for Cross-Company Code Transactions
├─ ⊞   Withholding Tax
├─ ⊞   Inflation
├─ ⊞   Correspondence
├─ ⊞   Financial Calendar
├─ ▢ ⊕ Use Business Transaction Events
├─ ⊞   Accounting Document Data Transfer
├─ ▢ ⊕ Delete Transaction Data
└─ ▢ ⊕ Maintain Authorizations

└─ ⊟ General Ledger Accounting
    ├─ ⊞   G/L Accounts
    └─ ⊟   Accounting Transactions
        ├─ ⊞   G/L Account Posting
        ├─ ▢ ⊕ Prepare Cross-Company Code Transactions
        ├─ ⊞   Open Item Clearing
        ├─ ⊞   Bank Account Interest Calculation
        ├─ ⊞   Document Reversal
        ├─ ⊞   Planning
        └─ ⊟   Closing
            ├─ ⊞   Valuating
            ├─ ⊞   Regrouping
            ├─ ⊞   Documenting
            └─ ⊟   Reporting
                ├─ ⊞   Sales/Purchases Tax Returns
                ├─ ⊞   Subsequent Tax on Sales/Purchases Debit
                ├─ ⊞   Withholding Tax: Reporting to Vendor
                └─ ⊞   Extended Withholding Tax: Reporting
```

FIGURE 8.7   (b) Settings for tax on sales/purchases in the IMG (© SAP AG)

```
            ├─ ⊞   German Foreign Trade Regulations
            ├─ ⊞   Statutory Reporting: Brazil
            └─ ⊞   Statutory Reporting: Argentina
        └─ ⊞   Carrying Forward
    └─ ⊞ Integration
    ├─ ⊞   Transfer G/L Account Master Data
    └─ ⊞   Information System
├─ ⊞   Accounts Receivable and Accounts Payable
├─ ⊞   Bank Accounting
├─ ⊞   Legal Consolidation
├─ ⊞   Consolidation Preparation
├─ ⊞   Asset Accounting
├─ ⊞   Special Purpose Ledger
├─ ⊞   Funds Management
└─ ⊞   Travel Management
├─ ⊞ Treasury
├─ ⊞ Controlling
├─ ⊞ Investment Management
├─ ⊞ Enterprise Controlling
├─ ⊞ Real Estate Management
├─ ⊞ Logistics - General
├─ ⊞ Environment, Health & Safety
├─ ⊞ Sales and Distribution
├─ ⊞ Materials Management
├─ ⊞ Logistics Execution
├─ ⊞ Quality Management
├─ ⊞ Plant Maintenance and Service Management
├─ ⊞ Customer Service and Customer Interaction Center
├─ ⊞ Production
├─ ⊞ Production Planning for Process Industries
├─ ⊞ Project System
├─ ⊞ Personnel Management
├─ ⊞ Personnel Time Management
├─ ⊞ Payroll Accounting
├─ ⊞ Training and Event Management
└─ ⊞ Basis Components
```

FIGURE 8.7   (c) Settings for tax on sales/purchases in the IMG (© SAP AG)

Assignment and structure of VAT Number

Since 1 January 1993, there have been no customs and excise checks at the internal borders of the European Union. Since then, a temporary rule for tax on sales/purchases has been in force for intra-community trade between traders. According to this rule, goods continue to be exempt as they cross internal community borders and a tax on sales/purchases burden is only imposed in the country of destination.

Intra-community trade is when a purchased object is delivered to a domestic purchaser from another EU member state in or from the remaining community territory, i.e. from another EU member state, that purchaser being in a tax-exempt area (e.g. a free port). This also applies when the trader (supplier) has previously imported the object into the community territory. The requirement is that the supplier of the object is a trader and is exporting the delivery within the framework of its company. The exception is the acquisition of a vehicle; in this case, the intra-community acquisition principle does not require that the vehicle supplier is a trader supplying goods or products within the framework of its company. In addition, the use of intra-community job processing is regarded as intra-community acquisition. Intra-community job processing occurs when the objects handed over by the principal, as a result of a general agreement, are used to manufacture an object with another function in the other community territory and this object is sent to the principal in its own country.

In order to enable implementation of this temporary value-added tax regulation, all those involved are assigned a VAT number. This must be applied for in writing. Instead of filling out a form, the applicant makes an application that details their name and address, tax number under which the applicant is registered for tax on sales/purchases, and the name of their regional tax authority, responsible for collecting tax on sales/purchases.

The VAT number is a combination of several letters and numbers. The first two digits are the letters that form the so-called 'national code' to identify the relevant member state in which the number is issued (e.g. GB = Britain). VAT numbers have a combination of a maximum of 12 numbers or letters after the national code. It is important that the VAT number is not identical to the tax number.

In the SAP System, you maintain the company's own VAT Number in the global settings for the Company Code (section 7.1.2). Figures 8.8 and 8.9 show where you enter this setting.

Who has to apply for a VAT number?

A VAT number is required by traders who take part in intra-community trade in goods and services. It is also required by legal entities, which are not traders, if they purchase objects on an intra-community basis that are not intended for the company. It is essential that each legal entity is only ever assigned one VAT number. This is particularly important for legal entities that are traders and purchase objects on an intra-community basis both for the company and for non-company areas. Legal entities that are not traders must (by law) pay tax as intra-community purchases on goods purchased from other member states if for the individual purchaser the total

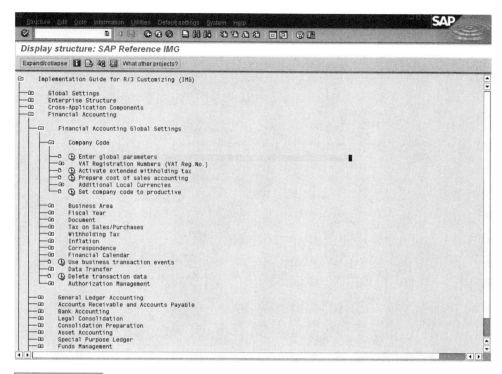

FIGURE 8.8 Global parameters for the Company Code (© SAP AG)

amount of remuneration paid for the acquisitions (net price without tax on sales/purchases) exceeded the amount specified by local tax authorities in the preceding year and/or is likely to exceed this amount in the current year.

Because VAT Number is set in Customizing, it is automatically used for orders. The contracting partner in other EU countries can therefore see that tax-free deliveries are possible. This also means that the partner can include the tax-free intra-community deliveries in its summarizing reports by entering the VAT Number of the persons/companies that place orders.

8.5.2 Basic settings

The basic Customizing settings for tax on sales/purchases include the calculation routine that contains the details required to calculate and post the tax on sales/purchases. The standard version of the SAP System already contains one or more predefined calculation routines for each country. Each calculation comprises several types of tax. These are called Condition Types in the calculation routine (e.g. initial tax, input tax). Each routine also specifies calculation regulations for these Condition Types. You should not change the default Condition Types and calculation routines. However, you should check that they are sufficient to meet your company's needs.

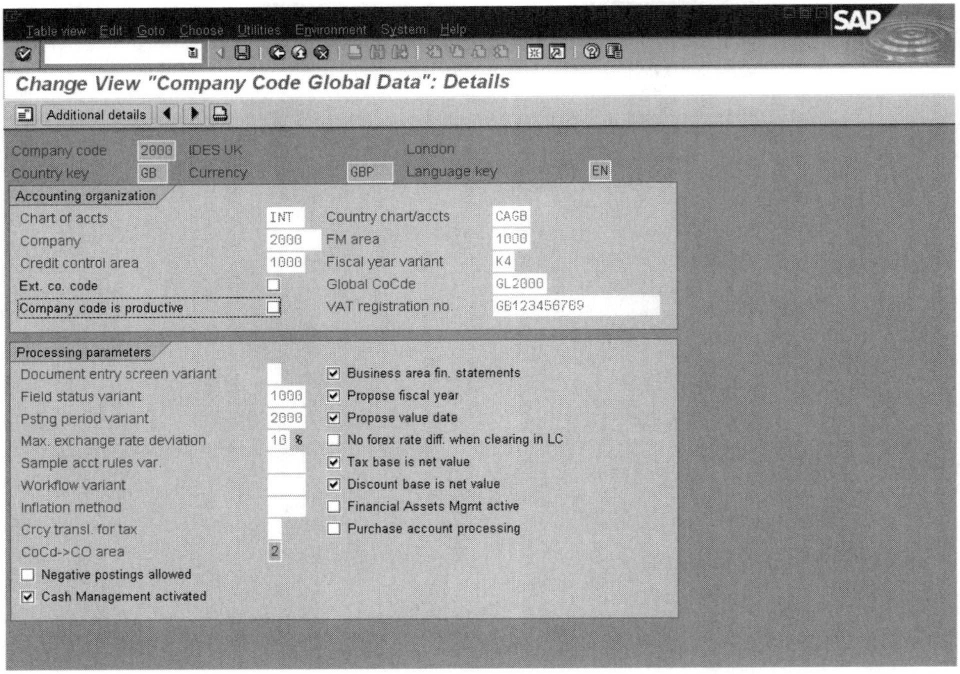

FIGURE 8.9 Maintaining a company's VAT Number (© SAP AG)

A calculation routine contains information about which amount is to be charged for the individual Condition Types. This may be the base amount (total of cost and revenue items) or a subtotal, and is specified in the 'frmTx' column.

The other basic settings for tax on sales/purchases in the standard version of the SAP System are default settings. You should only assign or check these settings, as the case may be.

From Release 4.0 onwards, the SAP R/3 System contains an option for processing tax returns for Warehouses, Sales Offices or Plants in foreign countries within the domestic Company Code. However, this function must be specifically enabled in Customizing.

8.5.3 Calculating the tax

Before the R/3 System can automatically calculate the trading tax for postings, you must define the tax on sales/purchases codes for each country. Each code represents one or more tax rates for different types of tax. The standard version of the system already contains the tax on sales/purchases codes for most countries. You should check these codes to ensure that they are correct (*see* Figure. 8.10).

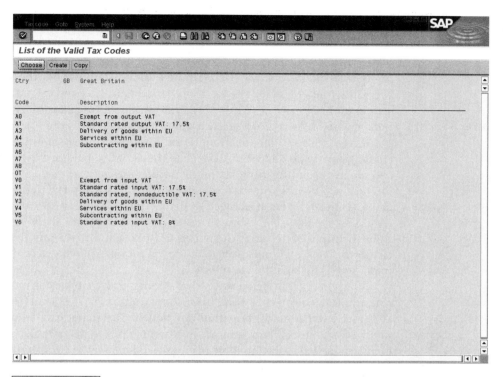

FIGURE 8.10 List of valid sales/purchase tax codes in the SAP R/3 System (© SAP AG)

You must take care not to delete or change the tax on sales/purchases codes or the associated definitions, as long as items with these tax on sales/purchases codes are stored in the system. If you did happen to, the tax amounts would appear with the incorrect tax rates in the corresponding returns and would also lead to incorrect amounts for payment transactions. For some countries, the standard version of the R/3 System already contains predefined sample tax codes.

8.5.4 Posting the tax

You need to specify the accounts to which the various types of tax are to be posted. The system requires these accounts so that it can post tax on sales/purchases automatically.

If a transaction covers several Company Codes, the standard procedure is that all the tax is only assigned and posted to the first Company Code. The tax due for other Company Codes is not taken into consideration.

8.5.5 Input tax and post-payment

Tax on sales/purchases is an assessed tax, i.e., it is determined by the tax authority (where required by law) and the trader, as tax debtor, receives a corresponding notice of tax assessment. The tax is determined for a certain period, the so-called taxation period (defined by law). The taxation period is usually the calendar year, but it can also comprise part of the calendar year (a month or quarter). This also applies to traders who are permitted to use a different fiscal year as the basis for calculation of profit. On expiry of the taxation period, the trader must submit a tax on sales/purchases return. The trader must calculate the tax to be paid or the surplus in its favour and report this in the input tax on sales/purchases return.

The tax return is regarded as the means of providing the defined amount of tax payable, though this is subject to inspection. The relevant tax authority is only required to establish the tax on sales/purchases payable if the tax return deviates from the input tax return. The return must be submitted using the appropriate official form. The trader must calculate the tax on sales/purchases in the tax return. The trader must also sign the tax return.

Initially, tax from deliveries, other goods/services, own consumption and intra-community acquisition in the taxation period has to be calculated. If relevant, tax amounts owed from other periods are added. The trader can deduct the deductible input tax amounts incurred in the taxation period (*see* sections 8.1 and 8.2). This also includes the deductible import tax on sales/purchases paid within the taxation period or to be paid by a certain day after the end of the advance return period (depending on the country's tax regulations).

If tax has been correctly calculated by a trader, the tax authority confirms this amount; otherwise it calculates the tax itself and states it accordingly. For example, the regulations regarding petty amounts could stipulate that a tax statement that deviates to the disadvantage of the person liable for tax is only considered if the deviation is at least €10.00. If the trader does not submit a tax return, the tax authority must estimate the tax. After the statement is issued by the tax authority and advance payments are deducted, there is a payment or rebate of the differing tax on sales/purchases amount, as the case may be.

The obligation to make advance tax payments is defined by local law. The advance payments are generally calculated by the trader in its advance returns and submitted to the relevant tax authority. In contrast to the annual return, the advance returns do not need to be signed by the trader; however, the advance return must be submitted on official forms. The forms are regarded as tax statements, though this is subject to inspection. The calculation of tax is regulated by law.

The standard version of the SAP R/3 System contains predefined tax forms. The system uses the posted Documents to generate any necessary advance returns (using country-specific reports). When this happens, the tax rates are established on a country-specific basis to define the tax codes.

CHAPTER 9

Withholding tax

9.1 THE PRINCIPLE

European countries such as Switzerland or Great Britain work with this kind of taxation. **Withholding tax** is assessed at the start of the flow of payment and is paid to domestic tax authorities by the payer and not by the legal taxpayer.

In some countries, withholding tax only has to be reported to the local tax authorities by a certain group of creditors. The periods for returns and settlement intervals are country-specific.

9.1.1 Example of calculation of withholding tax in the SAP R/3 System

In the SAP R/3 System you have to enter and balance the incoming invoice of a creditor who is obliged to pay withholding tax. The total amount of our example invoice contains a prior tax of 16% and shows a total of €116.00.

Suppose that the withholding tax rate is 20%. For withholding tax, the net amount is used as a basis, i.e. the tax on sales/purchases is not considered.

First, the total amount is booked into an expense account and the vendor account. You can have the prior tax calculated automatically by the system, or enter it manually. The R/3 System calculates the base withholding tax amount of €100.00 and recognizes the withholding tax code at the level of the Document item.

When the open item is balanced, the system automatically calculates the withholding tax of €20.00 and posts it to the Withholding Tax account. The creditor item is balanced. The amount of the invoice is reduced by the withholding tax and the sum of €96.00 is paid by the bank.

9.2 A TIME-DEPENDENT DEFINITION

Withholding tax may vary over time. You can define a period of validity for all settings in the SAP R/3 System to create a time-dependent definition for the settings.

9.3 'SIMPLE' VERSUS 'EXTENDED'

From Release 4.0 onwards, the SAP R/3 System provides two different methods of handling withholding tax: 'simple' and 'extended' withholding tax (*see* Figure. 9.1).

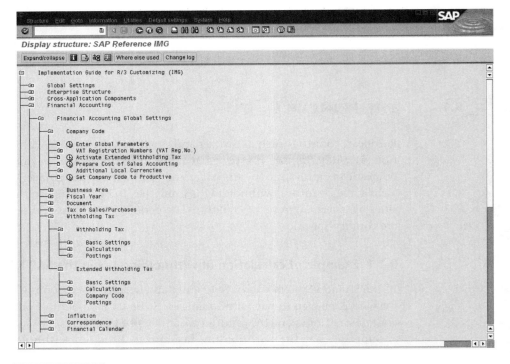

FIGURE 9.1 Withholding tax in SAP Customizing (© SAP AG)

9.3.1 'Simple' withholding tax

Simple Withholding Tax within R/3 (*see* Figure 9.2) supports:

- creditor withholding tax
- withholding tax calculation for payment
- one withholding tax code per creditor line

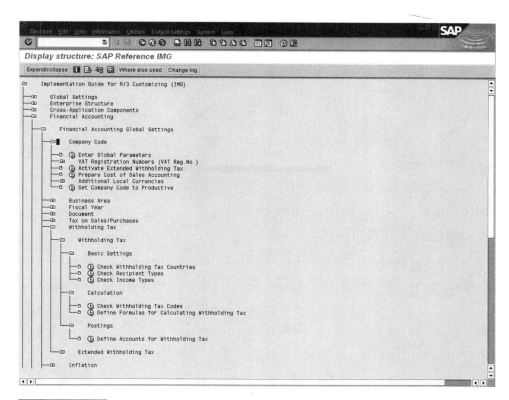

FIGURE 9.2   Customizing path for Simple Withholding Tax (© SAP AG)

9.3.2 'Extended' withholding tax

Extended Withholding Tax within the SAP R/3 System (*see* Figure 9.3) provides the following functions:

- several independent withholding taxes per creditor and debtor item
- proportional withholding tax for part payments
- extensions in the calculation of withholding tax
- calculation and posting of withholding tax when recording the invoice and on payment

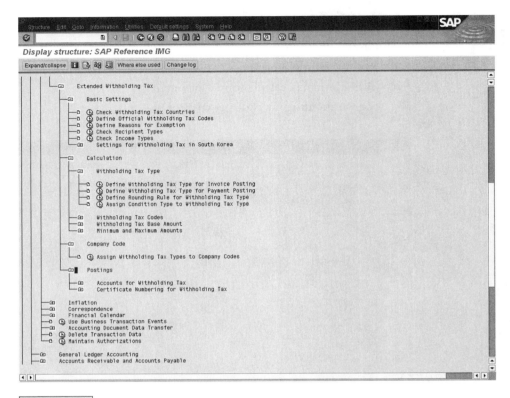

FIGURE 9.3 Customizing path for Extended Withholding Tax (© SAP AG)

CHAPTER 10

Current replacement cost and reinstatement value

In addition to the original acquisition costs or the original manufacturing costs, the SAP R/3 System can also record another, higher value for fixed assets. This is the current replacement cost.

The reason for the higher current replacement cost or an appreciation in value can lie, for example, in high rates of inflation. In some countries, trade laws allow the use of the current replacement cost as a reference base. In addition, in the case of technical equipment that is subject to rapid ageing, a more realistic, higher written-down current replacement cost can be reported.

Another reason for a higher value lies in the price calculation. In pricing policy it may be a good idea to calculate prices on the basis of current replacement cost in order to preserve the value of the goods or services over longer periods. You can also set an insurance value in the system in this way.

In the R/3 System, you can make legally correct postings for the depreciation required by external accounting and, at the same time, use joint accounting areas to record another value.

INFLATION

Inflation is a complex economic phenomenon that shows itself in many different ways and usually has several causes. The effects of inflation are equally multifaceted. Like the causes, the effects occur simultaneously and in combination.

10.1.1 Money value as a measure of inflation

Inflation is the change in the value of money in an economy. There are many different theoretical explanations of *money value*. If you assume that money has a function as a means of exchange, you quickly encounter the question of the purchasing power of money. The purchasing power of money describes its domestic value. Here, the prices for individual goods or services can fluctuate greatly; on average, the aim is to achieve a constant price level. The external value of money is determined by the exchange rate.

10.1.2 Types of inflation

Since the end of the Second World War, inflation has been the crucial factor in monetary imbalance in the economy of developed countries. Deflation has not occurred in most Western nations, which is why it will not be discussed further here.

Inflation is referred to either as 'low' or 'galloping', depending on the inflation rate. 'Galloping' inflation is also called *hyperinflation*. The rate at which inflation becomes referred to as 'low' or 'galloping' is not clearly defined.

In the United States, there was hyperinflation during the Great Depression. After the Second World War, there was hyperinflation in, for example, Greece, and even today some countries in South America are still struggling with this problem. This means that inflation is still a problem that must not be underestimated by companies that operate internationally.

A situation in which a continuous slight rise in the rate of inflation can be observed is called 'creeping' inflation. This development is typical of most Western industrialized nations in the period following the Second World War. In stable, Western nations, it hardly makes sense in a phase of creeping inflation to take inflation into account in their cost accounting.

The SAP R/3 System provides all the required technical options. As a general principle, only the financial accounting and/or internal accounting areas should take into consideration the fact that appreciation in value may only be noted up to the level of acquisition costs or manufacturing costs. Appreciation in value beyond this value is only possible in the Controlling function; it is prohibited in external accounting.

10.2 TECHNICAL PROGRESS

In industries with fixed assets that are subject to rapid technical change, technical progress may be a reason for reporting the value of fixed assets using a method that deviates from trade law or tax law. In day-to-day operations in such industries, the legal regulations can only be used to a limited extent to determine real prices and costs.

10.3 INSURANCE VALUES

Insurance premiums are often calculated on the basis of current replacement cost of assets and not on the current value of an asset. You can set and record alternative values for calculating Insurance Value in the asset master data record in the R/3 System.

10.4 INDEXATION

In the SAP R/3 System, you can set and write off indexed current replacement costs for fixed assets. The problem scenarios described above (inflation, technical progress and insurance values) can be determined using indexed sequences.

The definition of an *index sequence* can be based on two different procedures:

1 establishment of the current replacement cost on the basis of the replacement cost of the previous year

2 establishment of the current written-down replacement cost on the basis of the historical acquisition or manufacturing costs

The second variation is particularly suitable if there are no corresponding values for the previous year or if the current replacement costs have to be recalculated after importing old data (e.g. when the system is implemented).

The following factors are permitted in the Depreciation Area:

■ appreciation of the acquisition and manufacturing costs

■ cumulated depreciation of the historic values

The following postings must be made in the ledger accounts in the Depreciation Area:

■ depreciation

■ asset changes due to possible appreciation

■ asset changes due to asset movements (purchases)

The asset must be assigned a Depreciation Key in this Depreciation Area. This key must use the current replacement cost as a reference value. The Index Sequence Code must be entered in the asset master data record or in the Valuation Class. The Current Index Points must be entered in the Index Sequence at regular intervals.

Index classes have already been set up in the standard version of the SAP R/3 System. You only need to supplement and update these classes.

10.5   HANDLING INFLATION

The SAP R/3 System does not contain any predefined rules for Balance Sheet appreciation because this aspect varies greatly from country to country. In many countries, appreciation must be recorded in separate Depreciation Areas so that the value changes can be seen separately. Appreciation can be automated in the system or performed manually.

You should make a number of settings in Customizing so that the R/3 System posts both the Commercial Law Area and the proportional appreciation (value adjustment) automatically. The system automatically notes the Posting Date of the appreciation in the asset master data record.

CHAPTER 11

Individual financial statements

As already mentioned in section 4.1.2, the task of financial accounting (business accounting) is to create financial statements. The structures of financial statements are defined in the IMG (Implementation Management Guide). In SAP, you specify the relevant settings in General Ledger Customizing (*see* Figure 11.1). The structure shown in Figure 11.2 is one of the structures that is supplied with the standard version of the SAP R/3 System.

The system automatically works out the annual profit or annual loss when you start the report to create the Balance Sheet and P&L statement in General Ledger Accounting's application menu (Accounting | Financial Accounting | General Ledger | Information system | G/L account info system | Balance sheet/P+L) (*see* Figure 11.3).

You do not need to post the profit or loss manually. A user's task is to assign individual item designations (Fixed Assets, Current Assets, etc.) and to assign the corresponding accounts. This enables the reporting function to work out the annual profit or annual loss, depending on the situation that results from the balances of the assigned accounts. If an account is not assigned to an item, the R/3 System displays it separately under the Not Assigned item (*see* Figure 11.2).

The Retained Earnings account stores the profit or loss that is carried forward from previous years. Before this happens, you must assign this account to this item when you set up the financial statement version. You must also first define the Retained Earnings account and save it in the System under the appropriate item, as shown in Figure 11.4.

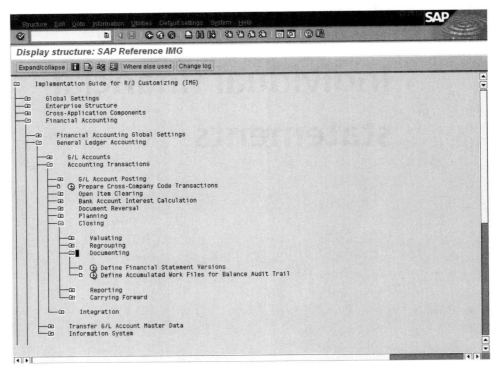

FIGURE 11.1   Defining financial statements in Customizing (© SAP AG)

The Retained Earnings account always depends on a Chart of Accounts (*see* Chapter 7). Figure 11.5 shows how you enter the Retained Earnings account in order to continue processing.

At the end of the fiscal year, to carry forward the balance of the P&L accounts to the Retained Earnings account, start the Balance Carried Forward program from the application menu. You do not need to post this data manually to balance the accounts. The balance carried forward is a technical SAP procedure that does not create any documents. This is because the account is credited in the new year when profits are assigned. You can manage more than one Retained Earnings account in this way.

You can use the Balance Sheet and P&L versions that are part of the standard SAP R/3 System as a template for creating your own financial statement version. In the R/3 System, you can create Balance Sheets and P&L statements for different specified organizational units – for example (group) Company, Company Code, or Business Area. You can also create the Balance Sheet and P&L statement in different languages, e.g. in the language used in the country of the Company Code or in the language set for the Company (group). You can also produce them in different currencies if the company group currency, index currency or hard currency has been stored along with the

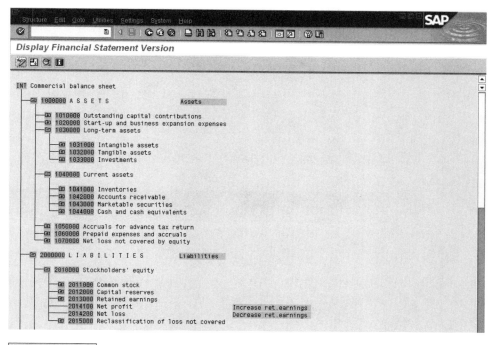

FIGURE 11.2 (a) Financial statement (standard version) (© SAP AG)

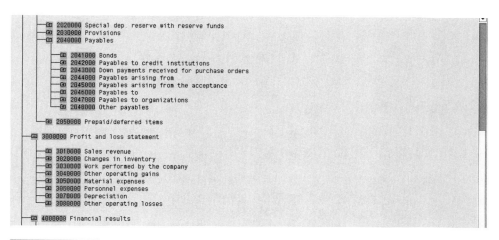

FIGURE 11.2 (b) Financial statement (standard version) (© SAP AG)

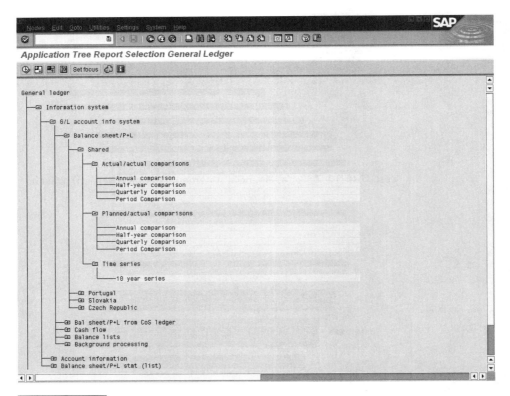

```
        4011000 Income from shares held in other companies
        4012000 Income from an agreement to transfer profits
        4013000 Income from other securities
        4014000 Miscellaneous interest and similar revenues
        4015000 Depreciation of assets and securities
        4016000 Expenses from transfer of losses
        4017000 Interest and similar expenses

      5000000 Extraordinary results
      6000000 Taxes
      7000000 Uses of profits and losses
      8000000 Accounts not assigned        Not assigned
      9000000 Notes to financial statements
```

FIGURE 11.2   (c) Financial statement (standard version) (© SAP AG)

```
Application Tree Report Selection General Ledger

General ledger
  — Information system
    — G/L account info system
      — Balance sheet/P+L
        — Shared
          — Actual/actual comparisons
              — Annual comparison
              — Half-year comparison
              — Quarterly Comparison
              — Period Comparison
          — Planned/actual comparisons
              — Annual comparison
              — Half-year comparison
              — Quarterly Comparison
              — Period Comparison
          — Time series
              — 10 year series
        — Portugal
        — Slovakia
        — Czech Republic
      — Bal sheet/P+L from CoS ledger
      — Cash flow
      — Balance lists
      — Background processing
    — Account information
    — Balance sheet/P+L stmt (list)
```

FIGURE 11.3   Starting Balance Sheet/P&L statement in General Ledger Accounting
(© SAP AG)

company code currency. (The **index currency** is the country-specific, artificial currency that is used for external financial reporting in countries that have high inflation; **hard currency** is a country-specific second currency used in countries that have high inflation.) Figure 11.6 shows the place in Customizing where you enter Additional Local Currency codes so that the System can handle this data correctly.

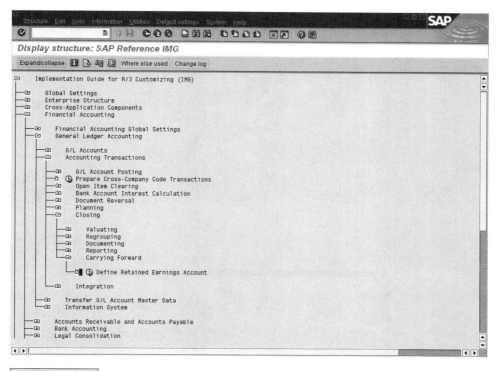

FIGURE 11.4 How to define the Retained Earnings account (© SAP AG)

When you create a version of the financial statements required, you can also create various Balance Sheet types (for instance opening and closing Balance Sheets). You can also enter additional details about the financial statement versions that are useful for management and specialized departments.

However, before you start defining a particular version, you must take a large number of factors into consideration. These factors affect the accounting techniques used during the fiscal year. To help you to understand and use these factors, the sections that follow contain descriptions of external accounting regulations and the rules used to structure financial statements formally. These sections also deal with general Balance Sheet and valuation methods and the individual items in Balance Sheets and P&L statements.

11.1 EXTERNAL ACCOUNTING REGULATIONS

Despite the modern trend towards economic internationalization and the continuous expansion of export trade and globalization that is led by large corporations, accounting regulations are still laid down on a national basis. This therefore means that they

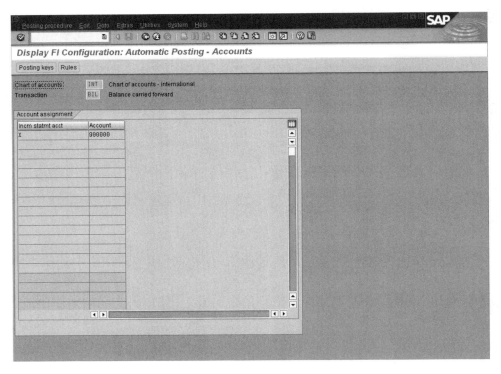

FIGURE 11.5 How to set up a Retained Earnings account in Customizing (© SAP AG)

have not been subjected to worldwide standardization. However, many efforts have been made to achieve some kind of uniformity. These are likely to continue to have an influence on trade law regulations in many countries and possibly even affect tax law as countries modify local standards to conform with international accounting standards. This is particularly necessary for a company seeking foreign funding.

To be listed on the New York Stock Exchange (NYSE), for example, companies are required to draw up financials based on the ***United States Generally Accepted Accounting Principles (US GAAP)***. In other countries, companies may need to draw up financials using ***International Accounting Standards (IASs)*** in order to be listed on various stock exchanges. In some countries, local accounting principles may also be required, forcing the company to draw up multiple financial statements. This makes using standards, especially those that concern national standardization, a crucial factor. This is why we recommend that, if the opening clause applies, European companies should draw up IAS closing accounts and not US GAAP accounts. Note, however, that SAP AG uses US GAAP reporting, since the company's stock is listed on the NYSE.

As a result of these developments, the sections that follow will explain these two financial accounting systems in more detail.

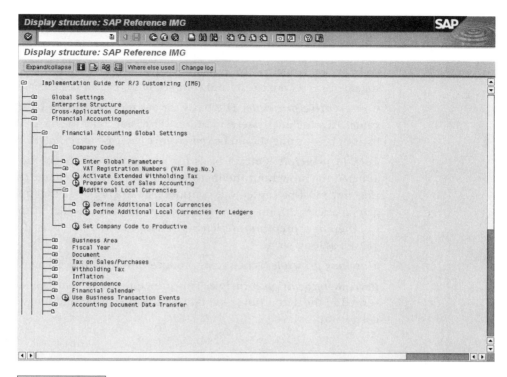

FIGURE 11.6   Setting the Additional Currency code in Customizing (© SAP AG)

11.1.1 US Generally Accepted Accounting Principles

For a stock-market quotation in many countries, it is necessary to submit annual accounts in accordance with the principles usual for that country. In the United States, for example, the annual accounts must be drawn according to US GAAP.

Accounting based on US GAAP does not follow clear laws and regulations. Instead, it is the result of rules and recommendations last published in 1972 in the Audit Guide, the principles of which still apply today. These principles are reflected in the *Statement of Financial Accounting Standards* published by the Financial Accounting Standards Board (FASB). The FASB is an independent private institution supported by the Securities and Exchange Commission (SEC), the United States' stock-exchange supervisory board. Its standards provide the primary source for GAAP. The FASB consists of seven full-time members of the professional organizations of American auditors.

Among other things, the idea behind accounting in accordance with GAAP is based on the desire to achieve a more even distribution of earnings and expenditures than is possible when using accounting for supervisory authorities. This is primarily intended to provide investors and lenders with a clearer picture of the profit they can expect. The following valuation principles in accordance with US GAAP support this aim:

■ *Going concern principle*. In the economic analysis of a company, it is assumed that the company will exist indefinitely.

■ *Disclosure principle*. Taking into consideration all the information known when accounts are rendered, this principle demands that the information in the financial statements is set out clearly and completely so that interested parties are not misled.

■ *Conservative principle*. The basis for accounting should be the best estimated value. This includes safety additions (Provision for Adverse Deviation, PAD). The basis of accounting should be *conservative but reasonable and realistic*.

■ *Lock-in principle*. Once a basis for accounting has been chosen, it should be adhered to throughout the lifetime of a business. To achieve this, a *loss recognition test* must be carried out continuously to check whether any new knowledge gained affects the amount to be paid by the policy holder. If this is not the case, i.e. there is a *premium deficiency*, changes must be made if this deficiency is viewed as long-term.

■ *Matching principle*. When costs produce earnings, they become an expenditure.

■ *Revenue-recognition principle*. This principle states that revenues are regarded as earned in the accounting period in which the corresponding goods or services are delivered/provided.

11.1.2 International Accounting Standards

The *International Accounting Standards Committee (IASC)* was set up in 1973. Its objective is to define internationally recognized standards in the field of external accounting, to publish these standards, and to promote their worldwide recognition and observance.

The IASs are mainly supported by the professional associations of auditors in approximately 120 countries. The controlling body of the IASC includes representatives of the EU, of the FASB and of the *International Organization of Securities Commissions (IOSCO)*. These representatives act as observers. IASs have already been defined for most balance-sheet and account-recording problems.

Accounting according to IASs follows a two-tier set of rules. The first level forms the framework that is the collection of principles used to define new standards. The IASC uses this as the theoretical basis for solving problems in accounting, account-balancing capability, and profit realization. The second level consists of the standards used to clarify specific accounting questions.

The standards are universally applicable, i.e. no distinction is made between individual financial statements and consolidated annual accounts or the size or legal format of a company.

11.2 | RULES THAT DEFINE THE FORMAL LAYOUT OF FINANCIAL STATEMENTS

11.2.1 Principle of layout

Annual accounts must be structured in accordance with generally accepted accounting principles. The purpose of this principle of layout is to provide a yardstick for interpretation. The generally accepted principles of accounting take precedence if commercial law does not provide a special ruling and interpretation yardsticks are needed to provide a suitable solution. The core of the generally accepted principles of accounting is derived from the principle of accuracy.

11.2.2 Components of annual accounts

The legal form and size of a company defines how accurately its annual accounts must be prepared.

Sole traders/partnerships, which do not have limited liability and do not have to apply the rules regarding publication, have a number of advantages over joint stock companies. Their annual accounts simply consist of the Balance Sheet and the P&L statement. In contrast, *joint stock companies* must also prepare supplements and an annual report.

Content of the supplement

The supplement allows the annual accounts to be structured flexibly because it gives a company various rights to choose whether items are listed in the Balance Sheet, in the Profit and Loss statement, or in the supplement.

Companies provide additional information about balance sheet line items in a supplement. Fixed assets, for example, can be described in more depth in the supplement. Here, the company can provide information regarding acquisition costs and on how the assets were depreciated. This information can be listed in an *asset history sheet* (*see* Section 11.7.2). Although this special regulation for joint stock companies means an increase in workload for the company, it also results in an improvement of external information.

A large amount of additional information is required in the supplement. This information could not be shown to this level of detail in the Balance Sheet and P&L statement alone, without making them cumbersome and less clear. The most important information to be listed is as follows:

- The supplement must include an explanation of the Balance Sheet and valuation methodology that has been used.

- The supplement must include an explanation of the principle used to convert foreign currencies. This gives a great deal of leeway in valuation, especially for international corporate groups. Any deviations in balance sheet and valuation methods must be specified. This is intended to make it easier to compare balance sheets.

- In the supplement, accounts payable must be classified according to their maturity. The supplements must also show how the accounts payable are secured.

- Financial obligations that do not appear in the accounts must be specified in the supplement. These include long-term debts, obligations with regard to environmental protection, and licensing agreements. These are latent obligations, not legal obligations. These obligations also include contingent liabilities and outstanding invoices for orders already placed (commitments). In practice, the commitments are generally only specified for investments.

- Revenue must be shown according to areas of activity and volume in regional markets.

- The effects of special fiscal regulations on the Balance Sheet must also be specified in the supplement.

The details contained in the supplement and its format will, of course, differ from company to company within the legal limits set.

Content of the annual report

The annual report must contain a description of the company's business and the company's situation that gives a true picture of the actual circumstances of the company. The report should contain a forecast for the area that is of great significance to the Balance Sheet analysis. This area includes:

- transactions of particular significance after the end of the fiscal year

- the forecasted development of the joint stock company

- research and development

It is important not to underestimate how useful an annual report can be in presenting a particular image of the company.

11.3 CLASSIFICATION REGULATIONS FOR THE BALANCE SHEET AND P&L STATEMENT

Sole traders/partnerships are not always required to use a fixed classification scheme for the annual accounts. This means that sole traders/partnerships only have to meet certain minimum legal requirements in accounting. For example, the Internal Revenue Service in the United States does not require companies with receipts under a certain level (US$250,000 as of 1999) to provide a Balance Sheet reconciliation with their year-end return.

Joint stock companies, on the other hand, are legally required to provide Balance Sheet information with their tax return. Additionally, they are required to adhere to local guidelines for Balance Sheet item classification and special P&L classification rules. Stock companies listed on stock markets are required to meet specific reporting guidelines. Companies listed on the US markets would thus be required to provide financials as defined by SEC regulations. Such regulations make it easier for investors to compare the financial positions of different companies.

At any time it is possible to create a more detailed classification than is legally prescribed.

Some countries, such as France and Germany, have legally prescribed classifications for items in the Balance Sheet and P&L statement. These countries have designated numbers for the financial statement items, which provides investors in these countries with a uniform financial statement layout.

There are two standard ways for classifying balance sheets. So we have the following:

- In European countries apart from the United Kingdom, the asset side is classified according to liquidity. The more difficult it is to convert assets into cash, the higher they are positioned in the classification. Real estate is placed in a very high position because it is an asset that is very difficult to convert into cash. The 'cash-type' items of the current assets can be converted quicker, which is why they are at the bottom of the Balance Sheet classification. This mirrors the investment strategies of investors in these countries, where long-term profitability is weighted more heavily than current profitability.

- In the United States and the United Kingdom, current assets such as cash, receivables, and inventories are listed first, since investors in these countries are more concerned with the current position of the company and the company's ability to pay short-term debt. Land, buildings and equipment are listed last on the asset side.

- The same principles apply to liabilities. In European countries apart from the United Kingdom, liabilities are classified according to maturity, with long-term liabilities appearing in the balance sheet before short-term liabilities. In the United States and the United Kingdom, reporting lists current liabilities before long-term debt.

11.3.1 Amounts specified in the annual accounts

In the eurozone, some countries allow for the preparation of financial statements in the local currency or in euros. There is an option, therefore, in such cases of choosing between preparing accounts in the local currency or in euros, within a transition period defined by the local laws governing the introduction of the euro. In these countries, each company can choose its own transition point within this defined period. In some European countries, the conversion will have been carried out on 31 December 2001, while in others it may be necessary to provide accounting information in two currencies for longer. The SAP euro-conversion tools enable the companies to meet these challenges in conformity with local regulations. For practical reasons and SAP performance reasons, however, a premature switch of currency is not recommended.

Calculations to the last decimal place are not required: amounts can be rounded up or down (full currency unit, thousands, millions). For reasons of clarity, the figures from the current year should use the same unit as the figures from the previous year.

Balance sheet and P&L items that do not figure in the current year and the year used as a comparison do not have to be shown.

11.3.2 Structural continuity

In countries with strict classification requirements, the classification of the Balance Sheet and P&L, with a few exceptions, has to be preserved. Deviations must be specified and justified in the supplement.

11.3.3 Specifying comparative figures

The figures from the previous year must be shown in the Balance Sheet. However, those figures can be changed if a variation is warranted, and this must also be justified in the supplement.

11.3.4 Supplementary classification for different branches of industry

In many branches of industry, annual accounts are prepared in accordance with various classification regulations that are set out for that particular industry. These regulations are supplemented by the classifications laid down for other industries.

| 11.4 | BALANCE SHEET AND VALUATION METHODOLOGY |

You must ensure that you understand the difference between the terms 'Balance Sheet Method' and 'valuation method'.

11.4.1 The Balance Sheet method

The **Balance Sheet method** involves the information that must be included as an asset or a liability in the Balance Sheet. If an object is described as an asset, it can be added to the Balance Sheet. This is then called 'an item that can be included in the Balance Sheet'. Not only do these criteria have to be taken into account, but there are also legal requirements prohibiting capitalization of capitalizable assets and permitting or demanding that of nonassets, which have to be complied with. As a result, a distinction is made between abstract Balance Sheet capability and concrete Balance Sheet capability.

Abstract balance sheet capability is present if an asset within the legal definition is involved. **Concrete balance sheet capability** is present if, under certain circumstances, there are capitalization regulations that differ from the capitalization principle, e.g. Balance Sheet prohibitions, Balance Sheet obligations, Balance sheet utilities, Balance Sheet rights of choice).

The prevailing opinion is that assets are characterized by their individual disposability and individual realization capability. The decisive factor for individual realization capability and individual disposability, and thus, in the final analysis, for the presence of abstract balance sheet capability, is whether capitalization criteria have been met. Based on local law, this usually includes the transfer of ownership.

The purpose of preparing a Balance Sheet is to protect creditors. As a result, only those objects that can potentially cover debts should be included in the Balance Sheet.

11.4.2 The valuation method

The *valuation method* defines how the items included in the current assets and liabilities are to be valued in the financial statement, i.e. the value at which they are reported.

The general valuation principles are regulated by various local laws. These general valuation principles are explained in more detail below.

- *Principle of consistency and comparability*. The consistency of the classification for the valuation methods and the uniform group of assets and debts is intended to ensure the comparability of the annual accounts of companies. This principle is supplemented to include specification of the previous year's figures in the Balance Sheet and P&L statement.

- *Principle of economic efficiency*. The principle of economic efficiency is also one of the general principles. It states that the costs for establishing the values in the Balance Sheet must not exceed the value of the information in each case. This can mean that, for example in consolidated accounts, smaller foreign group subsidiaries are not recorded or the financial statement figures are not specified to the exact penny.

- *Going concern principle for valuation*. Without this principle, certain asset values could not be reported at the value that they have for the company, but only at the market value. An example of this is a specialized machine in a company, which, due to the customizing carried out on it to meet the company's requirements, would sell on the free market for a lower price than its value to the company.

- *Principle of fixed-date individual valuation*. The requirement for individual valuation is the individual recording of the items in the Balance Sheet. The person/body preparing the balance sheet is thus under obligation to document, prove and, if applicable, justify the value of each asset and each debt in accordance with generally accepted accounting principles.

- *Principles of deferrals and accruals.* These are used to ensure that the appropriate profit for a period is established – that is, that the revenues and expenses are distributed over the fiscal year to ensure the comparability of financial statements.

For deferrals and accruals, various principles may be applied, such as the ***principle of caution***. The principle of caution takes the form of the ***realization principle*** (where profits may only be entered in the accounts when realized); on the other hand, this manifests itself as the ***principle of lack of parity*** (losses must be taken into account in the annual accounts if it is likely that they will be incurred). This makes it clear that the protection of debtors is the most important factor in the annual accounts, and so more weight is placed on the risks than on the opportunities in the valuation.

Other accounting principles do not allow the use of such principles, since accuracy takes precedence over possible risk factors.

The time that a profit is realized is defined in the realization principle as the point in time at which risk attached to the purchased goods changes hands and at which the seller has done all in its power to transfer the ownership rights to the purchased goods, i.e. the seller has fulfilled the obligatory contract. In reverse, this means that the signing of an obligatory contract does not yet represent an actual profit realization in the context of a balance sheet.

When an amount is reported on the asset side of the Balance Sheet, the realization principle means that it is linked to the acquisition or marketing costs (*see* sections 11.5.1 and 11.5.2) as an upper limit, depending on the amount involved. Ordinary depreciation can be derived using the realization principle; extraordinary depreciation could be calculated using the principle of lack of parity.

According to the latter principle, the conclusion of a contract can lead to a loss being entered in the financial statement (e.g. if any open transactions may lead to an imminent loss). In order to use the principle as a specific method of implementing the prudence concept, apply the lowest-value principle on the asset side and the highest-value principle on the liability side.

11.4.3 Balance Sheet utilities

Balance Sheet utilities form a subset of the items that cannot be assigned to the conventional Balance Sheet items. There is no legal definition for Balance Sheet utilities: their significance is implied from other legal regulations.

Items that are balance sheet utilities (so-called 'classical balance sheet utilities') are:

1. formation expenses
2. active latent taxes

These are not assets, but expenditures that can be entered as assets under certain circumstances and then have to be accounted for as expenditure in future periods, i.e. they are written off. ***Balance sheet utilities*** are all objects that are neither asset nor liability nor deferrals and accruals.

However, there are other classic Balance Sheet utilities in addition to those mentioned above. Table 11.1 gives an overview of some of them on the asset and liability sides of a Balance Sheet.

TABLE 11.1	Overview of Balance Sheet utilities

Assets	Liability or equity side
■ Formation expenses are to appear in the Balance Sheet as additional items in front of the fixed assets	■ Special items with reserves: to be shown in the Balance Sheet as additional items in front of the provisions
■ Latent taxes: to be shown separately as deferrals and accruals in the Balance Sheet	■ Unused expenditures for plant maintenance in the fiscal year: to be shown as provisions
■ Derivative goodwill: to be shown in the fixed assets in front of the tangible fixed assets	■ Expenditures such as large-scale repairs, plant maintenance, industrial reclamation only performed after one year, building renovation: to be shown as provisions
■ Expense-related customs duty and general tax on consumption (in the case of right of choice for reporting): to be shown as deferrals and accruals	■ Latent taxes as profit provisions if they do not lead to additional tax burdens in the future

11.5 VALUATION OF FIXED ASSETS

The *acquisition and manufacturing (purchase) cost principle* is the basic valuation principle used for fixed assets. According to this principle, the assets are initially reported using the acquisition or manufacturing costs as the maximum value. These costs are then allocated over the useful life of the asset, and so set the upper value limit for the asset.

The lower value limit for joint stock companies for the valuation of fixed assets and current assets is derived from the lower value items that result from a comparison of market value and book value at year end.

Ongoing acquisition and production costs are also applied as the highest-value principle, in accordance with US GAAP and IASs. The methods used in commercial law for ordinary depreciation (linear, output-related, declining-balance method) are widely used in countries throughout the world.

There are three areas in which an exception is made and the acquisition and production costs principle does not apply. These are:

1 *Free-of-charge acquisition.* Here, the company can choose whether (or not) to enter this item in the balance sheet. If the object is entered in the balance sheet, the company's profit increases.

2 *Exchange (barter).* Here, the current market value as a unit value of the asset exchanged is reported as the acquisition cost.

3 *Grants/subsidies.* Just like a free-of-charge acquisition, the company can handle this item as one that creates profit or one that does not affect profits. If this item is handled in such a way that it does not affect profit, the original acquisition

costs are reduced by the amount of the grant/subsidy, and this therefore reduces the company's profit. However, the reduction does not have any further effects because the amount of depreciation reduces to the benefit of profit in subsequent years. However, if this procedure is used, problems may arise in cost accounting in separating the items mentioned here from accruals. This is why, in most cases, a special item with reserves is created.

11.5.1 Acquisition costs

Acquisition costs are defined as the expenditures incurred to purchase an asset and to make it ready for use. The acquisition costs for an asset include the purchase price, the expenses (e.g. transport costs and commissioning costs) and the subsequent acquisition costs (in the case of real estate, for example, this might be the local improvement assessments or drain connection costs). Price reductions in the acquisition price need to be deducted from this.

There is no fundamental difference at the international level with regard to valuation.

11.5.2 Manufacturing costs

Manufacturing costs are legally defined as 'expenditures incurred through the usage of commodities and services for the manufacture of an asset, its extension or for an improvement going far beyond its original condition'.

The lower limit of manufacturing costs is the direct cost, i.e. those costs that are directly attributable to the assets. These direct costs include direct material costs, direct manufacturing costs and special direct costs of manufacturing. The upper limit is primarily formed by the overhead costs of the material and manufacturing area, the general administrative costs, expenditures for social facilities, expenditures for voluntary social benefits (e.g. bonuses for anniversaries), expenditures for company pensions, and attributable interest for borrowed capital. The selling expenses must not be reported under any circumstances. The broad valuation field of manufacturing costs between lower and upper limit means that the manufacturing costs serve as a parameter for action as regards Balance Sheet policy.

Some international standards require the reporting of material and manufacturing overhead costs. According to IAS for example, the valuation of non-output-related administration overhead costs is prohibited.

Inclusion in the cost price of interest on borrowed capital

The valuation of manufacturing costs to include the interest on borrowed capital is generally prohibited; only the interest incurred during the period of manufacture may be included in the calculation. This right of choice also applies to the acquisition cost of an asset. If this right of choice is used, an explanation is required in the supplement.

11.5.3 Fixed valuations

Fixed valuations can also be reported for fixed assets if the following criteria are met:

- The total valuation is of minor importance.
- The quantity, the value and the composition are subject to only slight fluctuations.
- The fixed assets are replaced regularly.

Neither the IASs nor the US GAAP permit fixed valuations in principle. Nonetheless, in cases of minor importance there would be no fundamental violation of the principle of correctness, always assuming that the fixed valuation is a close approximation to the actual attributable value.

11.5.4 Ordinary depreciation

Ordinary depreciation is depreciation that is set across the useful life of the asset. The methods of depreciation are based on various laws and regulations, including tax laws. The following methods are commonly used:

- *Straight-line depreciation.* The depreciation amount remains constant across the useful life (regulated in so-called depreciation tables).
- *Declining-balance depreciation.* The depreciation amount is reported as a percentage of the asset's remaining value. The consequence of this is that the depreciation amount decreases from year to year.

Many countries have simplified their rules for determining depreciation in the year that the asset is acquired (if the asset is acquired in the first six months of the fiscal year, the full depreciation rate can be reported, but if the asset is acquired in the second half of the fiscal year, half the depreciation rate can be reported) and may even allow for full depreciation on low-value assets (the Internal Revenue Service in the United States, for example, allows such calculations).

In the SAP R/3 System, you must set the maximum depreciation amount for low-value assets in Customizing. Figure 11.7 shows the Customizing path for this setting.

Depending on which value of Company Code is involved, you need to enter the amount manually in Customizing (see section 7.1.2). Figure 11.8 shows how you do this.

You must also set company-specific depreciation rates in Customizing. Figure 11.9 shows where you enter this data.

As the scheduled depreciation of an asset is always based on its useful life, assets that are not subject to wear and tear, e.g. real estate, cannot be depreciated. You can use different depreciation methods for individual Balance Sheet items and even for individual assets. To comply with IAS and US GAAP, you should select the depreciation method that corresponds to the useful life of an asset. You should also check the depreciation period regularly.

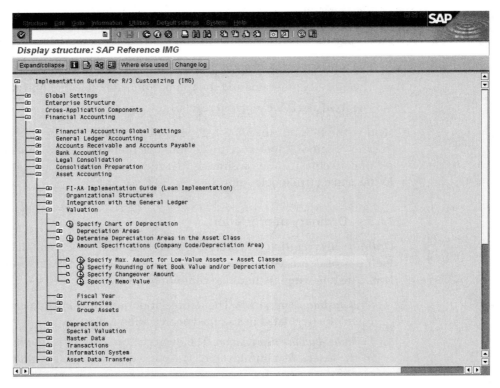

FIGURE 11.7 Setting the maximum amount for low-value assets in Customizing
(© SAP AG)

11.5.5 Extraordinary depreciation

Extraordinary depreciation is to be calculated in the case of intangible assets as well as usable and unusable fixed assets, if the reduction amount is a one-time occurrence. Extraordinary depreciation is generally shown separately in the Profit and Loss statement or explained in the supplement.

You must not mix up extraordinary depreciation with a reduction in the useful life of an asset. In the case of extraordinary depreciation, the entire remainder value is distributed across the new useful life and there is no continuous value reduction.

Extraordinary depreciation is set out in the IAS and US GAAP. The factor that is of particular importance here is the revenues/earnings realized on the market (also known as profitability value).

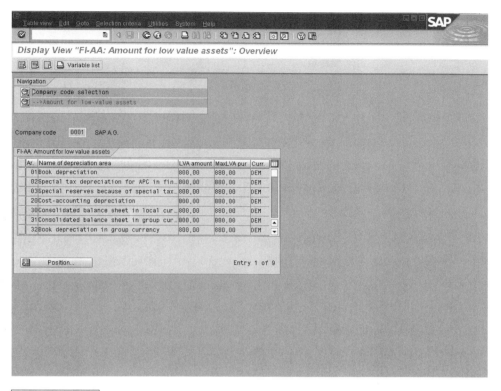

Display View "FI-AA: Amount for low value assets": Overview

FIGURE 11.8   Entering the maximum amount for low-value assets in Customizing
(© SAP AG)

11.6   VALUATION OF CURRENT ASSETS

11.6.1 Production costs

The same points apply to the production costs of current assets as to the production costs of fixed assets. For more information, please refer to section 11.5.2.

11.6.2 Valuation simplification methods and collective valuation methods

Local laws may allow companies to use a simplified valuation method for certain items of their current assets when they prepare their annual accounts. The aim of this is to reduce the time and effort involved in preparing annual accounts. The most important methods are:

■ *Average valuation.* This is the most commonly used method. It establishes the inventory value of raw materials and consumables, either at one point in time or continuously (weighted average value), from the opening inventory plus acquisitions minus retirements.

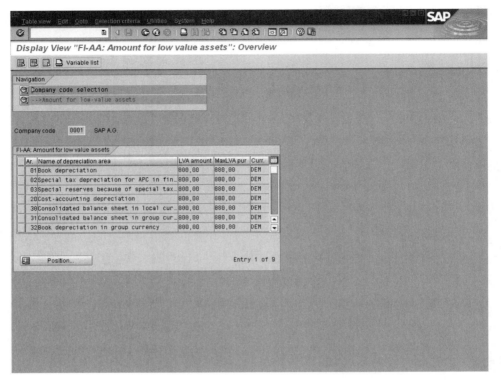

FIGURE 11.9 Setting depreciation rates in Customizing (© SAP AG)

- *Consumption sequence procedure.* LIFO (last in, first out), FIFO (first in, first out), LOFO (lowest in, first out) and HIFO (highest in, first out) are four options. Internationally, the average method, the FIFO method and the LIFO method are permitted. The HIFO method is not permitted. In the case of the LIFO method, other information regarding the choice of method and the effects on the annual reports must also be provided.

- *Fixed value method for raw materials and consumables.* The same requirements as for fixed assets apply here (*see* section 11.5.3). Fixed value reporting is not permitted for international reports.

- *Group valuation.* Inventory assets that are identical, or have the same value, can be combined into a group. You can then use the weighted average value to report them. You can also use group valuation for international reporting.

11.6.3 Depreciation

For current assets, you calculate (extraordinary) depreciation at the lower exchange or market price for the Balance Sheet date. If no exchange or market price is available, you must reduce the amount to the lower applicable value. In this case, you can derive the lower applicable value either from the purchase or sales market. For manufacturing companies, the value of raw materials and consumables is derived from the purchase market, depending on the level of manufacturing maturity (sales maturity). In this case, you use the replacement value or reproduction value. You derive the values of commodities, semi-finished and finished goods from the sales market.

11.6.4 Principle of loss-free valuation

You cannot use the realization principle to create a proportional realization of profit. The valuation of semi-finished goods is referred to as the ***completion of contract method***. The only exception to this is when the long-term completion of orders forms a significant proportion of business activity. In this case, you can create a proportional realization of profit. This method is called the ***percentage of completion method***. This method has the advantage that you can use it to calculate profit periodically.

The percentage of completion method, and therefore the partial realization of profit, are contained in both the IAS and US GAAP.

Finally Figure 11.10 shows another overview of the options you can use to report and valuate the assets and liability sides of a balance sheet.

Overview of reporting and evaluation options

Capitalization options

- Assets purchased
- Goodwill purchased for a charge
- Plant maintenance and expansion expenses
- Discount of accounts payable
- Low value assets

Options to accrue

- Provision for expenses in quarters 2 to 4 of the next year
- Other provisions for expenses
- Special items with reserve

Valuation options

- Calculation of manufacturing costs
- Goodwill purchased for a charge
- Valuation simplification methods or collective valuation methods
- Ordinary depreciation
- Extraordinary depreciation with anticipated temporary reduction in value of fixed assets
- Extraordinary tax write-offs
- Extraordinary depreciation with reasonable commercial judgement

---

FIGURE 11.10   Overview of reporting and valuation options (© SAP AG)

BALANCE SHEET ITEMS

Before you can include an asset in the Balance Sheet, you must be able to assign it to the operating assets. On the asset side of the Balance Sheet you must then identify this asset either as a current asset or a fixed asset.

Assets are specified as *fixed assets* if they 'have the purpose of permanently serving the business'. If this permanent service to the business does not apply, the asset is a *current asset*. In the case of fixed assets, companies show the development of the individual items of the fixed assets as shown in the context of the asset register in the balance sheet or in the supplement (*see* section 11.7.2).

The liability side of the Balance Sheet shows the negative counterparts of assets. These include debts, equity capital, prepaid expenses, and deferred income. From a legal point of view, all liability items (including accounts payable and provisions) that are not equity capital or prepaid expenses and deferred income are regarded as debts. The principle of completeness requires that all debts are shown as liabilities.

The most important aspects of the individual Balance Sheet items in assets and liabilities are discussed in the remainder of this section.

11.7.1 Formation expenses

Formation expenses are the costs incurred in setting up, or significantly extending, in-house and sales organizations. In particular, these expenses refer to the cost of setting up a (new) business input in order to start production. A company can decide whether or not to carry this Balance Sheet utility as an asset (*see* section 11.4).

Formation expenses in the Balance Sheet usually correspond to the original self-generated goodwill. The primary aim of this item is to avoid start-up losses. It can therefore be seen as an artificial element that is used to make the balance sheet look better.

You cannot include expenditure for founding the company and acquiring capital in the balance sheet. These expenditures include:

- for joint stock companies, any expenses incurred when setting up the company as a legal entity
- expenses incurred in procuring share capital (prospectus, court and notary costs, printing costs of shares)

As formation expenses are nonassets, there is a limitation on profit distribution for this item. Profit generated by capitalizing this item as an asset must not be distributed. However, you can carry out a partial capitalization. If the item has been capitalized, an annual depreciation of at least 25% must take place. The development of the item must be reported in the asset register.

US GAAP allows capitalization or, as the case may be, prescribes capitalization if a benefit is likely in the future. Legal costs, costs for choice of location, moving costs,

costs for personnel recruitment and similar start-up expenses may be amortized over a maximum of 40 years. However, they are usually amortized over 10 years. As yet, the IAS principles do not contain any special regulations about this.

11.7.2 Fixed assets

In addition to Balance Sheet classification, local law may require that the development of the individual items of the fixed assets be shown. The asset history sheet is used for this purpose.

Basic structure of the asset history sheet

The asset history sheet:

- shows the development of individual fixed asset items and the formation expenses item
- is only required for joint stock companies
- can be placed either in the Balance Sheet or in the supplement
- is prepared using the gross method

You must determine the values for formation expenses as well as for fixed asset items separately and list them in the following sequence:

1   Historical acquisition and production costs
2   Acquisitions
3   Retirements
4   Transfers
5   Depreciation adjustment of the fiscal year
6   Depreciation (cumulative)
7   Remainder value up to 31.12. of the fiscal year
8   Remainder value of the previous year
9   Depreciation of the current fiscal year

In the menu of the Asset Accounting application component, the information system contains a report (FIAA-21) that you use to call an asset history sheet (see Figure 11.11). The asset history sheet always applies to a specific Company Code.

The asset history sheet has two main purposes. It is a useful tool to help you interpret the balance sheet analysis, and it is also a way of calculating the annual results reliably. It helps you understand where changes come from and to see how reliable the statements in the Balance Sheet and Profit and Loss account actually are. For example, you can use the asset history sheet to detect whether the person who drew up the Balance Sheet disguised poor operating results by using sales figures to liquidate undisclosed reserves and convert them into earnings.

You must first define the asset history sheet in the Customizing application component in the R/3 System (*see* Figure 11.12).

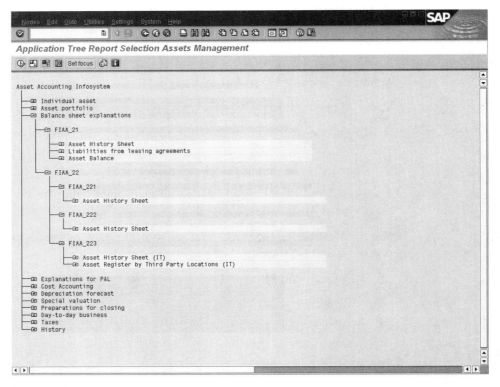

FIGURE 11.11 Calling up asset history sheets (© SAP AG)

The standard version of the SAP R/3 System already contains several asset history sheets. You can use these without changing them (*see also* Figure 11.13):

- Total depreciation
- Acquisition values
- a 13-column asset history sheet
- Transferred reserves
- Special items

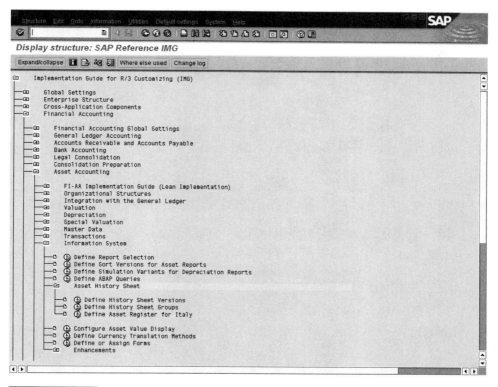

FIGURE 11.12   Setting up the asset history sheet in Customizing (© SAP AG)

Double-click on the version of the asset history sheet you require to view its structure (*see* Figure 11.14).

Intangible fixed assets

You must not capitalize any intangible assets that were acquired free of charge. These are self-generated intangible assets. Expenditure for patents, copyright, the acquisition of know-how and developed software may be a large proportion of overall business activity, and in some cases these expenses form the foundations of a business. However, the value of these self-generated assets is not lost; instead, it is reflected, for example in public limited companies, in the stock market quotation or the purchase price of the entire company. For some companies, the prohibition of capitalization leads to excessive debts and, as a result, the liquidation of the company.

The general principles for fixed assets also apply to the capitalization of (derivative) intangible assets that were acquired for a charge.

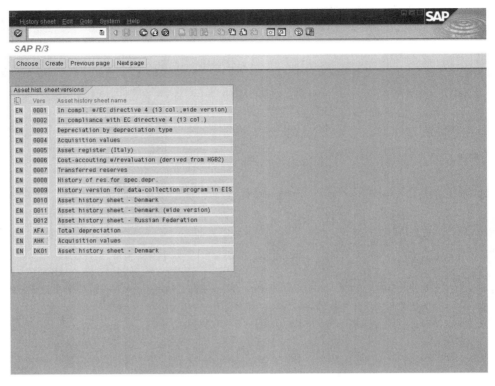

FIGURE 11.13 Versions of the asset history sheet already present in Customizing for the standard R/3 System (© SAP AG)

However, in international reporting, a company is obliged to capitalize all intangible assets, no matter whether they are free of charge, if they can be regarded as assets. This particularly applies if you can clearly identify an intangible asset's useful life. However, because it often happens that no clear identification can be made, the IAS and US GAAP have a capitalization option for self-generated intangible assets.

Research and development costs

Research and development costs, associated with the aquisition of know-how, generally cannot be capitalized: they are regarded as current expenditures.

This capitalization is usually also prohibited by international standards. However, companies are obliged to capitalize development costs that have a clearly definable value with regard to future earnings (which is a more theoretical capitalization option).

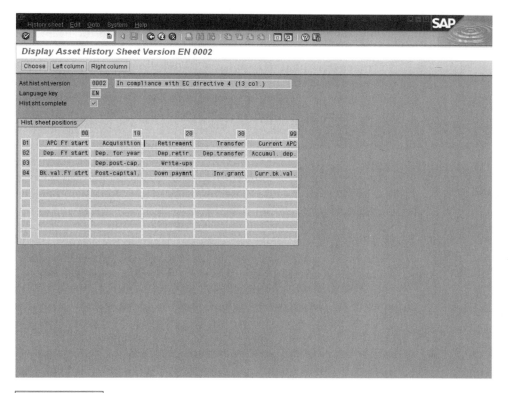

FIGURE 11.14   Structure of version 0002 of the standard asset history sheet (© SAP AG)

Goodwill

Goodwill is also an intangible asset. As we have already explained, this is why only the goodwill acquired for a charge may be reported in the fixed assets. Derivative goodwill is the difference between the purchase price – or part ownership – of a company and the (proportional) equity capital of that company. Here, equity capital is defined as the difference between assets and liabilities (in the sense of borrowed capital).

As explained in section 11.4, goodwill is one of the Balance Sheet utilities, because it is not obviously an asset but may still be reported.

IAS and US GAAP prohibit the capitalization of goodwill. However, derivative goodwill must be capitalized. The goodwill is the difference between the amount of the purchase price and the *fair value* of the assets and liabilities. The fair value must be set according to the intended use by the purchaser. This can lead to assets and liabilities being revalued.

Non-money assets (fixed assets) are always reduced if negative goodwill is present. Any remaining amount is referred to as *negative goodwill*. It is then reported in the Balance Sheet as *negative deferred income* and depreciated over a maximum of five years.

To explain goodwill further, a worked example is given, where the equity capital of a company that has been taken over is US$60 000 in the Balance Sheet. If, for example, the purchaser of the company pays $100 000 to take over the company, the difference is $40 000. This difference arises from the commercial Balance Sheet equity capital of the company that was taken over. However, the equity capital of this company must not be derived from its Balance Sheet but from the current value of its assets and debts. For this reason, the assets and liabilities are revalued and the balance sheet is prepared again, from the point of view of the purchaser. As a result, the undisclosed reserves and burdens of the company taken over are disclosed.

We now assume that $25 000 must be attributed to the equity capital in the commercial balance sheet (of $60 000). This value has been adjusted because $25 000 has been uncovered as undisclosed reserves (the difference between Balance Sheet values and higher market value) for real estate, buildings, etc. This results in a goodwill of $15 000 equal to $100 000 (purchase price) – $60 000 (equity capital from the commercial balance sheet) – $25 000 (undisclosed reserves within the balance sheet).

The next step is to check whether the calculated difference, from the point of view of the purchaser, still contains assets that can be capitalized which could not be capitalized by the company that was taken over. These can be, for example, self-generated intangible assets of the company that was taken over, because these assets were not reported in the Balance Sheet of the purchased company. From the point of view of the purchaser, which also purchases the intangible assets when it purchases the company, these are not self-generated intangible assets. Instead, they are purchased intangible assets that must be capitalized by the purchaser. Our example contains this kind of item, that is to be valued at $5 000. For this reason, the difference item is reduced to $10 000, equal to $100 000 – $60 000 – $25 000 – $5 000).

This remaining value of $10 000 is called goodwill. The purchaser can choose to capitalize it if it requires (and it must capitalize it for tax purposes). If the capitalization option is used, the equity capital in the purchaser's Balance Sheet is changed to the purchase price of $100 000. To do this, the $100 000 of the purchasing company is set instead of the book equity capital of $60 000 of the purchased company. This equity capital is created by the capitalization of undisclosed reserves, intangible assets and the goodwill of the company that was taken over. If the capitalization option is not used, the goodwill must be written off completely in the year of purchase. In this example, this reduces the profit in the fiscal year to $10 000, which in turn reduces the equity capital of the purchasing company to $90 000.

11.7.3 Down payments in the Balance Sheet

Down payments that are made

Down payments are mainly made for products that are not actually in stock and for services from suppliers or those obliged to fulfil contracts. These payments are a commercially useful way of evenly distributing advance financing to vendors and customers across the manufacturing period.

Down payments made must be reported in the Balance Sheet according to their use. These include:

- down payments for intangible assets
- down payments for tangible assets
- down payments for inventory, including down payments for future expenditure items such as materials, external services and plant maintenance

You should note that down payments to affiliated companies and associated companies must normally be reported under Accounts Receivable from affiliated companies and associated companies.

In the SAP R/3 System, you enter down payments in a separate account (a reconciliation account). You set up this account in Customizing (*see* Figure 11.15).

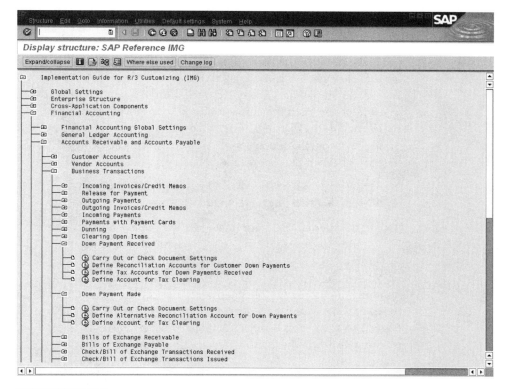

FIGURE 11.15 Down payments made (and received) in the Balance Sheet (© SAP AG)

The reconciliation account forms a link between the subledgers in which you enter any down payments and General Ledger accounting where the Balance Sheet is created. You must set the Tax Account for input and/or value added tax (tax of purchases/sales), depending on how the down payments are to be made (*see* section 11.7.4).

Down payments that are received

Similar to down payments made, down payments received (payments on account) are usually received for the purpose of financial balancing in the case of services provided by customers on a long-term basis. **Down payments received** occur when no exchange of services or fulfilment of the contractual service has yet taken place. You must often set up bank guarantees, which may not be reported in the balance sheet (as contingent liabilities). Down payments are not entered in the books when the down payment request is sent, but only when the payment arrives.

The down payments received are reported on the liability side of the Balance Sheet, under Accounts Payable. The reporting method you select defines the layout of the Balance Sheet. This is because the open depreciation of the down payments on inventory makes the Balance Sheet shorter. The ratio of equity capital to borrowed capital changes as a consequence.

Any down payments received from affiliated companies and associated companies must be reported in the corresponding Accounts Payable.

In the SAP R/3 System, you enter down payments received in a separate account (again, a reconciliation account). You set up this account in Customizing in a similar fashion to down payments made (*see* Figure 11.15).

Input tax on down payments made

Down payments made are posted in Accounts Payable. These payments are based on vendor invoices. However, the payment is not posted until the bank account is debited.

You can always select either gross or net reporting, i.e. you can use either the gross amount (including tax on sales/purchases) or the net amount to capitalize the down payment made. However, down payments made are shown in the Balance Sheet and linked to the corresponding Balance Sheet asset items (*see above*). As net reporting is obligatory for these asset items, down payments made are generally reported as net amounts.

However, an exception to this is down payments to affiliated companies and associated companies. These are reported gross under Accounts Receivable (*see* section 11.7.4).

Tax on down payments received

There is another capitalization option for prepaid amounts and deferred income (as legally defined in Europe). This option is available for tax on sales/purchases for amounts that do not apply to down payments received. Down payments received are regarded as prepayments on the part of the person ordering (the customer), placing the company compiling the Balance Sheet under obligation to fulfil contracts later.

The down payments received can be entered as liabilities either with the gross amount (including VAT) or the net amount, as follows:

- *Gross method.* If, for example, a company preparing a Balance Sheet has received a down payment of €115, including 15% VAT, the gross method uses the following postings in accounts receivable:

    – Cash €115 (debit) and Down Payment Received €115 (credit)

    – VAT Down Payments (Expenditure) €15 and Accounts Payable (where relevant) €15

    By capitalizing the tax on sales/purchases expenditure as a deferred item, the expenditure is neutralized, which conforms to the character of tax on sales/purchases as a transitory item. The postings are:

    – Deferred item €15 and VAT on Down Payments (Expenditure) €15

- *Net method.* With the net method, the example is booked directly as income-neutral as follows:

    – Cash €115 (debit) and Down Payments Received €100 (credit)

    – VAT €15 (credit)

In day-to-day operations, the net method has prevailed, as the advantage lies particularly in the valuation of the down payment received from stocks. If you use net Balance Sheet reporting you do not need to convert the amount to the net value that corresponds with net reporting of the inventory.

11.7.4 Accounts Receivable and Accounts Payable

Receivables from goods and services, including their value added tax, are posted to the accounts receivable ledger. These receivables are shown as gross values (with value added tax) in the Balance Sheet.

Payables for goods and services, including input tax, are posted to the Accounts Payable ledger. They are reported as gross values in the Balance Sheet (with input tax).

Differentiation of receivables after maturity

Accounts Receivable are defined as 'assets for which the incoming payment is usually expected in the near future'. In order to make short-term liquidity easier to under-stand, you should mark all Accounts Receivable that have a maturity term of more than one year. The differentiation is usually shown in an Accounts Payable register in the supplement to the annual accounts. The R/3 System automatically reports all Accounts Receivable within a year separately, because you must also report the total of receivables.

The SAP R/3 System automatically regroups Accounts Receivable if you specify the accounts (for the maturity term below or above one year) into which they are to be divided in Customizing. To create annual accounts, call the Regroup function from the application menu. You make the appropriate settings in Customizing at the positions shown in Figure 11.16.

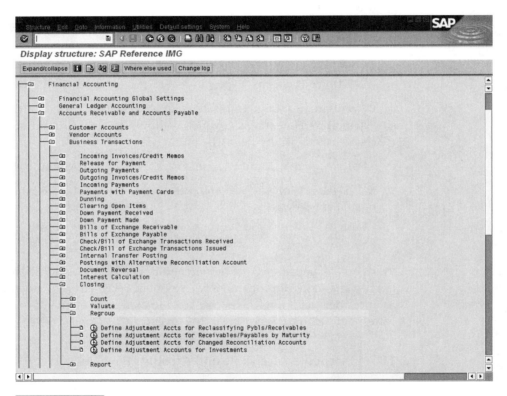

| **FIGURE 11.16** | Regrouping in Customizing (© SAP AG) |

11.7.5 Other accrued assets and liabilities

These two Balance-Sheet items are accrued business transactions. In legal terms, an accrued transaction is a business transaction that does not happen until after the closing date for annual accounts. This means that the revenue/payment is only due after the Balance Sheet date. To ensure that you can determine the current profit, you must assign costs and revenues that relate to the accounting period but have not been recorded.

Accruals are the counterpart of the transitory prepaid amounts and deferred income, when payment is made before earnings, i.e. a payment is made in the old fiscal year for a transaction in the new fiscal year. You enter these payments as Other Payable or Other Receivable items. You cannot enter them in the 'Prepaid Amounts and Deferred Income' Balance Sheet item because this is only used for transitory deferrals and accruals.

If the accrued amounts have any importance, you must specify them in the supplement.

11.7.6 Prepaid amounts and deferred income

Prepaid amounts and deferred income (in addition to assets and debts) are adjustment items that are used to distribute specific figures over a particular time period. They ensure that profit is determined in accordance with the principles of allocation. They are called *transitory prepaid amounts* and *deferred income*.

Deferrals and *accruals* are defined as revenues or expenses incurred on the accounting Key Date, and they represent earnings or expenditures from a different period. The result is that prepaid amounts and deferred income can be reported if the expense (payment) is due input to the date of the financial statements and the expenditure is only incurred a certain time after the date of the annual accounts. Similarly, prepaid amounts and deferred income can be reported as an asset if the income (payment) is due input to the date of the annual accounts and the income is only earned a certain time after the date of the annual accounts.

Tax on sales/purchases on down payments

This special type of deferral and accrual has already been discussed in detail in section 11.7.3.

Loan discount, share discount, share premium

The requirement of principle for the capitalization of items such as these is that the repayment amount of a liability must be higher than the amount of the expense.

The loan discount is interest paid in advance. Here, the borrower must enter the higher repayment amount as a liability and can report the amount of the difference as prepaid amounts and deferred income. Alternatively, the borrower can account for the expenditure in the Balance Sheet in place of even distribution over the fiscal year by dissolving the deferrals and accruals immediately, creating income in the year that the loan is taken.

Tax regulations might, however, require capitalization if the item is entered as a liability.

11.7.7 Equity capital

Equity capital is a residual figure that remains after assets and debts have been balanced. Equity capital is divided into a fixed component, the subscribed capital (*see below*), and a variable component that changes continuously over the course of time.

Equity capital can take a negative value. If the amount is negative, you must enter it on the asset side of the Balance Sheet. For example, this may be caused by an excessive Balance Sheet debt (when assets no longer cover the debts and therefore reduce the equity capital). However, this does not take undisclosed reserves (if allowed by law) into consideration. For this reason, you should not mix up this situation with the company's actual excessive debt.

Equity capital is not simply a residual figure; it also represents the company's liable capital. The equity capital has, as regards liability for losses, lower liquidation preference in the case of creditor claims. As a result, if the company goes into liquidation, creditors are paid first, before the providers of equity capital. In contrast to borrowed capital, the company is provided with equity capital on a permanent basis.

Subscribed capital

Subscribed capital is the capital to which the liability of the company owners, in the case of company liabilities to creditors, is to be limited. You must report subscribed capital (nominal capital, stock capital) at its nominal amount. This is the amount specified in the company articles (statutory capital) and entered in the commercial register. Subscribed capital does not have to be completely sold. If it is not, the subscribed capital remains unpaid.

The total amount of subscribed capital must be shown in the owner's equity section of the Balance Sheet. If capital is to be obtained on a subscription basis but has not yet been paid in full, this is entered as unpaid subscribed capital. This means that the unpaid subscribed capital is regarded as a type of Account Receivable from the company's owners, independent of whether the stock has already been called or not. The unpaid subscribed capital is either entered as a deduction from owner's equity (contra equity approach) or as subscription receivable in the asset section of the Balance Sheet. Although this choice is available, the contra equity approach is generally used. The United States' SEC requires the contra equity approach because of the risk of collectability.

If you use the *gross method*, you can post amounts on the asset side in front of the fixed assets in the Subscribed Capital Unpaid item. In this case, you must identify the called subscribed capital as a percentage of the total.

If you use the *net method* to prepare the Balance Sheet, you can deduct the uncalled, outstanding deposits on the liability side from the Subscribed Capital item. You show these figures in the liability section of the balance sheet. You must then enter the remaining amount in the Called Capital item in the main column. In this case, the specified Subscribed Capital Unpaid must also be shown under Accounts Receivable and designated accordingly.

Capital reserves

In the Balance Sheet, you enter as capital reserves any other deposits that are present in addition to the subscribed capital. These deposits include:

- share premium for the issue of shares or stock above the nominal amount
- other additional payments that are used to replace an increase in the subscribed capital (statutory)
- capital substitution in the form of loans and rights of use

Profit reserves

Profit reserves are generally not permitted. However, the SAP R/3 System includes this option to accommodate countries that have this allowance. These reserves are divided into the following categories:

- *Legal reserves*. Legal reserves are only regulated by law in the case of public limited companies and commercial partnerships limited by shares.
- *Reserves for own shares and shares of majority stockholders*. Reserves for own shares are intended to neutralize the ownership of own shares or group shares. Otherwise, there is a risk of entering self-generated goodwill in the balance sheet when you value the company's own capital. The reserves can be formed by, or transferred from, existing profit reserves, from the annual profit or loss, or (according to prevailing opinion) from capital reserves. The reserves for own shares and shares of majority stockholders cannot be distributed. They therefore act as a limit on profit distribution to the amount of the value of the company's own shares.
- *Legal profit reserves*. These include other free reserves that are permitted – or required – according to company articles.
- *Other profit reserves*. These include other free reserves that are not required by law or regulation.

11.7.8 Annual profit/loss and Balance Sheet profit

The term 'Balance Sheet profit' is used in the context of the way the annual profit is used. It can be used for:

- the allocation of reserves (legal, statutory, free reserves) where allowed by local regulations

- the accumulated profit or losses carried forward
- profit distribution

If you set the corresponding Balance Sheet item from the annual profit when you prepare the Balance Sheet, you can use the annual profit for reserves and profits carried forward. For this reason, the Balance Sheet profit is usually the amount that is to be provided for profit distribution (dividends), and is usually marked to show that it will leave the company soon. This is why, to help you establish the amount of equity capital, you must decide whether Balance Sheet profit is to be reported as borrowed capital.

The 'distribute-and-retrieve method' plays a significant role in helping you assess Balance Sheet profit. This method distributes the Balance Sheet profit and then later – in most cases due to increased flexibility in comparison with nominal or stock capital – returns it to the equity capital as capital reserves. This method of restructuring equity capital is mainly used because of its tax advantages: it reduces the corporation tax burden.

- Reduction of tax-rate burden to the distributions rate
- Tax credit of the tax on distributed profits, especially if the shareholder, for whatever reasons, does not pay corporation tax

However, the danger of conflicting interests means that the 'distribute-and-retrieve method' is the only practical option if a company does not have many owners.

11.7.9 Capital-substitution loans and rights of use

In bankruptcy proceedings against a private corporation, loans or rights of use paid by the company to company owners in the past (rents, licenses, patent fees, etc.) can be handled as that private corporation's equity capital. The background to these capital-substituting loans and rights of use is the idea that an entrepreneur is under an obligation to provide the company with sufficient capital (if economically in a position to do so) for it to operate effectively. In the case of granting loans and assigning rights of use, it is a *prima facie* argument supporting the economic solvency of the company owner.

11.7.10 Corporation tax on the equity capital

Corporation tax is applicable to a number of elements of a company's resources, thus:

- *Subscribed capital.* No corporation tax is included in the nominal capital, no matter whether the capital has been paid in or not. The nominal capital, which cannot be distributed, is not classified as equity capital for corporation tax purposes.
- *Capital reserves.* Capital reserves do not attract corporation tax either. However, because the capital reserves can be distributed, they are reported in the tax classification of the usable equity capital as equity capital. Capital reserves, in this sense, are not allowed by most international accounting standards.

- *Legal reserves*. Legal reserves are formed from the annual profit, and therefore attract an undiminished corporation tax burden if corporation tax is due in that fiscal year.

- *Reserves for own shares*. Reserves for own shares were formed from annual profit after tax, or from other profit reserves. This means they attract an undiminished corporation tax burden. However, if these reserves were formed from the reallocation of capital reserves, they do not attract corporation tax.

- *Statutory reserves and other profit reserves*. These reserves are retained profits on which the full amount of corporation tax has been paid.

- *Annual profit/Balance Sheet profit*. Corporation tax is calculated on the basis of the planned use of the annual profit.

- *Non-taxable earnings*. Non-taxable earnings, such as investment grants, are exempt from corporation tax.

- *Corporation tax on profit distribution*. If profits are distributed, the shares of equity capital with the greatest corporation tax burden are those that will be used first.

11.7.11 Special items with reserves

If allowed by law, liability items formed from income and earnings for tax purposes are also shown as special items with reserves (reversal authority) in the financial statements. If special items with reserves were entered in the Balance Sheet, the supplement to the financial statements must contain an explanation of how they were formed.

In addition to non-taxable reserves, joint stock companies can also set the permitted special depreciation and increased depreciation in the special items as an alternative to a direct reduction of the fixed assets.

Special items with reserves are items that are entered in the Balance Sheet between the equity capital (open reserves) and the borrowed capital (provisions). This Balance Sheet item represents a mixed item that is partly equity capital – often assumed at a flat rate of 50% – and borrowed capital to the amount of the share of tax to be covered from this item.

11.7.12 Fiscal law value adjustments (special depreciation)

Special depreciation can either be directly reduced for the fixed assets or the difference to normal depreciation can be set in the special items and allocated over the useful remaining life of the asset.

11.7.13 Provisions for pensions

There is often an obligation to set up provisions for promised company pensions (direct promises), whereby the basis of the calculation and thus the amount of the provisions is generally not regulated by law. For this reason, it is better to refer to the generally accepted accounting principles. The generally accepted principles of accounting correspond to a mathematical insurance calculation with the following essential components:

- age of the person entitled to the pension and, where applicable, the spouse entitled to the pension
- claim in the event of an insurance case (e.g. 50% of last salary)
- number of years of company service
- age when the claim was initially granted
- discount factor

Pension provisions are generally increased on an annual basis, but this is only used in the long term. In this case, pension provisions are expenditures that do not affect expenses, for these expenditures are available to the company as liquid capital until the pensions are actually paid.

11.7.14 Provisions for taxation

Advance payments usually have to be made for some operating taxes, such as corporation tax, trade tax or real property tax. These payments are based on the last tax assessment. The actual expenditures are calculated at the end of the year. The result is balanced against the advance payments made and reported as Anticipated Tax in the tax reserves. A claim for tax rebate is reported under Other Assets.

For assessed income and tax on sales/purchases for which the amount has been established, the amount is entered in the Balance Sheet under Other Liabilities and not under Provisions for Taxation.

Tax deferral as a liability

If tax is deferred as a liability, the taxable profit is initially lower than the commercial profit. If this is a temporary deviation, i.e. the deviation can be reversed in the succeeding years, there is an obligation to report tax deferral as a liability. The provision for tax deferrals as a liability is to be shown separately in the Balance Sheet or in the supplement.

Tax deferral as an asset

If tax is deferred as an asset, the taxable profit is initially higher than the commercial profit. If this difference can be reversed in later fiscal years, with a corresponding negative difference, there is a reporting option for showing it as an asset. The prepaid amounts and deferred income must also be shown separately as an asset in the Balance Sheet and in the supplement.

A tax deferral item is cleared when the corresponding increased or reduced tax burden takes effect, or when it is likely that this will no longer happen.

11.7.15 Residual time to maturity of Accounts Payable

Similar to Accounts Receivable, you must also supply details of residual times to maturity for Accounts Payable. Accounts Payable items are shown separately according to maturity. For example:

- up to 1 year
- 2 to 5 years
- over 5 years

This separation is usually carried out in the Accounts Payable Adjustment account. This account must appear in the Balance Sheet or in the supplement.

The SAP R/3 System automatically regroups payables if you have specified the accounts to which the payables are to be assigned in Customizing. The principle is the same as that for regrouping receivables. You make these settings at the place shown in Figure 11.17.

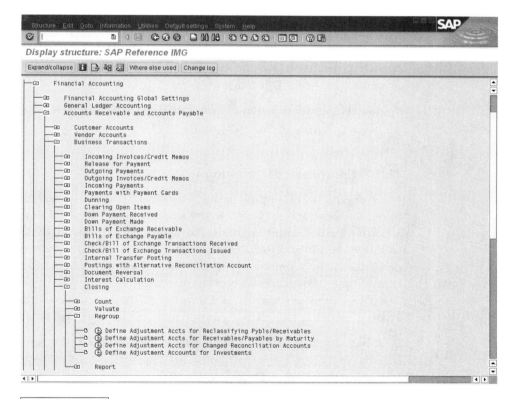

FIGURE 11.17 Regrouping Accounts Payable (© SAP AG)

THE ITEMS IN THE PROFIT AND LOSS ACCOUNT

The expenditures and earnings recorded for a certain period are set against one another in the Profit and Loss account (*see also* section 4.1.2). In contrast to the Balance Sheet, which refers to a certain point in time (namely the Balance Sheet date), the Profit and Loss account is an account that refers to a period of time. You can structure the Profit and Loss account in the following two ways:

- in report form
- in account form

The report form is prescribed for stock companies. You can set it up as 'total cost type of short-term results accounting' or as 'cost of sales type of short-term results accounting'. These are each described further below.

11.8.1 Total cost type of short-term results accounting

If you use the total cost type of short-term results accounting method, you report the total earnings and expenditures of the entire fiscal year. This means that the total cost type of short-term results accounting is period-related and does not require there to be any relationship between expenditures and sales revenues.

This accounting method is traditionally used in European countries to determine operating results. It has the following advantages over the cost of sales type of accounting: it means you can:

- directly transfer expenditures from financial accounting
- report inventory / asset changes directly

11.8.2 Cost of sales accounting

The cost of sales accounting method includes sales revenues and only those expenditures that were incurred to create the sales revenues in the calculation. Expenditures are also classified according to operating functional areas (production, sales and distribution, administration). This means that period-related expenditures (sales and distribution and administration costs) are reported in parallel with product-related expenditures (production costs of the goods sold).

Cost of sales accounting is the method that prevails worldwide in external accounting. It has the following advantages over the total cost type:

- It has a higher level of international acceptance (e.g. for foreign financing).
- It also provides additional information because material and personnel expenses are specified in the supplement.

However, before you can implement cost of sales accounting, you must establish an effective operational accounting system with cost centre and cost element accounting (*see* section 4.1.3).

If you use cost of sales accounting you should divide material expenditure into precise categories, according to material and external services. You also need to subdivide personnel expenditure into wages and salaries, social benefit costs, and pensions. These must all be entered in the supplement to the financial statements. This means that you must also use the total cost type short-term profitability analysis. This involves a great deal of additional time and effort if local regulations require the use of total cost accounting.

11.8.3 Description of items in the total cost or cost of sales accounting methods

The total cost or cost of sales accounting methods have similar items in the report form. However, they do not involve the same procedures. For example, if you use the total cost type of short-term results accounting, the Other Operating Charges item exists and includes (for instance) rents; if you use cost of sales accounting, this item is spread across the general administration costs, depending on the distribution to individual cost centres.

Three items are worthy of special mention:

- *Sales Revenues (in the P&L statement).* In this item, you can only enter the revenues of usual business, i.e. revenues from cost and income accounting. Sales revenues are the net values of the products or services that have been sold. These include packaging and delivery costs. Sales revenues must be reduced to allow for cash discounts, quantity discounts, loyalty bonuses and other bonuses.

- *Other Operating Income.* You use this item to report earnings that cannot be reported under any other earnings item.

- *Depreciation on Current Assets* (insofar as this exceeds the usual amount of depreciation in a joint stock company). This item includes special depreciation, e.g. tax depreciation. You cannot enter normal depreciation such as depreciation on raw materials, consumables or accounts receivable in this item.

- *Income from Participating Interests.* This includes dividends from joint stock companies, profit shares from partnerships, interest from loans with profit participation, etc. You must report earnings from participating interests in affiliated companies as subitems, marked as 'of which'. Alternatively, you can report them separately in the supplement to the financial statements.

The remaining items in the Profit and Loss account are self-explanatory. As mentioned at the beginning of this chapter, you do not need to make many settings in Customizing in the R/3 System for annual reports. However, if you do not have the appropriate commercial knowledge, there is a danger that your annual accounts will contain incorrect data.

CHAPTER 12

Consolidation

Drawing up consolidated accounts is more complicated than drawing up individual financial statements. This is because it involves more than one company and requires the consolidation of legally independent companies.

A number of legally independent companies that are managed by one management structure is called a *group*. You use addition and allocation (consolidation) procedures to create consolidated accounts from individual financial statements. Consolidated accounts consist of a Consolidated Balance Sheet and supplements to the group accounts.

The following section explains the background business knowledge you need to draw up consolidated accounts. The most important Customizing settings are also described below, and Figure 12.1 shows where you make the Customizing settings in the SAP R/3 System.

12.1   GROUP TYPES AND STRUCTURES

The 'leading' company in a group is called the ***parent company***. The subordinate branches of the group are called ***subsidiaries***. These also include indirect shareholdings (known as ***second-tier subsidiaries***) of the parent company. The parent company draws up the consolidated accounts.

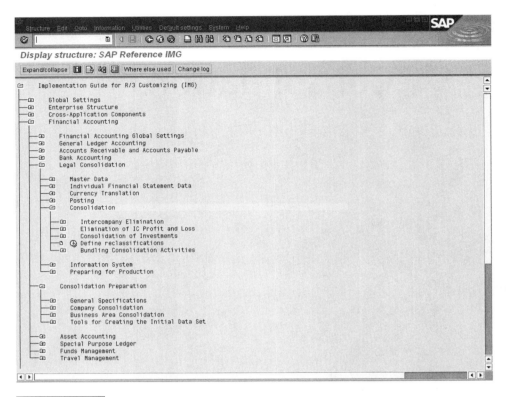

FIGURE 12.1 Consolidation in Customizing (© SAP AG)

Figure 12.2 shows the different types of corporate group:

- *Horizontal group*. In a horizontal group, a company has shares in similar operations in the same branch of industry. This increases its market share in a specific segment. An example of a horizontal group in Europe would be the VW–Audi–Seat–Skoda group.

- *Vertical group*. A vertical group consists of companies that manufacture at earlier, or later, stages in the production process. This reduces costs, because all the processes for one product can be streamlined under one management structure and some of the profit margins in preceding stages can be removed. An example of a vertical group is the Pearson Group.

- *Conglomerate group*. In a conglomerate group, all the companies are grouped under one management team (e.g. a sole trader or partnership) without creating a relationship of dependency between the individual companies. In many cases, group assets are managed by a holding company that is set up for this purpose. In practice, there are not many conglomerate groups nowadays.

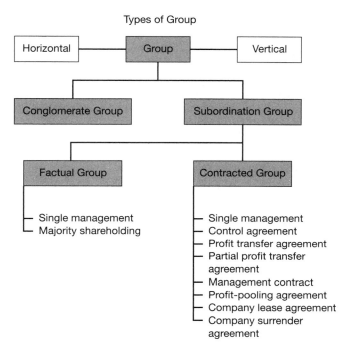

Types of Group

Types of group (© SAP AG)

■ *Subordination group.* A subordination group consists of legally independent companies that are controlled by one company. The controlling company manages the group.

Subordination groups can be created in two ways:

1 In a *factual group*, one company obtains the controlling interest or shareholder majority in another company by buying shares. This creates a relationship of dependency.

2 A *contracted group* is created when a company makes agreements with other companies that restrict the legal and/or economic freedom of these companies. In a contracted group, we can assume that there is a single management level. The contracts generally mean that the controlling company can even issue instructions that are to the disadvantage of the subordinate company if this serves the purposes of the group.

The following types of contracts are relevant in the context of a contracted group:

■ In a *control agreement*, the subordinate company transfers its management operations to the controlling company.

- In a *profit transfer agreement*, the subordinate company is obliged to transfer all the profit it generates to the controlling company. This is called 'financial integration' and, as a rule, the parent company also accepts any losses that are made.

- The *management contract* is a type of profit transfer agreement.

- In a *partial profit transfer agreement*, only part of the subordinate company's profit is transferred. The remaining profit remains in the company.

- In a *profit-pooling agreement*, all the profit is transferred and redistributed by the controlling company as part of its cash management procedures.

- A *company lease agreement* means that the entire company is leased to another company. This second company runs the first on its own account and under its own name.

- A *company surrender agreement* is similar to a company lease agreement. In this case, although the company does not operate under its own name it still operates on its own account on the basis of powers of attorney granted by the surrendering company.

12.2 CONDITIONS FOR CONSOLIDATION

The features that define a group are generally defined by law. Table 12.1 lists possible features that might define a group, as a non-country-specific example.

TABLE 12.1 Group definition features – examples	
■ Majority of shares or votes	■ Majority of voting rights
■ Controlling influence of any kind	■ Controlling influence in the sense of voting rights majority, right to occupy management positions, control agreement
■ In the case of single management of the controlling company (also in the sense of a conglomerate group)	■ Existence of a subordination group in the case of a conglomerate group only if there is a single management from a joint stock company
■ Group with mutual shareholdings	■ The conditions are defined by law

There is likely to be a requirement to draw up consolidated accounts when some or all of the criteria specified in Table 12.2 are met.

TABLE 12.2	**Duty to draw up consolidated accounts – example reasons**
■ Single management by a parent company of at least one subsidiary	■ The parent company is a sole trader/ partnership
■ The parent company is a joint stock company	■ 5000 employees on average
■ The shareholding is at least 20 % and is permanent	

Exemptions from a duty to prepare consolidated accounts, depending on the size of the group, are regulated by law. Furthermore, subsidiaries in countries in the European Union that are also parent companies do not need to prepare consolidated accounts if the foreign parent company has its headquarters within the EU and it includes the local subsidiary, with all its second-tier subsidiaries, in its own consolidated accounts and group management report.

12.3   AIMS OF CONSOLIDATED ACCOUNTING

Consolidated accounts have the same information function as individual financial statements. They should represent the actual circumstances of the assets, financial and earnings situation of the group, while observing the generally accepted principles of bookkeeping and accounting. Protecting creditors (and protecting shareholders) is of primary importance here.

The fundamental difference between an individual financial statement and a set of consolidated accounts is that the consolidated accounts only have to be presented to the board of directors and the Annual General Meeting of shareholders of the parent company. This means that the consolidated accounts have no legal function and are therefore of no legal consequence since all subsidiaries are responsible for tax reporting. Nevertheless, the consolidated accounts auditors check the consolidated accounts as to whether the generally accepted accounting regulations have been adhered to during preparation.

As is the case with the individual financial statement, the national regulations governing consolidated accounts vary greatly. For this reason, the European Union has initiated a harmonization of the regulations for the global consolidated accounts in the form of the Seventh EU Directive. This has affected local tax laws in EU countries. For example, in order to make it easier for internationally operating groups in Germany to obtain capital, for which consolidated accounts are required according to international law (US GAAP, IAS), the German parliament passed new laws in 1998 making it easier to raise capital. This law means that groups that have to draw up consolidated accounts according to international law are not required to submit additional consolidated accounts according to German regulations.

12.4 INTERNATIONAL THEORIES FOR CONSOLIDATED ACCOUNTS

The unity theory and proportional consolidation are two very different consolidated accounting methods that are used internationally.

12.4.1 The unity theory

Nowadays, the *unity theory* is the most widely used consolidated accounting theory. It assumes that the legally independent companies in a group form an economic entity. As a consequence, the Balance Sheet and/or Profit and Loss accounts of a group must contain all the assets, debts, expenditures and earnings of the companies involved.

You must create a clearing item so that the shares of other company owners of the subsidiary's equity capital can be seen in a consolidated financial statement.

12.4.2 Proportional consolidation (or parent company) theory

The economic entity of the grouped companies is more strongly defined in the *proportional consolidation theory*, also known as the *parent company theory*. Here, consolidated accounts are only interpreted as extended accounts of the controlling company. They show the asset shares or profit shares of the subsidiaries to be assigned to the controlling company. This means that all the assets, debts, expenditures and earnings of the subsidiaries are only included to the extent of the proportion of ownership.

This theory also makes it possible to omit reporting of minority shareholdings and to include the current assets and liabilities only to the extent of the percentage of the majority shareholding in the consolidated financial statement. Otherwise, their shares of the profit (minority shares of the profit) are reported separately.

12.5 THE CONSOLIDATION CODE

Figure 12.3 shows the consolidation code in accordance with graduated consolidation.

The first stage of graduated consolidation is when you include subsidiaries in the consolidated accounts. The parent company–subsidiary relationship was explained in Section 12.1. It requires the single management of the subsidiary by the parent company. In the case of full inclusion of the subsidiary, full consolidation is required, i.e. the consolidation of capital and debt as well as expenditure and earnings, and thus the elimination of internally generated profit and loss in the fixed and current assets.

In a second step, you include those companies that are owned by two or more parent companies at the same time, i.e. joint ventures. The parent companies are independent of each other and have the same rights in the joint venture. The part-

Content of Consolidated Accounts

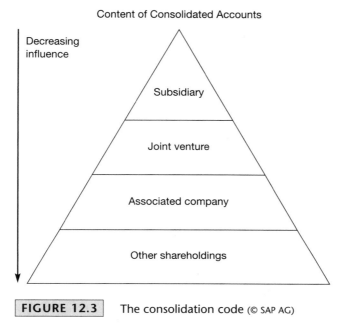

FIGURE 12.3   The consolidation code (© SAP AG)

nership is intended to enable permanent, shared management and control. The inclusion of joint ventures is either by means of proportional consolidation or using the equity method.

The equity method is a simplified form of full consolidation and uses the same principles. In equity consolidation, the individual financial statement data of the company involved is not included in the consolidated accounts. Only the changes to the equity capital of these companies are taken into consideration. If you use the equity consolidation option, the joint venture is regarded as one of the associated companies.

According to US GAAP, you cannot apply proportional consolidation for joint ventures. However, IAS regulations have an option that allows you to do this.

In the third stage, you include associated companies, also referred to as equity companies. These are companies over which a corporate group exercises major influence because of its share ownership. Although the associated company is included in the consolidated accounts, it does not become an affiliated company but remains an equity company.

Other shareholdings include shareholdings with a percentage share of less than 20 per cent. These shareholdings are reported in the accounts at their acquisition cost. There is no consolidation.

12.6 GENERAL PRINCIPLES FOR DRAWING UP CONSOLIDATED ACCOUNTS

To reliably eliminate internal group relationships (and thereby eliminate interim profit and loss) you must always draw up the consolidated accounts on the date on which the parent company creates its annual accounts. This is known as the uniform key date. If the date of the accounts of one of the companies included lies more than three months prior to the date of the accounts of the parent company, you must create interim accounts for the interval between the consolidated accounts and inclusion of the subsidiary in the consolidation.

To draw up consolidated accounts, you need a uniform accounting system and a uniform Balance Sheet classification scheme. This is the situation if the SAP R/3 System is implemented throughout the entire group. However, if the group contains companies that are legally required to use different classification schemes – for instance in the case of foreign subsidiaries, banks, industrial companies or insurance companies – the data must be transferred between the schemes. The classification regulations that apply for the individual financial statement also apply here (*see* Chapter 11).

Now that the general legal background of consolidation has been described, the following section explains the process of consolidation and the Customizing settings you require. The individual points will be worked through on the basis of the process diagram shown in Figure 12.4.

12.7 MAINTAINING MASTER DATA IN CUSTOMIZING

You enter the settings in the following places (*see* Figure 12.5):

- *Currencies*. You maintain all the currencies used in the group in 'Currencies'.

- *Companies*. Companies are subsidiaries, joint ventures and associated companies or other participants. These can be identified using an alphanumeric key and be included in the consolidated accounts. You can also set up companies that do not belong to the consolidation code. The reasons for inclusion and exclusion are defined and regularly updated.

- *Subgroups*. The subgroup comprises the companies that belong to a parent company. SAP requires this group for the consolidation of the group. The subgroup can correspond to the overall group. You must not change the subgroup at random, because this will cause inconsistencies when you carry forward the balance. In the subgroup (this applies to conglomerate groups), one or more companies are identified as the parent company.

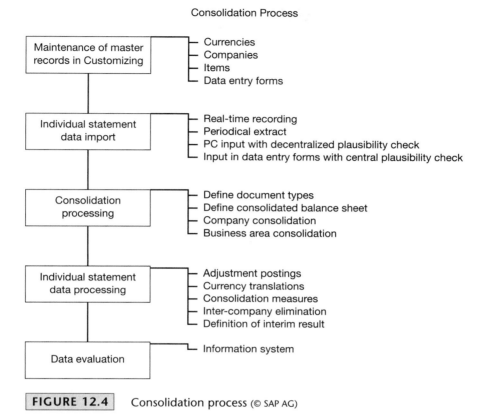

Consolidation Process

FIGURE 12.4 Consolidation process (© SAP AG)

■ *Financial statement items.* The financial statement item numbers are the central consolidation term used for processing consolidation in the SAP R/3 System. Financial statement items can be financial statement items from the Balance Sheet and Profit and Loss statement that are relevant to accounting. They can also be static information and benchmarks. If a group uses different Charts of Accounts, a uniform group financial statement item catalogue must be defined for the consolidation.

To standardize how data is entered in all companies, data entry forms have been defined for the SAP R/3 System in order to specify the data required for consolidation. You make the relevant settings in 'Individual Financial Statement Data' (*see* Figures 12.6 and 12.7).

Data can be entered as follows:

■ If the subsidiary also uses the SAP R/3 or R/2 Systems, you can use direct through-posting (real-time recording) in the consolidation area. This can take place monthly or quarterly to create quarterly financial statements (periodic extract).

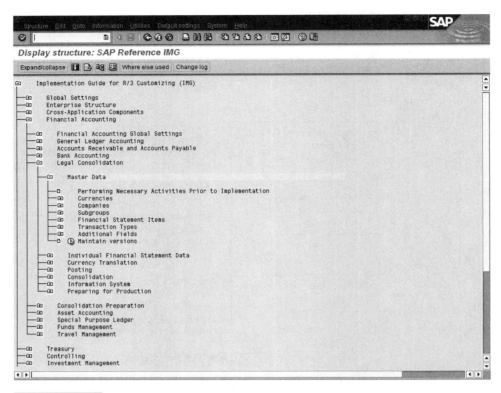

FIGURE 12.5 Consolidation master data in Customizing (© SAP AG)

▓ You fill out the data entry forms in the database systems such as MS-Access, dBASE or ORACLE, and then upload the forms into the relevant SAP System. Decentralized plausibility checks can be carried out here. You can also automatically transfer financial statement items that are in different data entry forms into other data entry forms after you enter them in one data entry form. This avoids the same data being entered twice on different data entry forms, and thus inadvertent inconsistencies.

▓ You enter data entry forms that have been filled out by the consolidation code directly. In this case, the plausibility check is carried out centrally.

12.8 CONSOLIDATION PREPARATION

Preparation for consolidation takes effect through the screen shown in Figure 12.8. Individual aspects are described further below.

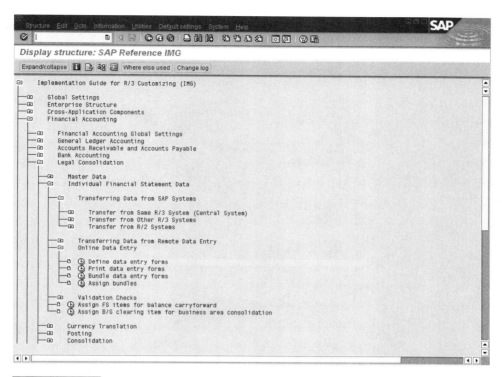

FIGURE 12.6 Defining data entry forms in Customizing (© SAP AG)

12.8.1 Defining Document types

Posting Documents are used to record all changes in values of individual financial statements in the system within the framework of consolidation. As this data is recorded in a separate application component area, it guarantees that the individual financial statement data can still be evaluated later on. This means, for example, that adjustments to the Consolidated Balance Sheet in accordance with US GAAP can be marked with the document type 'US'.

12.8.2 Defining the Consolidated Balance Sheet and P&L structure

The standard version of the SAP R/3 System already contains a structure. You can either use this structure as a template or supplement it with your own modifications. You then assign the operative accounts to the item keys to identify that these accounts are to be included in consolidation.

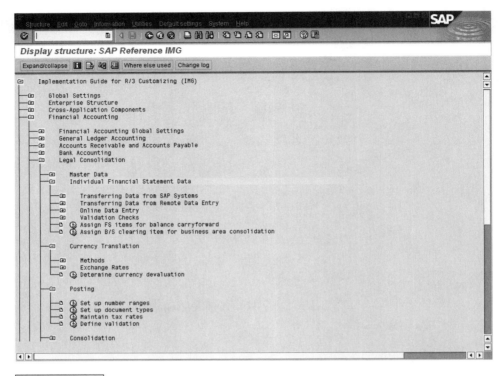

FIGURE 12.7   Transferring financial statement data in Customizing (© SAP AG)

12.8.3 Company Consolidation

Company Consolidation is a SAP tool. You use it to create consolidated accounts on
the basis of legally independent companies. A client's Company Codes are usually
legally independent companies.

You must update the Company Numbers in the Customer and Vendor master data
records and in the General Ledger account to allow the system to automatically
assign partner company accounts for transactions within the group.

12.8.4 Business Area Consolidation

You can only use Business Area Consolidation together with Company Consolidation. You cannot carry out Business Area Consolidation without assigning the master
data and defining the Document types required for Company Consolidation.

In Business Area Consolidation, financial statements are drawn up for individual
Business Areas. In this case, the internal relationships between the consolidation
units of these Business Areas are eliminated.

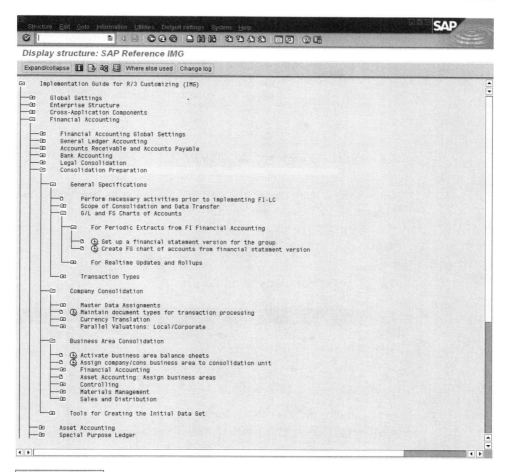

FIGURE 12.8   Preparation for consolidation in Customizing (© SAP AG)

12.8.5 Individual financial statement data processing

At the end of a fiscal year, you must start the balance Carryforward program in the General Ledger accounting application menu in the FI module. Here, the balances of the accounts for the individual financial statement are carried forward. This is carried out for all financial statement items concerned in the balances of adjustment and consolidation postings.

12.8.6 Adjustment postings

Adjustment postings are used to adapt the company's individual financial statements to the uniform accounting and valuation procedures used within the group.

12.8.7 Currency translation

Foreign companies usually record their individual financial statement in the appropriate company currency (e.g. French companies currently do so in French francs, and will do so in euros). In the SAP R/3 System, you can translate the currency for each individual company if a conversion method has been set in the Company master data record.

12.9 CONSOLIDATION ACTIVITIES

One of the advantages of the SAP R/3 System is its highly automated consolidation procedures. Users do not need to enter consolidation postings manually. Instead, these postings are automatically generated by the system when you enter the elimination type you require.

12.9.1 Inter-company elimination

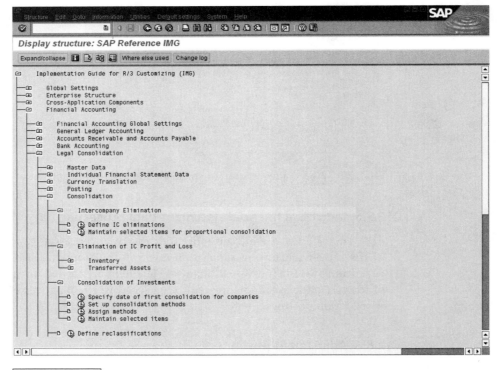

FIGURE 12.9 Inter-company elimination in Customizing (© SAP AG)

In SAP terminology, inter-company elimination is the consolidation of debts as well as the consolidation of expenditure and earnings. These concepts are grouped together under this term because the procedures are carried out in the same way. Figure 12.9 highlights the main screen where this process is initiated.

Debt consolidation

As a group is a fictional, uniform company, within which no external relationships are possible, all the Accounts Receivable of the companies in the group that come from other group companies are offset against the corresponding Accounts Payable.

Consolidation of expenditure and earnings

Expenditures and earnings incurred from business relationships between the companies in a Consolidation Code must always be eliminated if the economic relationships are not of subordinate significance. Only relationships to third parties are reported in the group P&L statement.

12.9.2 Elimination of inter-company profit and loss

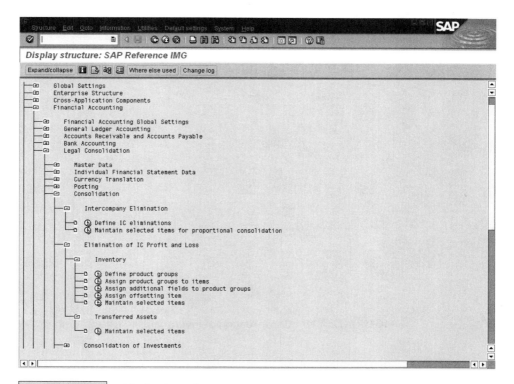

FIGURE 12.10   Elimination of inter-company profit and loss in Customizing (© SAP AG)

Inter-company profit and loss is eliminated by product group (*see* Figure 12.10). These product groups are created by grouping individual products together. The standard version of the SAP R/3 System already contains product groups that have been set up for financial statement items in the inventory. These product groups are designed to illustrate the supply and service relationships of the company. Here, the book values are corrected by the incidental expenses and valuation adjustments so that a difference to the group manufacturing costs can be calculated. You post changes to previous periods by entering a corresponding offsetting item in Customizing. This then affects the net income.

In accordance with the unity theory of consolidated accounting (*see* section 12.4.1), the sale of fixed assets between companies in a Consolidation Code is handled as if there were only a shift of assets between plants. Inter-company profit or loss must be reversed. This also affects the net income.

12.9.3 Capital consolidation

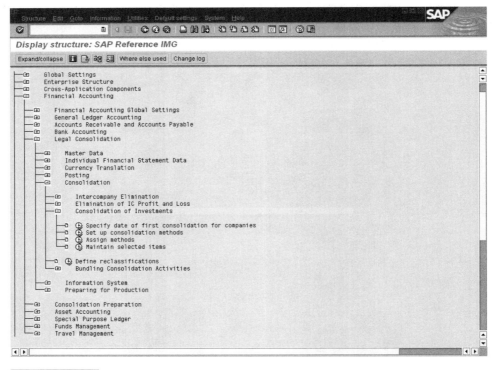

FIGURE 12.11 Consolidation of investments in Customizing (© SAP AG)

The consolidation of investments is used to offset the proportional capital of a subsidiary with investment book values of the parent company.

The standard version of the SAP R/3 System includes consolidation methods for full consolidation, grouping of interests, proportional consolidation and equity valuation, with the variants 'book value method' and 'revaluation method' or 'capital share method' to meet various legal requirements. Furthermore, the selected items required for consolidation of investments are already set (*see* Figure 12.11).

When the book value method is used to consolidate investments, the investment book value at the parent company is offset against the equity capital that results from the book values of the current assets and liabilities.

If the revaluation, or capital share method is used, the subsidiary's equity capital is revalued with the market values of the current assets and liabilities. This is carried out in a new Balance Sheet. This is the Revaluation Balance Sheet, which contains all the undisclosed reserves and debts (where allowed by local laws). If you use this variant, you must take the principle of acquisition cost into consideration, i.e., the subsidiary's equity capital must not exceed the acquisition costs of the shareholding.

You must make the appropriate settings in Customizing to specify which capital consolidation method is used in the group. You then assign the variants to these methods. Once you have done this, you must specify whether any resultant income-creating goodwill is written off over several years or if it is to be offset against, for example, reserves.

You must also enter the method (proportional or full) to be used to eliminate undisclosed reserves as part of investment consolidation.

12.9.4 Reclassifications

Reclassifications are transfers between Balance Sheet items or P&L items. You might need to do this at the level of individual financial statements (adjustment postings) if, for example, the usual business activity of the individual company is different from that of the group or if parts of the inventory have been entered in the individual financial statement as finished goods although they are semi-finished goods from the point of view of the group. In this example you must reclassify finished goods as semi-finished goods.

12.9.5 Data evaluation

The consolidation information system already contains a wide range of predefined evaluations. However, you can add your own evaluations to these when required. After you open the report you require, these evaluations are displayed on screen where you can edit them.

CHAPTER 13

The FI-AA Asset Accounting module

13.1 BASIC PRINCIPLES AND OVERVIEW

Just like other areas of financial accounting, asset accounting is also defined by legal regulations and guidelines. These include the valuation regulation for preparing a Balance Sheet correctly on the Balance Sheet date, and also the postings within a year, such as acquisitions and retirements of fixed assets or the handling of orders for assets.

13.1.1 Asset Accounting organizational units

Similar to the Financial Accounting module, the SAP R/3 System Asset Accounting application component contains the following organizational units (as shown diagrammatically in Figure 13.1). Each is described further below.

- Client
- Company Code
- Business Area
- Cost Centre (CO)
- Plant (Logistics)

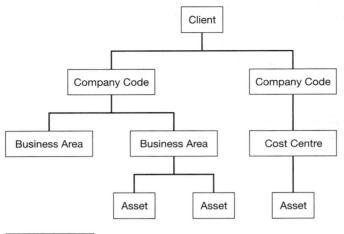

FIGURE 13.1 Organizational units in the Asset Accounting Component (© SAP AG)

Client (group)

The Client is the top organizational unit in the SAP R/3 System. As a general rule, the client is legally equivalent to the group (*see* Chapter 7).

At group level, assets can be evaluated across Company Codes. At group level, a separate asset history sheet (*see* section 11.7.2) can be kept. The movements within a group are recorded in the group asset history sheet as transfers whereas, from a financial accounting point of view, these are disposals or acquisitions for the relevant company.

Company Code (subsidiary)

A Company Code (*see* section 7.1.2) is a legally independent business unit within a client (*see* section 7.1.1) that prepares its own financial statements. The assets of a company are its fixed assets.

Assets are assigned to one Company Code and managed by this code for the period during which they are assigned to it. When you customize the System, you must set up and maintain Asset Accounting views in Financial Accounting.

Business Area

Business Area (*see* section 7.1.3) is used as the basis for preparing Balance Sheets and Profit and Loss statements within a Company Code. However, the Business Area is not subject to the legal requirements that apply to the Commercial Accounts of a Company Code. The Business Area provides another means of creating new classifications and providing more information. The assets can be

- assigned to business areas
- automatically posted for the business area
- transferred between the individual business areas

Cost Centre

You can set up a cost centre – a Controlling organizational unit (*see* section 4.1.3) – in every asset master data record. In most cases, an asset is only assigned to one cost centre. However, in the R/3 System you can distribute an asset across several cost centres. A corresponding distribution to cost centres is carried out in cost centre accounting.

All postings, such as acquisitions and disposals or even interest and depreciation, are automatically transferred to cost centre accounting. You can use forecasted costs to help plan cost centres.

Plant

The plant (*see* section 7.2.1) is an organizational unit in the Logistics area and does not have a function in Asset Accounting. However, the integration of the application components within the SAP R/3 System means that there *is* a connection: an asset can be assigned to a plant. Assets can be shifted between individual plants. The plant can play a role as an organizational unit in evaluations.

13.2   FIXED ASSETS

For large companies, the fixed assets of the Balance Sheet are classified according to the following scheme:

- intangible assets
    - franchises, commercial copyrights and similar rights and values as well as licences for them
    - goodwill
    - down payments made
- tangible assets (*see also* Figure 13.2)
    - real estate, leasehold rights and buildings, including buildings on non-owned real estate
    - technical plant and machinery
    - other assets, fixture and fittings
    - down payments made or assets under construction

■ investments

  ■ shares in affiliated companies

  ■ loans to affiliated companies

  ■ investments

  ■ loans to companies in which there is a shareholding interest

  ■ securities involving long-term investments

  ■ other loans

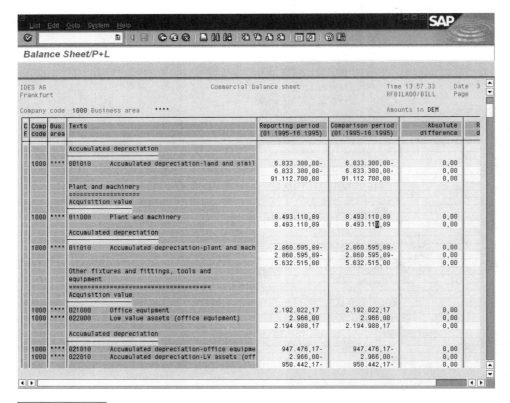

FIGURE 13.2   Balance Sheet and P&L statement in the SAP System (© SAP AG)

The precise contents and valuation methods for these categories are explained in Chapter 11.

TERMS USED IN ASSET ACCOUNTING

13.3.1 Assets

The terms 'economic assets' and 'assets' are virtually identical. If objects are *tangible fixed assets*, they meet these criteria:

- independent valuation capability
- economic values
- long-term usability

13.3.2 Real property and plant facilities

The difference between real property and plant facilities can be significant for taxation.

Taxable real property establishes the standard value that is used as the basis for assessing the various types of tax. *Real property* comprises real estate, buildings, other components and accessories. In contrast, machines and any kind of fixtures and fittings that belong to a plant are called *plant facilities*. As fixtures and fittings are only used for commercial activities, they are not part of real property.

13.3.3 Physical inventory

Companies are obliged to include assets that they have created themselves or purchased in an inventory list (*see* section 4.1.2). An exception to this is low-value assets. These can either be included in the inventory and then depreciated in the same way as other assets, or they can be reported immediately as an expenditure.

Every asset must be defined and recorded in a separate Asset master record (*see* Figure 13.3). Each asset must be clearly identifiable. Other ways of classifying fixed assets in the SAP R/3 System are described in Section 13.15.

13.3.4 Asset history sheet or inventory list

Local law may require an annual physical inventory of the assets. The assets are recorded in an inventory list (via an asset history sheet).

The asset history sheet must contain all assets until they are eliminated from the company (*see* Figure 13.4). If they have already been fully written-off, they must be listed in the asset history sheet with a book value of zero. The standard version of the SAP R/3 System contains an asset history sheet with a line and column layout in accordance with the fourth EU Directive.

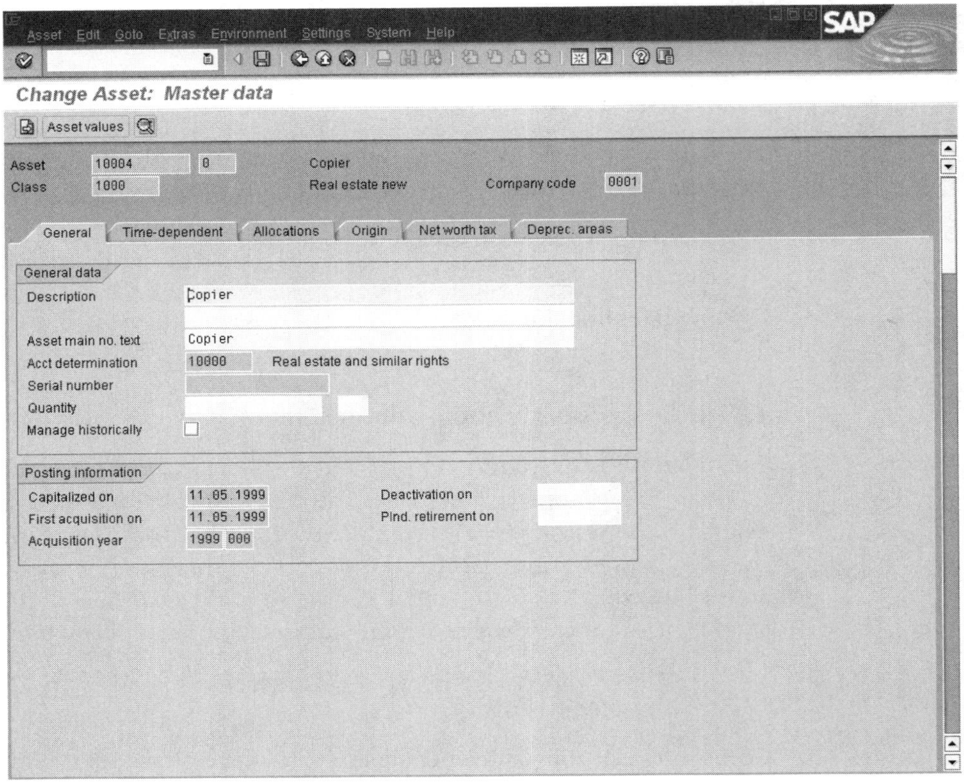

FIGURE 13.3 General data and Posting Information used in Asset master record
(© SAP AG)

An annual inventory can be replaced by continuous co-posting of acquisitions and disposals (retirements) in the inventory list. And then, on the Balance Sheet date, the inventory list must show the following:

- the precise designation of the asset
- the balance sheet value on the balance sheet date
- the date of acquisition or manufacture of the object
- the acquisition or manufacturing costs of the asset
- the retirement date, insofar as the object has been retired in the current year

Section 11.7.2 contains a detailed description of how to create an asset history sheet.

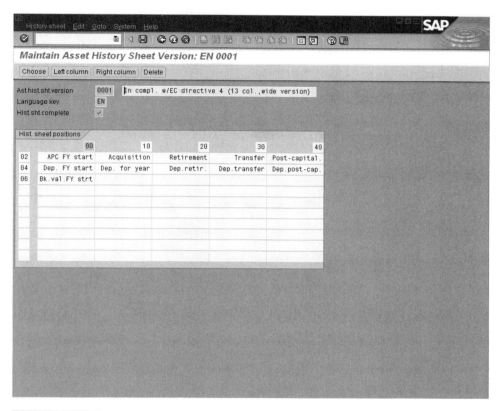

FIGURE 13.4   Maintaining the asset history sheet in Customizing (© SAP AG)

13.4   ASSET ACCOUNTS

Asset Accounting is managed in the same manner as Accounts Payable and Accounts Receivable: using Financial Accounting subledgers in the SAP R/3 System. For this purpose, each Asset Account must be assigned an asset class, which in turn is assigned to a reconciliation account in the General Ledger account (*see* Figure 13.5).

To ensure that the posting procedure in Asset Accounting runs smoothly, you must follow these rules:

- Asset Accounting uses the Chart of Accounts (*see* section 7.1.8) defined for the Company Code.

- The corresponding accounts are defined in the Chart of Accounts of the Company Code.

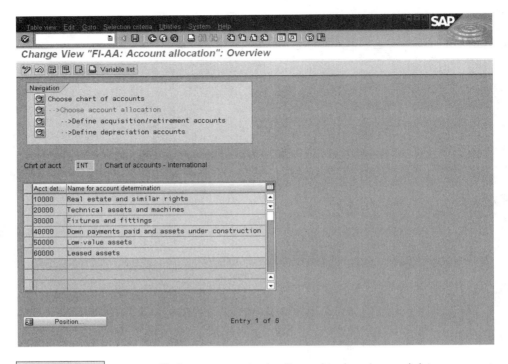

FIGURE 13.5 Reconciliation accounts in the General Ledger (general data – account determination) (© SAP AG)

■ The various asset classes are linked to corresponding General Ledger Accounting reconciliation accounts.

13.5 INTEGRATION WITH THE CONTROLLING MODULE

If you are using the CO (Controlling) module, any postings made in Financial Accounting can use the double-entry accounting technique (*see* section 7.7) to trigger postings in Controlling. Cost elements that correspond to the expenditure accounts in Financial Accounting are set up in Cost Accounting. With more information about account assignments (particularly additional account assignments), it is possible to take other aspects of costing into consideration.

You can maintain the following organizational units as part of overhead cost accounting:

- Cost Centre
- Order
- Project

13.6   USEFUL LIFE

Useful Life determines the period of depreciation and the depreciation method used for a particular asset. The depreciation methods permitted by law are supplemented by a series of depreciation tables for certain sectors, e.g. for the chemicals industry.

13.7   INVENTORY RULES FOR FIXED ASSETS

Tangible fixed assets are recorded in Asset Accounting. For tangible fixed assets, just as for purchased software, postings are made to the Asset account when these items are acquired, and the assessed value during their useful life is adjusted when they are disposed of. This is how the inventory is determined on the Balance Sheet date. Random spot-checks are carried out regularly and systematically for all tangible fixed assets.

Intangible assets and investments can only be determined by means of a book inventory. These assets are recorded in the corresponding subledgers (see section 7.9). The inventory on the Balance Sheet date is drawn up using the data in these subledgers.

13.8   CLASSIFICATION OF FIXED ASSETS

In the SAP R/3 System, fixed assets are classified at the following levels (*see also* Figure 13.6):

Each is described further below.

- Financial statement level
- Classifying level
- Asset-related level

13.8.1 Financial statement level

The classification at this level can itself be shown in a three-tier hierarchy of classes:

1 *Financial Statement Version.* The R/3 System supports several financial statement versions, e.g. the commercial statements, statements for tax calculation or calculation financial statement variants. These are connected, as shown in Figure 13.7.

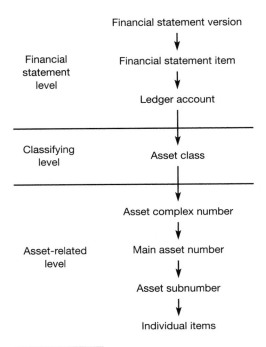

FIGURE 13.6   Classification of fixed assets (© SAP AG)

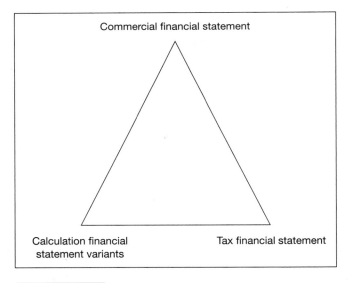

FIGURE 13.7   Financial statement versions (© SAP AG)

2 *Balance Sheet Item.* The Balance Sheet item is a grouping-together of several General Ledger accounts that are combined into one Balance Sheet item.

3 *General Ledger Account.* The General Ledger accounts are linked to the assets via Asset Class, as shown in Figure 13.8.

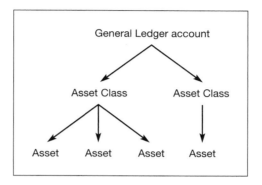

| **FIGURE 13.8** | Ledger Account (© SAP AG) |

Asset Class

In the SAP R/3 System, Asset Classes such as Vehicles, or Fixture and Fittings (*see* Figure 13.9) have both a classifying function and a controlling function.

The controlling functions are:

- number assignment by the system
- assignment of reconciliation accounts in the General Ledger (account determination) for Balance Sheet items
- control and layout of the screen
- default values from the SAP R/3 System
- default setting of useful life
- default setting of depreciation type

Account Assignment Key

One of the most important functions of Asset Class is its connection to the corresponding General Ledger account in Financial Accounting. The Account Assignment Key links the Asset Class and the reconciliation account in Financial Accounting.

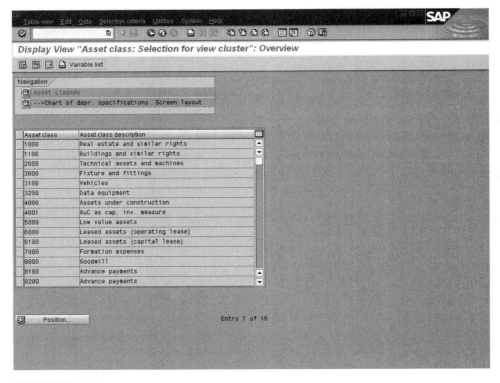

FIGURE 13.9 Display showing the Asset Classes in each Depreciation Area (© SAP AG)

Control parameters

A range of additional control parameters for Asset Class provides a number of control options for each class. You use these options to:

- control the screen layout in the Asset master data record
- control field properties in the Asset master data record
- control the assignment of the main asset number

Default values

The fields in a screen can be given default settings that are plausible commercial values. It is a good idea to set default values for the fields at the Asset Class level. Asset Classes are defined at the Client level; this means that they are relevant for all Company Codes (subsidiaries).

Asset Class structure

An Asset Class consists of three sections:

1 *header (control parameters).* The header contains the parameters used to maintain master records and account determination.

2 *master data section.* The master data section contains the various specifications of an asset master data.

3 *valuation data section.* The valuation section contains the settings for the default values used for depreciation. Several valuation data sections can be assigned to each Asset Class so that country-specific settings can be taken into consideration (*see* Figures 13.10 and 13.11).

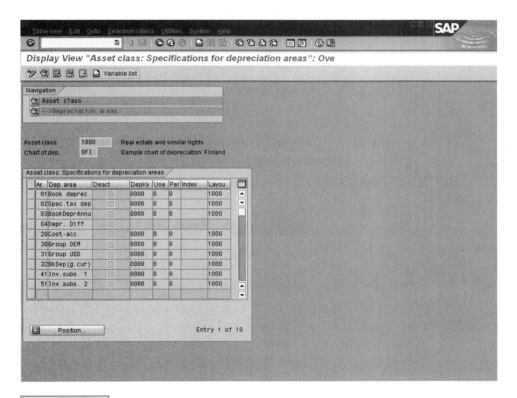

FIGURE 13.10   Components of Depreciation Areas (© SAP AG)

13.8.2 Classifying level

The classifying level is used to structure assets. Asset Classes make it possible to use both a business level and a legal level. Each asset must be assigned to an Asset Class.

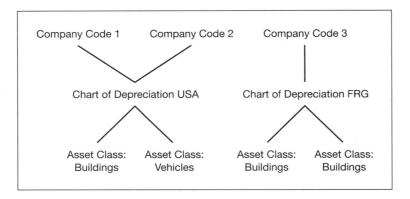

FIGURE 13.11   Asset Classes used in the Charts of Depreciation (© SAP AG)

13.8.3 Asset-related level

If asset-specific criteria are used to classify the data, up to four additional levels can be defined:

- Asset Super Number (asset complex/economic unit)
- Main Asset Number (individual asset)
- Asset Subnumber (part asset /separate post-capitalization)
- individual items

13.9   FUNCTIONS OF ASSET CLASSES

Asset Classes control the functions of the Asset master data records, as follows:

- *Default values.* Default values are stored in the master data record of an Asset Class. This means that an Asset Class functions as a reference and makes Asset master data records easier to create.
- *Screen layout rules.* The Asset Class controls the screen layout as well as the field properties of an Asset master data record. This means that a decision is made whether to display or hide particular fields. If a field is displayed, it is specified as a mandatory field or an optional field.
- *Assignment of numbers.* You can control how numbers are assigned in each Asset Class. This assignment does not affect any other classes.
- *Evaluation criterion.* If you use SAP reports to create evaluations, the Asset Class is usually used as a selection criterion. You can run calculations for typical characteristics within an Asset Class.

13.10 PLANT MAINTENANCE FOR FIXED ASSETS

The way that fixed assets are classified from an accounting point of view is completely different from the way required from the Plant Maintenance (PM) module point of view. In Asset Accounting, you cannot classify fixed assets according to technical location or equipment. When you enter the FI Asset Number in the master data record of the technical location or equipment, the Asset Accounting data is integrated with the data from the Plant Maintenance (PM) module. This means, for example, that plant maintenance orders that must be capitalized in the PM module can be capitalized into assets. If required, you can also jump directly from Asset Accounting (Financial Accounting) into a screen for a machine's technical area.

13.11 ASSET TYPES

In addition to Current Assets, a range of other asset items appears in the Asset section of the Balance Sheet:

- intangible assets
- tangible assets
- investments

The transition from tangible assets to investments is seamless. The following principle applies: the faster an asset can be liquidated (sold), the more likely it is to be referred to as an investment.

13.12 SPECIAL FORMS OF FIXED ASSETS

In addition to the asset types listed in section 13.11, you can also define other, special forms of fixed assets in the SAP R/3 System (see Figure 13.12). These are describrd further below and are:

- assets under construction
- low-value assets (LVAs)
- leased assets

13.12.1 Assets under construction

Assets under construction are a special form of tangible assets. They are not very different from other assets listed in the asset master data record. They are shown in the Balance Sheet as a separate item, and therefore need separate account assignment in the Asset Class.

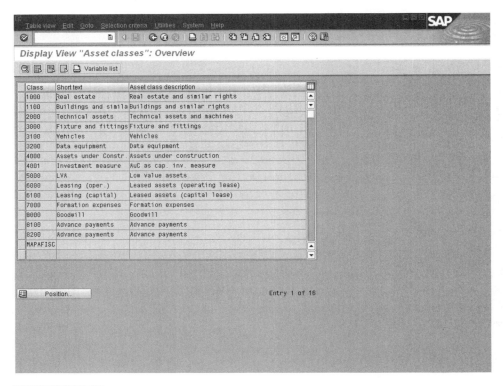

FIGURE 13.12   Special forms of fixed assets (© SAP AG)

Administration

In the SAP R/3 System, the master data records of assets under construction are managed in the same way as those of other assets. If necessary, you can manage several assets under construction collectively in one Asset master data record. On completion (of construction), you can distribute the individual items to the usable assets.

Depreciation

Standard depreciation on assets under construction is not permitted in many countries. However, you can carry out special commercial depreciation by using the Asset Class. Depreciation Key is set by the Asset Class.

Down payments

The Down Payment movement-type group must be enabled before you can post down payments. You must also define its assignment to the corresponding General Ledger account. The key for negative acquisition and manufacturing costs must be enabled so that you can make credits to the capitalized asset account at a later point in time.

Administration of individual items

In the case of particularly large-scale investments, you can use open item administration to administer assets under construction on an individual item level. The Asset Class controls how the individual item administration is activated when a corresponding master data record is created.

13.12.2 Low-value assets (LVAs)

Low value assets can be written off in full in the year of their acquisition or, as the case may be, directly in the month of acquisition. In the SAP R/3 System, a special Depreciation Key is set up for low-value assets. The Customizing settings for low-value assets were explained in section 11.5.4.

Maximum Value

As the permitted maximum amounts differ from one country to the next, a Maximum (permitted) Value is maintained at Company Code level. The check against that maximum value can take place as early on as recording of the order, or later when the actual acquisition is posted. If the check takes place when the acquisition is posted, deductions such as cash discounts can be taken into account.

Individual check

In the SAP R/3 System you can carry out individual checks on the total amount of incoming goods against the value set in the Company Code (for the administration of individual items).

Quantity check

You can also carry out a quantity check as an alternative to the individual check. If you carry out a quantity check, the total sum of all assets is divided by the number of assets. The result is checked against the Maximum Value set for the Company Code.

13.13   DEPRECIABLE AND NON-DEPRECIABLE FIXED ASSETS

13.13.1 Depreciable fixed assets

In the SAP Asset Accounting application component, Asset Classes are used to structure machines and technical plant. Asset Class controls the screen layout. You can only maintain very limited amounts of technical information in an Asset master data record's text box: more detailed technical information – for example, maintenance intervals – can be stored through the PM (Plant Maintenance) module.

13.13.2 Non-depreciable fixed assets

The valuation of real estate and shareholdings takes place either on the basis of the acquisition costs, or the partial value, or a value between acquisition costs and the partial value. In the R/3 System, real estate and shareholdings are also displayed in asset master records.

13.14　REPRESENTATION OF ASSETS

Assets can be simple assets, as well as very large-scale production systems. To represent the main section of an asset, the R/3 System uses a 12-digit Asset Number. A four-digit subnumber is used to represent the auxiliary components of an asset, where the subnumber '0000' is assigned as the standard setting in the R/3 System, even without subdivision into partial assets. For example, a car is assigned a main Asset Number, and a retrofitted car stereo or mobile phone is given a subnumber.

You can create additional subnumbers for each main number. Each subnumber leads the R/3 System to a separate Depreciation Area. Individual movements are posted directly to the subnumber as individual items for each Depreciation Area.

13.14.1 Single-entry assets

Single-entry assets are represented by individual Asset master records. As already mentioned, the default subnumber for the Asset master record is '0000'.

When an asset is shown as a single-entry asset, certain restrictions must be taken into consideration:

- depreciation and book values from previous accounting periods cannot be sorted by the year of acquisition
- later acquisitions cannot be depreciated independently

13.14.2 Assets with partial assets

If an asset consists of several partial assets, it may be a good idea to record the individual partial assets separately, both from a technical point of view and from a commercial viewpoint. The mobile phone in the example just given can therefore have a different value from the car in which it is installed.

You may want to split an asset into partial assets for the following reasons:

- separate value development of the individual asset parts
- different controlling assignment of the partial assets (separate cost centres)
- investment support is posted as a subnumber with negative values
- technical splitting of an asset (possibly taking PM requirements into consideration)
- additional entries

Partial assets can be recorded and depreciated separately. If you make additional acquisition entries, you must create a separate subnumber for each acquisition entry year. A setting in the system means that this form of acquisition posting may be mandatory.

13.14.3 Additional entries

You can specify subnumbers yourself or have them assigned internally by the system (*see* Figure 13.3). When you set up subnumbers, you can also set up a separate structure – for instance, they can be sorted according to acquisition years.

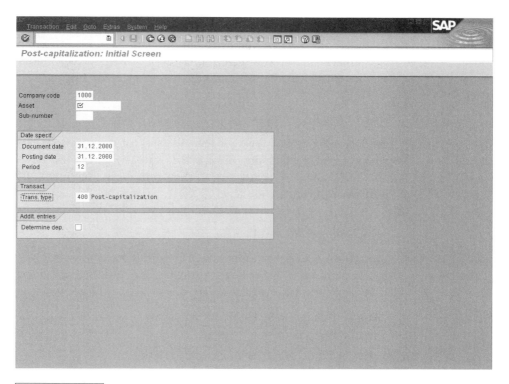

| **FIGURE 13.13** | Additional entries (© SAP AG)

13.14.4 Depreciation parameters

Asset Class uses the screen structure control to define whether partial assets can be depreciated separately. If the valuation and depreciation parameters are identical to those for the main Asset Number, the main number is used to carry out uniform depreciation.

13.14.5 Asset Super Number

Asset Super Number groups together several main Asset Numbers into one economic unit. You use Asset Super Numbers in the following cases:

- when asset depreciation is carried out as part of Real Estate Administration such that the individual assets are grouped into a single economic unit
- when large manufacturing complexes consist of several assets, in which circumstance the Asset Super Number can be used as another structuring feature which makes it possible to carry out an evaluation for the overall asset complex.
- when tax regulations in a country stipulate this

Asset Super Number can be set in the associated assets. The number then acts as a sorting criterion. When you carry out evaluations in Asset Accounting, you can use Asset Super Number as a selection criterion. The Logistics Plants must specify the structure of the Asset Number and the Asset Super Number.

13.14.6 Asset Complex

Asset Complex groups together several assets for depreciation. This is a requirement in commercial law in some countries. However, you may also have to group together individual assets for tax reasons. In the Controlling function, you can also use Asset Complex as a classification level.

13.14.7 Negative assets

Negative assets have been mentioned at several points in previous chapters. The Asset Class determines whether negative acquisition and manufacturing costs are permitted in each class. Areas where negative assets *are* used include:

- the collection of investments on separate assets or on subnumbers of an asset (a negative partial asset)
- the collection of credits on separate assets

It is generally not permitted to carry investment support measures and credits on one number.

13.15 THE ASSET MASTER DATA RECORD

The Asset master data record contains all the long-term data relating to an asset:

- item-related master data
- depreciation data
- organizational master data

In the SAP R/3 System, Asset master records describe independent assets in the way required by tax regulations. You must create an Asset master record in the R/3 System for each asset. These assets are listed individually in the inventory list and described accurately.

Asset aquisitions can only be posted when the Asset master data record has been created in the R/3 System.

13.15.1 Structure of the Asset master data record

The asset master data record is always divided in two areas:

- general master data with different field groups
- depreciation data with different depreciation dates

13.15.2 Master data in Asset Accounting

The general section of the Asset master data record contains information about an asset. The data used to evaluate the asset is located in the Depreciation Data section. Background information and depreciation data is shown in the field groups:

- general specification
- details of account assignments
- inventory data
- posting information
- time-dependent index
- evaluation groups
- investment support measures
- depreciation areas
- asset values
- information of asset administration
- real estate information

- insurance data
- leasing terms
- information for Plant Maintenance

You can store additional information in the appropriate text box in all the field groups listed above. And each of the groups is described further below.

General specifications

You maintain the designation, the quantity and the unit in the General Specifications field group (*see* Figure 13.14). If low-value assets are listed in a collective account, it is important that you maintain the quantity and the unit.

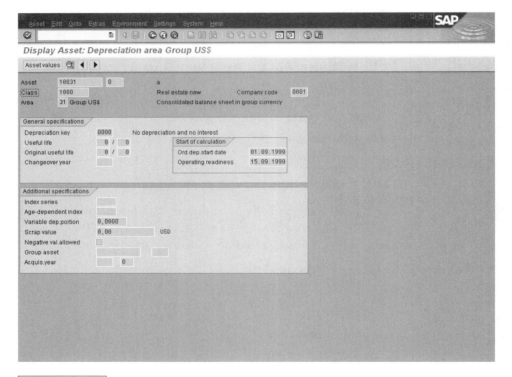

FIGURE 13.14 Displaying an asset: general data

Account assignment entries

If Asset Accounting is organized using the Materials Management (MM) module's Purchasing function, you can carry out the Liability Check and Budget Administration functions when the asset is ordered.

Inventory data

You enter the date of the last physical inventory in Inventory Data and add information about the inventory. If the Include Asset field is activated, the asset is included in the inventory list.

Posting information

In addition to Activation Date that is set automatically by the SAP R/3 System, you can store other specifications, such as Deactivation Date or Order Date.

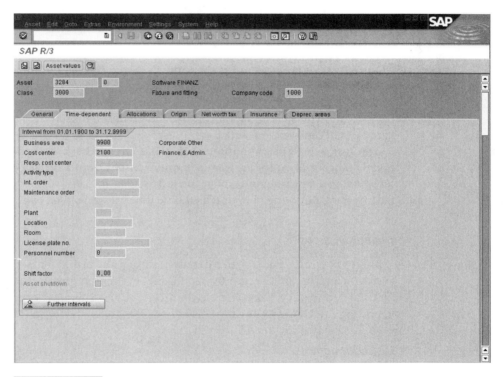

FIGURE 13.15   Displaying an asset: time-dependent data (© SAP AG)

Time-dependent index

Some business assignments change in the course of their service lives. It is a good idea to save any historical data if the organizational assignment or form of use changes, so that you can provide complete information about an asset and its use (*see* Figure 13.15).

You can save the following data on a time-dependent basis in the Asset master data record:

- Business Area
- Cost Centre responsible
- type of goods/services) (Activity Type)
- Internal Order
- Plant Maintenance Order
- Plant/Location/Room
- Car Licence Number/Personnel Number
- Shift Factor
- Asset Shutdown

If several values are present for the same field, the R/3 System indicates this with an asterisk (*) after the relevant field.

You can use specific 'Valid from' and 'Valid to' dates to record data without gaps. If data for an Asset master data record is requested, the display always depends on the date in each case.

You can select any time interval that has already been updated so that you can update it again. If you want to re-determine entries from a certain point in time, you must define a new time interval in the R/3 System. Initially, the existing field contents are transferred into the newly defined time interval so that you can change them.

Evaluation groups

Evaluation groups control the detailed evaluation of fixed assets. In the SAP R/3 System, you can define up to five additional evaluation groups. You can set up these fields as mandatory fields (required entry) and use them as sorting criteria within Reporting (*see* Figure 13.16).

Depreciation Areas

You can set the depreciation parameters for each Depreciation Area of a Chart of Depreciation in the Asset master data record. You can branch from the Asset data into the individual Depreciation Areas (*see* Figure 13.17).

Insurance data

As the entries for insurance are often insufficient, you can maintain additional data in the R/3 System. You can list alternative valuation options as well as Type, Insurance Companies and Agreement Number data. The system uses index series to automatically determine the insurance valuation without you having to maintain a separate depreciation area for the insurance value (*see* Figure 13.18).

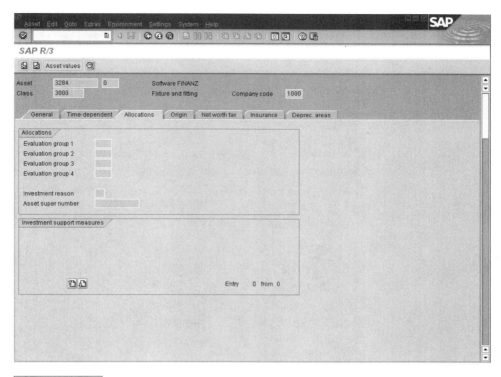

FIGURE 13.16   Displaying an asset: allocations

13.15.3 Number assignment to Asset master data records

Asset Numbers can be assigned internally by the R/3 System or externally by the user. In the case of external number assignment, the user is responsible for number assignment. However, the R/3 System ensures that no duplicate numbers are assigned. Asset Number always consists of the main Asset Number and the subnumber '0000'.

13.15.4 Changing Asset master data records

You will need to change an Asset master data record if it has been reorganized or if asset data was entered incorrectly. To update Asset master data records, use the Change Asset menu item.

13.15.5 Deactivating Asset master data records

As a rule, an asset has only a limited economic and technical life expectancy. However, the economically meaningful service life does not have to correspond to the technical service life. It may also happen that an asset is no longer required and is

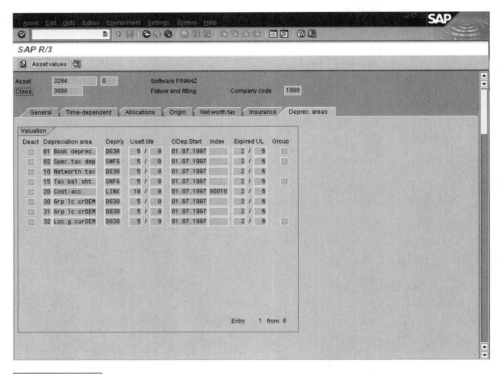

therefore sold. When you post an asset disposal/retirement, the R/3 System automatically deactivates it in its Asset master data record. You can, of course, also make changes manually if required.

13.15.6 Deleting Asset master data records

If an asset has already been ordered and therefore set up in the system, you must delete it from Asset Accounting if the order is cancelled. It may also sometimes happen that an Asset master data record has been set up in the wrong Asset Class and therefore must be deleted. You can only delete an Asset master data record if no postings have been carried out for that asset; otherwise, this may cause inconsistencies in the system.

13.15.7 Blocking Asset master data records

If an Asset master data record has been 'locked', it can no longer be posted to. A Blocking Code is used for assets under construction to prevent any additional acquisition postings to the asset. However, you can still carry out transfers and retirement postings even if the Blocking Code is set.

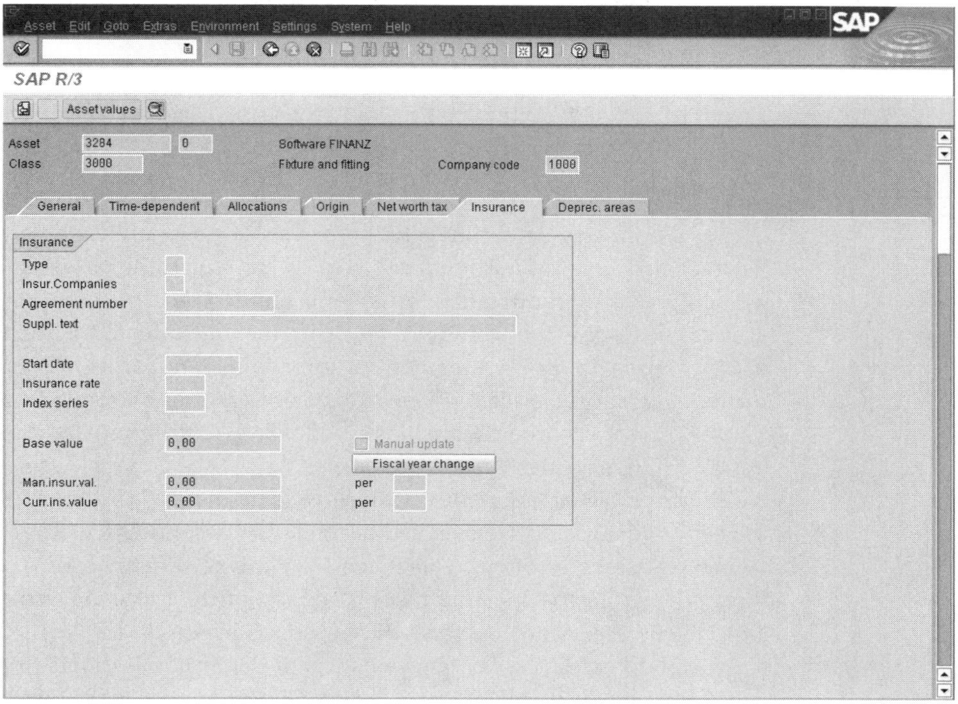

FIGURE 13.18 Displaying an asset: insurance (© SAP AG)

13.16 VALUATION

In the SAP R/3 Asset Accounting application component, each Company Code is assigned a Chart of Depreciation for the valuation of fixed assets. In turn, several Depreciation Areas are integrated in a Chart of Depreciation. A Chart of Depreciation can be assigned to several Company Codes.

13.16.1 Chart of Depreciation

A Chart of Depreciation contains all the Depreciation Areas used in a Company Code. As the legal regulations vary in each country, separate Charts of Depreciation are used. The Chart of Depreciation controls the following:

■ Depreciation Areas
■ Depreciation Key

- properties of the movement types
- investment support measures

Each is described further below.

Depreciation Area

Depreciation Area determines the properties of the commercial law, tax law or other depreciation areas of a Company Code. In particular, the commercial and tax regulations can vary significantly from one country to the next. A large number of Company Codes from different countries are consolidated within the same Group. Each country has its own regulations for valuing companies. To achieve uniform valuation, you should only apply one Chart of Depreciation for each country.

You can set up other Depreciation Areas (e.g. Costing) in addition to those used to meet legal requirements.

The commercial law Depreciation Area is hard-coded in the R/3 System. It controls how individual assets are assigned to the ledger accounts. The values are controlled by Account Assignment Keys, which can have different definitions in each Depreciation Area. To ensure that posting takes place smoothly, the same currency must be used both in the Company Code and the Depreciation Area.

In certain cases, the tax law valuation or depreciation differs from the commercial law valuation or depreciation. The Tax Depreciation Area shows separate valuation approaches and depreciation, so that it can reflect the different methods.

Depreciation Key

Depreciation Key defines the depreciation method and the depreciation rates.

Type of movement

The type of movement represents the type of business transactions in the R/3 System.

Investment support measures

Investment support measures can be reported as negative acquisition and manufacturing costs. They can be handled separately in each Company Code.

Reference Charts of Depreciation

The standard version of the R/3 System contains country-specific Charts of Depreciation for many different countries. This contains the maximum amount of information, and it can be reduced to suit your particular requirements. You should first copy the Charts of Depreciation and then modify the copy.

13.16.2 The Controlling function

Cost Accounting procedures used in a company often handle valuation in a different way from the way it is handled in commercial law or tax law valuation. No legal regulations need to be observed in imputed valuation. For example, unlike in commercial law or tax law valuation, the following costs can be used as a basis:

- imputed costs
- replacement values above acquisition costs
- other operating costs

13.16.3 Derived Depreciation Areas

In addition to the true Depreciation Areas mentioned so far, you can also manage 'derived' Depreciation Areas. Derived Depreciation Areas consist of up to four true Depreciation Areas. The differences between the commercial law and tax law depreciation areas can be shown in a third, derived Depreciation Area.

13.16.4 Group valuations

As a rule, valuation within a group's Company Code differs from the valuation used in the Company Codes themselves. This is why a group must carry out its own valuation. A separate valuation must be carried out if assets are sold between the individual subsidiaries of a group.

13.16.5 Different currencies

In international groups, the subsidiaries use currencies that are not the same as the group currency. In the case of two Company Codes, which are identical apart from the currency, you can determine the currency difference and therefore the differences caused by different valuations.

13.16.6 Investment support measures

It is a good idea to create separate depreciation areas for investment support measures in the asset classes. This allows you to carry out the following:

- checks when support is received
- evidence of retention periods in the case of asset transfer or retirement, and correct posting of the investment support.

13.16.7 Annual closing of accounts – fiscal year change

The SAP R/3 System distinguishes between annual accounts and fiscal year change. The annual statements of the old fiscal year are usually drawn up several weeks after the new fiscal year has started.

Fiscal year change

In the R/3 System, the fiscal year change means the start of a new fiscal year. You cannot make postings to assets in a new fiscal year until after the fiscal year change. The earliest possible date for the fiscal year change is in the last month of the old fiscal year.

If the fiscal year change has been carried out, the R/3 System continues to allow postings in the old fiscal year. In this case, the old fiscal year may not yet be concluded. This has the advantage that postings to assets in the old fiscal year are also taken into consideration in the new fiscal year. The values of both acquisitions and retirements of access are correctly posted in the new fiscal year.

In the R/3 System, you can carry out a test run of the fiscal year change (*see* Figure 13.19).The test run indicates the totals of all assets. It also generates a log for the assets that are not correctly posted. The system creates a stock of work from these error messages, and the R/3 System displays the error messages as long texts.

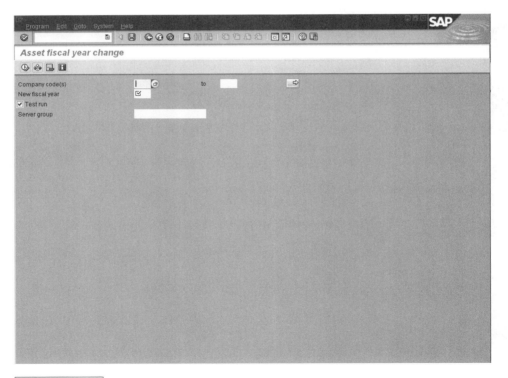

FIGURE 13.19 Initiating a test run for a fiscal year change (© SAP AG)

From an accounting point of view, a fiscal year change means that the annual closing procedures have not yet taken place. This only happens when the annual closing program has been run, after which you can no longer make postings in the old fiscal year.

Year-end closing

The fiscal year is concluded when the books are closed. No more postings can be made.

In accordance with country-specific requirements, end-of-year reports consist of the annual Balance Sheet, the Profit and Loss statement, and the supplement to those financial statements.

In order to prepare the annual reports the Asset Accounting application component has a number of tasks. Examples are:

- depreciation simulations
- changes and adjustment postings
- a check of the asset history sheet
- a check of the evaluations of the asset valuation

As seen from the list immediately above, you can simulate various depreciation processes in Asset Accounting in the R/3 System (*see* Figure 13.20). Here, you can simulate and check valuation parameters, and you can change them if required. You may also have to adjust the values at this point in time.

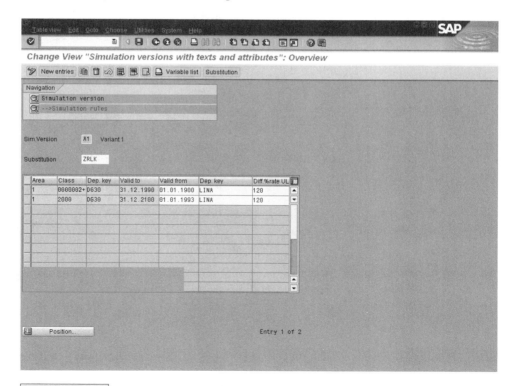

FIGURE 13.20 Depreciation simulation (© SAP AG)

If the depreciation simulations show that changes are required, you can modify the actual posting accordingly. You can also make adjustments due to incorrect postings.

If, for whatever reason, a fiscal year has been closed too early and late postings still have to be made in the old fiscal year, you can reopen a closed fiscal year. Indeed, you can open individual Business Areas or the entire Company Code at a later stage.

Year-end closing program

The year-end closing program carries out all the tasks involved in closing the fiscal year. If the fiscal year is closed, no further postings or adjustments can be made. The year-end closing is only possible in the following fiscal year. If, for example, the annual reports for 1999/2000 are drawn up in the 2000/01 fiscal year, the next fiscal year that can be closed is 2000/01.

The year-end closing program automatically checks a range of criteria without which no year-end reporting would be possible. The program checks whether:

- errors occurred when the depreciation was calculated (e.g. an incorrectly defined calculation key)
- the planned depreciation was fully posted to the General Ledger
- the stocks of the depreciation areas to be periodically posted were fully posted to the General Ledger
- all the assets acquired in the fiscal year are also already activated (residual value regulations) – but as this check is irrelevant for assets under construction, you can deactivate it for the appropriate Asset Classes.
- all incomplete assets have been completed

13.17   DEPRECIATION

The R/3 System logs every posting and every change in value of an asset. It uses this data to automatically calculate the planned depreciation of this asset.

13.17.1 Planned and manual depreciation

As the current valuation is continuously recorded in Asset Accounting, planned depreciation – the amount of which is continuously adapted – is stored in the system. The different depreciation methods and periods are also taken into consideration here. The SAP R/3 System automatically posts the depreciation amounts to the General Ledger accounts.

In addition to the planned depreciation described above, you may have to carry out manual depreciation. Manual depreciation is usually extraordinary depreciation or transfers from reserves. In principle, you can carry out manual depreciation for every type of depreciation. As manual depreciation is irregular and cannot be planned, this depreciation cannot be set systematically (*see also* section 11.5.5).

13.17.2 Time and amount of depreciation

The R/3 System contains all necessary depreciation periods, such as months, quarters, half-years or years. You can select the appropriate Depreciation Cycle in each Depreciation Area. As a rule, in commercial law a depreciation run is initiated once or twice a year; in contrast, costing via the Controlling usually carries out monthly depreciation runs.

13.17.3 Additional Account Assignment Objects for the Controlling module

Since the SAP R/3 System is an integrated system, the primary postings in financial accounting also provide data for the Controlling module. Additional postings are made to Controlling Objects. The additional Account Assignment Objects are, for example:

- Cost Centres
- internal orders
- types of goods/services
- Plant Maintenance Orders

Controlling evaluates these objects and provides additional control information. In turn, you can also define separate additional Account Assignment Objects for the various Depreciation Areas.

13.18   REORGANIZATION AND ARCHIVING

In theory, the R/3 System can store data indefinitely. However, it is a good idea to archive the data from previous years, for instance using the archiving tool supplied by iXOS. In this context, reorganization means deleting old data from the system.

When you carry out reorganization, the total figures from previous years should be kept in the system for comparisons and evaluations (*see* next section) and only the individual items should be reorganized. You can re-import the archived data into the R/3 System as part of an audit (*see* section 5.9).

13.19   THE ASSET ACCOUNTING INFORMATION SYSTEM

The standard version of the SAP R/3 System already contains a great number of evaluation options. You can supplement the standard reports with other reports to meet your individual requirements.

13.19.1 The report tree

The report tree and its branches structure the reports available in Asset Accounting (*see* Figure 13.21). The report tree contained in the standard version of the SAP R/3 System can be changed and restructured at any time. You can use the standard reports as templates when developing your own reports.

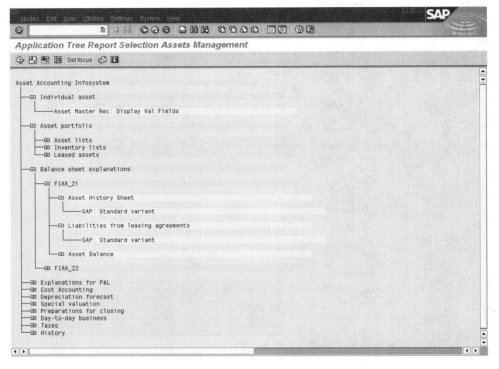

| **FIGURE 13.21** | Report tree for Asset Accounting (© SAP AG) |

In the standard reports, you can set the navigation to follow the required degree of detail and the sorting method. You can carry out the following evaluations in the reports:

- individual and totals evaluation (where totals can be expanded by double-clicking on the line)
- evaluations across any number of Depreciation Areas
- evaluations in variable stages and sort versions
- evaluations sorted by amount or restricted to a specified number of largest amounts

You use the Set Focus and Generate List toggles to customize the report tree.

13.19.2 The asset history sheet

The SAP R/3 System provides country-specific asset history sheets (*see* Figure 13.22) that correspond to commercial and tax regulations. You use the settings in Customizing to modify these sheets to your own requirements. The lines and columns in the asset history sheet are freely definable. The asset history sheet is the central means of evaluation, both within a year and as part of the annual accounts.

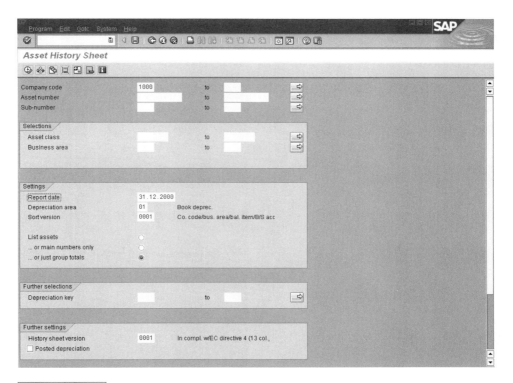

FIGURE 13.22   Asset history sheet (header screen) (© SAP AG)

You must enter the relevent Depreciation Area, the sort version, and the history sheet version in the Asset History Sheet specifications screen. You must first define a sort version if you have not yet maintained one.

Further detail is entered in a subsequent detailed screen (*see* Figure 13.23).

You will find further information on this topic in section 11.7.2.

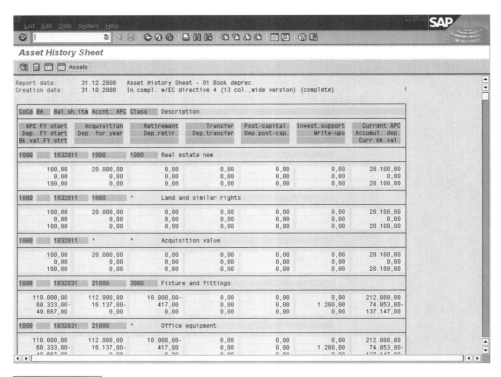

FIGURE 13.23 Asset history sheet (detailed screen) (© SAP AG)

13.19.3 Simulation

In Asset Accounting, simulation calculation is used in planning to make it possible to represent each of the different value developments for various parameters (*see* Figure 13.24). Simulation is frequently used for planning asset values, as follows:

- for different depreciation methods
- for different asset movements
- in the case of changes in the depreciation area

By changing parameters, the simulation shows an asset value development over the entire period of depreciation, so that future depreciation scenarios can be planned. This can also take future investments into consideration.

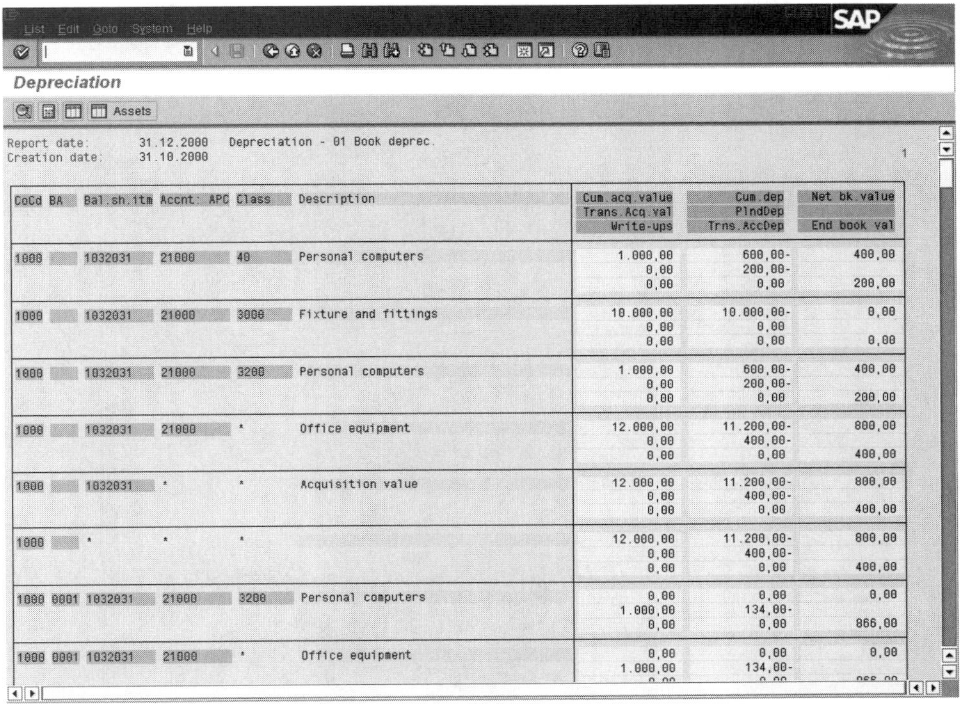

Report date: 31.12.2000 Depreciation - 01 Book deprec.
Creation date: 31.10.2000 1

CoCd	BA	Bal.sh.itm	Accnt: APC	Class	Description	Cum.acq.value Trans.Acq.val Write-ups	Cum.dep PlndDep Trns.AccDep	Net bk.value End book val
1000		1032031	21000	40	Personal computers	1.000,00 0,00 0,00	600,00- 200,00- 0,00	400,00 200,00
1000		1032031	21000	3000	Fixture and fittings	10.000,00 0,00 0,00	10.000,00- 0,00 0,00	0,00 0,00
1000		1032031	21000	3200	Personal computers	1.000,00 0,00 0,00	600,00- 200,00- 0,00	400,00 200,00
1000		1032031	21000	*	Office equipment	12.000,00 0,00 0,00	11.200,00- 400,00- 0,00	800,00 400,00
1000		1032031	*	*	Acquisition value	12.000,00 0,00 0,00	11.200,00- 400,00- 0,00	800,00 400,00
1000		*	*	*		12.000,00 0,00 0,00	11.200,00- 400,00- 0,00	800,00 400,00
1000	0001	1032031	21000	3200	Personal computers	0,00 1.000,00 0,00	0,00 134,00- 0,00	0,00 866,00
1000	0001	1032031	21000	*	Office equipment	0,00 1.000,00 [illegible]	0,00 134,00- [illegible]	0,00 [illegible]

FIGURE 13.24 Depreciation simulation (© SAP AG)

CHAPTER 14

Special-purpose ledgers

14.1   SPECIAL-PURPOSE LEDGERS VERSUS STANDARD LEDGERS

In the SAP R/3 System, you can supplement the ledgers in the standard version with other ledgers that can set up individual evaluation systems. You may have to do this if different aspects, for example commercial and technical values, are to be represented together in an evaluation but SAP does not provide that evaluation in the standard system. You can also use special-purpose ledgers when you are not using the Controlling module but you want to carry out Cost Centre Accounting or when there are other control requirements.

14.1.1 Standard ledgers

The standard SAP R/3 System contains the following standard ledgers:

- General Ledger
- Consolidation account
- Profit Centre account
- Reconciliation Ledger

14.1.2 Special-purpose ledgers

Depending on the information you want to obtain, you must plan the layout and structure of data tables carefully to obtain the report option you require. To achieve this, you can take data from other SAP applications and import it from external systems into the special-purpose ledgers. Before the data comes into the tables in the special-purpose ledgers, it is validated and may even be changed. Figure 14.1 shows a diagram of the extent to which SAP modules are integrated with one another, the interfaces to other systems, and the functions of the special-purpose ledgers.

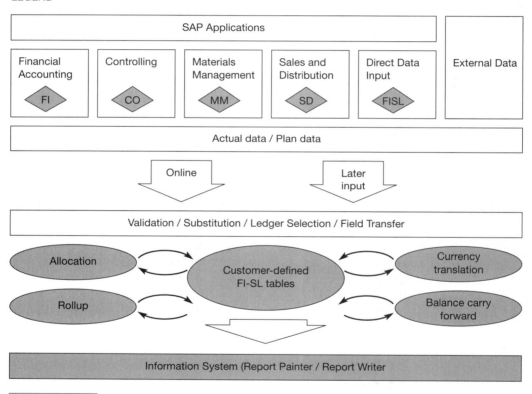

FIGURE 14.1 Integration of the special-purpose ledgers (© SAP AG)

You can use the standard R/3 evaluation tools (the Report Painter and the Report Writer in a row/column structure) to evaluate the special-purpose ledgers. You can use queries for one-time evaluations.

Advantages of the special-purpose ledgers:

Special-purpose ledgers have certain advantages over the standard ledgers, as follows:

- Existing database structures can be extended to include customer-specific requirements in order to meet individual business requirements.

- The contents of the ledgers can be structured in a flexible manner because, on an individual basis, you can specify which business transactions are to be posted to the special-purpose ledger.

- Adjustment postings can be made without difficulty.

- You can set up separate special-purpose ledgers for group Charts of Accounts and country-specific Charts of Accounts.

- In the special-purpose ledgers, you can define separate accounting periods to show fiscal-year variants.

- The validation and substitution functions make it possible to manipulate the data that is transferred to a special-purpose ledger.

- Data from other SAP applications and external systems can be totalled and distributed individually.

- You can use the special-purpose ledgers to set up a reporting system that applies across several applications and organizations.

Special purpose ledgers are purely receiver systems in which data is only received. They do not provide data for other applications in the system.

In general, when you plan a special-purpose ledger you should take care that there are no evaluation tools already provided in other SAP modules for setting up the evaluation; otherwise, you may create unnecessary work. The Controlling module in particular contains a wide range of tools for creating Cost Accounting reports.

Special-purpose ledger database tables

The standard version of the R/3 System contains several special-purpose ledger database tables. These tables cannot be used directly; they simply act as examples. However, you can customize copies of these tables to meet individual requirements. The special-purpose ledgers consist of a partial quantity of data that is kept in a special-purpose ledger database table. You can group together individual database tables to form table groups. The individual dimensions used here can come from different applications of the SAP System or other systems. The total of the individual dimensions produces the Coding Block of a database table for the special-purpose ledgers (*see* Figure 14.2).

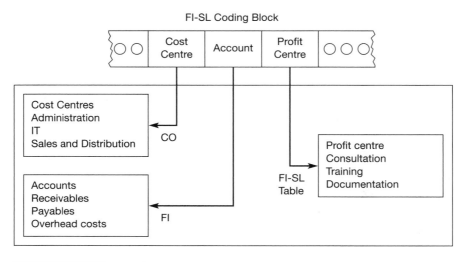

14.2   SPECIAL-PURPOSE LEDGER MASTER RECORDS

The master records of the special-purpose ledgers determine the structure of the relevant database table. Each ledger has up to 16 different criteria, which in technical terms represent up to 16 dimensions of a table. The special-purpose ledgers consist of a subset of tables. You can also assign one or more separate ledgers to any database table. In the ledger, you define which dimensions of a Coding Block are included in a special-purpose ledger.

You can specify whether or not a business transaction is posted to the special-purpose ledger. You can either post all business transactions into a single ledger or post an individual business transaction in several special-purpose ledgers. The Integration Manager regulates how a business transaction is posted to the special-purpose ledgers. The transfer conditions are stored in the Integration Manager. They are apportioned according to market criteria such as regions, product features, or organizational units. Figure 14.3 shows the structure of special-purpose ledgers and database tables.

The reports that are created on the basis of the various special-purpose ledgers access the same dataset and select the data according to requirements. When you define special-purpose ledgers, it is better to define several small ledgers instead of one large one. This keeps the number of datasets low, because a separate data record is generated for each combination of the dimensions. Several small special-purpose ledgers allow the R/3 System to run faster than one large special-purpose ledger.

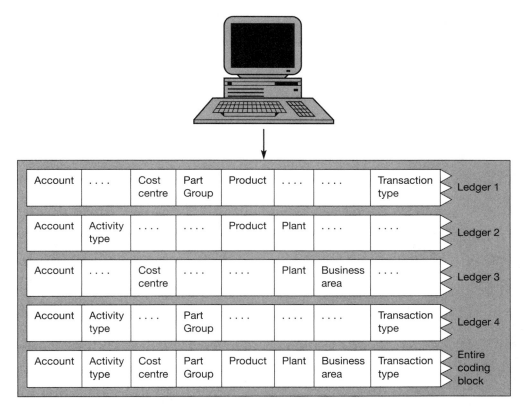

FIGURE 14.3   Special-purpose ledgers and an entire Coding Block (© SAP AG)

There are a number of possible reasons for using several special-purpose ledgers at the same time:

- reports in several currencies (up to three currencies per table, e.g. transaction currency, local currency and group currency)
- several business calendars and fiscal-year variants
- different evaluation criteria of the dataset

Local Company Code data is saved in a local ledger. The data of a global Company or the data of Company Codes that are assigned to a Company are saved in global ledgers. (*See also* Chapter 7.)

14.2.1 Field Transfer

The Field Transfer function controls how data is transferred into the special-purpose ledgers. Field Transfer contains stored information about which dimensions are filled in the database table by a business transaction. You can only define Field Transfer for special-purpose ledgers; you cannot do so in the standard ledgers of other applications.

14.2.2 Procedures

The Integration Manager is the interface for posting from other SAP applications or other systems into the special-purpose ledgers. It controls whether the system posts a business transaction to the special-purpose ledgers, and how it does so, if applicable. The distribution of the business transactions is carried out on the basis of individual business criteria. For the sake of simplicity, you can gather individual business transactions and groups together. A group can then be assigned to a ledger.

14.2.3 Posting Periods

Before you can use special-purpose ledgers, you must first define the Posting Periods in the system. The SAP R/3 System requires Posting Periods so that it can post the individual postings correctly in the right period for the special-purpose ledgers. A business transaction can also be transferred into different periods in several ledgers. For example, special-purpose ledgers can be configured for weekly evaluations and other ledgers can be configured for monthly evaluations. Theoretically, you can create up to 366 special-purpose daily ledgers. Posting Periods do not necessarily have to match the posting periods used in the Financial Accounting module; in this case, however, you must ensure you set certain settings correctly so as to meet your requirements.

14.2.4 Versions

You can keep different versions of each special-purpose ledger. For this purpose, the following different data record types are available in the special-purpose ledgers:

- actual data
- planned data
- actual data (allocation)
- planned data (allocation)

The different versions can be identified by different data record types and different version numbers. For example, this means that you can define different plan versions that are determined on the basis of different assumptions. The standard System already contains several Versions; you can add your own Versions to them at any time, as required.

You can also keep different Actual Versions in the R/3 System. The different Actual Versions mean that you can carry out different consolidation variants.

14.2.5 Validation and Substitution

When data is posted into special-purpose ledgers, almost all of it is validated. You can define specific validation rules in the R/3 System, because it is often the case that no general set of rules can be applied and stored. The data is validated before it is posted in the special-purpose ledger so that only checked data comes into the ledger. The validation is carried out using Boolean logic.

In Customizing, you can specify what is to happen if the validation rules are not complied with. A warning may appear or you must correct the input. In the case of data correction, you can replace the entered values with other values. For example, Cost Centre descriptors can be renamed in this way when they are posted to a special-purpose ledger.

14.3   FUNCTIONS

14.3.1 Sets

Before you can use special-purpose ledgers, you must first define sets. Sets are used in many components of the ledgers. A *set* is a range of values of a dimension in a database table or the sum of certain values of a dimension (*see again* Figure 14.2).

In Figure 14.2, for example, a set within the cost centre could be the range 100–199 for Administration Area. Another example could be the cost centres from 200 to 299 for the IT Area.

Sets are maintained centrally and can therefore be used alongside each other in all modules.

14.3.2 Functions in special-purpose ledgers

A special-purpose ledger includes the following functions, each of which is described further below:

- Planning
- Posting
- Periodical tasks
- Information System
- Master Records
- Tools

Planning

Planning in the special-purpose ledger function means the input, distribution and posting of data. The data can be entered at varying detail levels (*see* Figure 14.4).

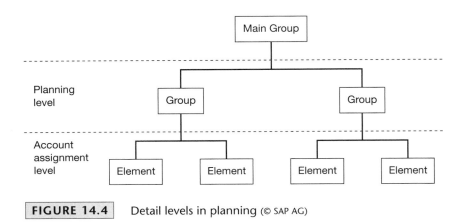

FIGURE 14.4 Detail levels in planning (© SAP AG)

As already mentioned above, you can set up different plan Versions to take account of, and represent, different assumptions. Planning can be carried out in different currencies. You can use the Copy function to apply old, planned or actual Versions as templates for current Versions, which can then be changed accordingly after copying. The number of possible plan Versions is unlimited.

Posting

Posting in the special-purpose ledgers can take place in different ways:

- *By importing data from another SAP application.* Before data is imported into a special-purpose ledger, it is always validated first and, where applicable, substituted. If data is transferred from another SAP application, the data is posted, usually in real time, into one or more special-purpose ledgers on the basis of the rules set in the Integration Manager. The Document Number from the original SAP application is also adopted by the special-purpose ledger.

- *By means of direct input (for adjustment postings).* As a rule, the posting of entries into the special-purpose ledger takes place from other SAP applications, as shown above. However, you can also enter data directly into a ledger. This may happen because:

  - the posting is only to take place in the special-purpose ledger

  - different Versions of documents are to be posted

  - additional currencies are to be entered manually

  - statistical quantity postings are to be made

  - Documents have a balance that does not equal zero

These postings, which are to some extent incorrect from an accounting point of view, can be made in the special-purpose ledger without risk, because it is purely a receiver system and therefore does not pass on any data. Data that is entered directly in the special-purpose ledgers has to be marked appropriately and can therefore be easily identified at a later date.

■ *By import of data from external systems.* The third form of data import is data import from external systems. This requires interface programs. Several program examples are supplied with the standard system because it is not possible to deal with all possible interfaces. You must first copy the programs and then modify them to your own requirements.

Periodical tasks

As a general rule, Documents are posted online in the special-purpose ledgers so that they are available in real time. However, there are also a few tasks that are performed only periodically. These include:

■ Allocation

■ Rollup

■ Currency Translation

■ Balance carry-forward

■ Data Import

■ Archiving

The **Allocation** task is used to allocate or distribute amounts from a sender to a number of recipients. During Allocation, all the values are recorded in an Allocation Account and then allocated to recipients. With distribution, there is no detour via the Allocation Account: the amounts or quantities are distributed directly by the senders to the recipients. Sets are also used when working with allocation and distribution (*see* Figure 14.5).

The values can be allocated in three different ways:

1 *Fixed amount method.* The recipients receive fixed amounts or quantities.

2 *Fixed proportion method.* The recipients each receive a specified percentage.

3 *Dynamic method.* As in the case of the fixed proportion method, the recipients each receive a specified percentage. The amount of the set is determined dynamically on the basis of the sets read from the recipients.

When you create evaluations, the Report Painter or Report Writer reads the data required for the evaluation from all the ledgers that contain the required data. If the ledgers to be read contain a great deal of data, the reaction times are very long and the System and network loads are high. **Rollups** save frequently required data in totalled and compressed form. Rollup ledgers save the data from several other ledgers.

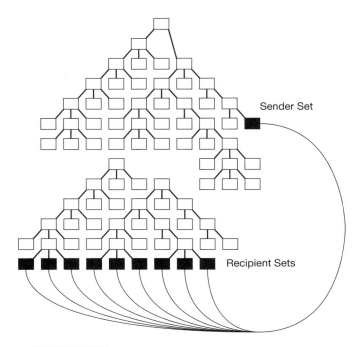

Sender Set

Recipient Sets

The standard version of the R/3 System contains a ***Currency Translation*** program that can be used to convert amounts that have already been posted.

The ***Balance Carry-forward*** function is used to transfer balances from accounts from the previous fiscal year into the new fiscal year. This function enables the carrying forward of Asset accounts as well as that of Profit and Loss accounts.

The standard version of the R/3 System contains some sample ***Data Import*** programs for importing data from external applications. As these programs only act as examples, you must first copy them and then modify them to meet your requirements.

Archiving is used for information that you no longer need in your production system. When data is archived, it is deleted from the SAP database and placed in a file. You can then transfer this file to an archive system for storage. The data can be accessed as needed.

Information System

The Information System function works with the Report Writer and Report Painter tools. Both tools have similar functions. The Report Painter is easier to use; for example, you do not need to know about the set technique. Data is displayed in tables, where you can specify each column and line.

Master Records

The start of this main section, at 14.2, contains a detailed discussion of the master data in special-purpose ledgers.

Tools

The Tools function consists of the following:

- *Sets*. These are frequently used in special-purpose ledgers. The structure of a set has already been described in section 14.3.1.

- *Diagnosis*. This function can be used to test and check the System to see how and where a Document is posted in the special-purpose ledger or why a Document is not posted in a ledger.

- *Evidence List*. Evidence List can be used to display the contents of a table or to print the contents.

- *Ledger Statistics*. The Ledger Statistics action logs the number of postings in a database table.

CHAPTER 15

Travel management

TAX-RELATED HANDLING OF TRAVEL COSTS

15.1.1 Business trips (domestic)

Expenses

In the case of domestic business or official trips, employees are generally entitled to a tax-free daily or flat-rate amount for expenses. The Travel Management module allows you to define the rates allowed by legal regulations and those provided to employees by the company.

You can, for example, set up methods for calculating how long a trip is, thus determining the amount an employee receives. If several business or official trips take place on one calendar day, the absence times on this day are added together. If the business trips or official trips do not include overnight stays, which are deemed to start at 4 p.m. and ending at 8 a.m. on the following calendar day, the absence times could once more be added together. The day could thus be regarded as one or two days of absence, depending on how a 'day' is defined. Should the employee be reimbursed at a higher rate than allowed by country-specific regulations, this amount is often subject to income tax.

Although accounting principles may allow for business travel expenses, tax law may not allow the complete write-off of such expenses. In the United States, for example, usually only 50 per cent of dining expenses are tax-deductible.

Accommodation costs

For employee business trips, the employer can reimburse the accommodation costs at a flat rate without receipts if the employee received the accommodation for non-business-related reasons free of charge or at a reduced rate. You can define this in the Customizing function to meet local regulations and company guidelines.

Vehicle costs

Flat-rate amounts can be specified for vehicle expenses incurred by employees on business trips and business owners when using private cars on business trips.

15.1.2 Business trips (abroad)

Board and lodging costs

In the case of business or official trips abroad, expenses for board and lodging may be taken into account in the form of flat-rate tax-free daily allowance. In contrast, accommodation costs are deductible either for the amount of the receipts or, without individual receipts, at a flat rate for accommodation expenses. The daily or flat rate may be defined at a different rate depending on the country visited. If several countries are visited on a trip on a given day, you can define the rate used in the country last visited as the applicable rate.

Day travel (abroad) for a number of days

If the trip abroad involves a number of days, daily rate can be based on the country that was reached prior to midnight local time. If, on the date of return travel from abroad, the place reached by midnight is in the home country, the daily or flat rate of the last place of work could be used. Such calculations are country-specific and can be defined in the Customizing function for each country.

Tax-free daily or flat-rate amounts

Some home countries have specific daily rates that are tax-free. In certain cases, the amount may vary depending on the country visited. You can set up tables in the SAP R/3 System to capture this information and make it available for taxation calculations.

OVERVIEW OF TRAVEL MANAGEMENT IN SAP R/3

Since Release 4.0, the Travel Management module is a part of Financial Accounting instead of Human Resources Management. This makes it possible to handle all aspects of business trips, from application to approval all the way to posting the trip costs. This mirrors international accounting standards.

As the R/3 modules are so closely integrated, when this data is recorded in Travel Management it is also posted directly through to Financial Accounting for correct posting and payment of the trip-cost reimbursement. The corresponding Cost Centres are also debited in Cost Centre Accounting within the Controlling module. The integration of Human Resources Management with Wages and Salaries means that the correct tax is deducted from the reimbursed trip costs.

The Travel Management functions in the SAP R/3 System must be enabled before you can use them. Here, we recommend that you create a project IMG for Travel Management and then that you enable the Travel function at that location. This step means that the environment needed for Travel Management is generated automatically.

The following IMG sketch shows where Travel Management is located in Customizing and explains the master data for Travel Management.

15.2.1 The master records of Travel Management

Before you can update the master records, you must set the number ranges for Trip Numbers (*see* Figure 15.1). These numbers can either be assigned internally (Number Range 01) or externally (Number Range 02). SAP recommends that you use number range 01 (internal number assignment).

If you use internal number assignment, the SAP R/3 System automatically assigns a consecutive number from the specified number range for each recorded trip. When you define the number range, make sure that the ranges of the individual Human Resources Management areas do not overlap.

If you have selected external number assignment (Number Range 02), the person recording the travel data must specify the trip number. This may result in incorrect data input.

15.2.2 Trip Provision Variants

In Trip Provision Variants, the rules for reimbursement and tax-free amounts (*see also* section 15.1) for each country are specified for Travel Cost Accounting. We recommend that you define a separate travel regulation Variant for each reimbursement rule.

The standard version of the SAP System already contains three Trip Provision Variants for the United States and one each for Belgium, Denmark, Germany, Great Britain, Japan, The Netherlands, Austria, Switzerland and Spain.

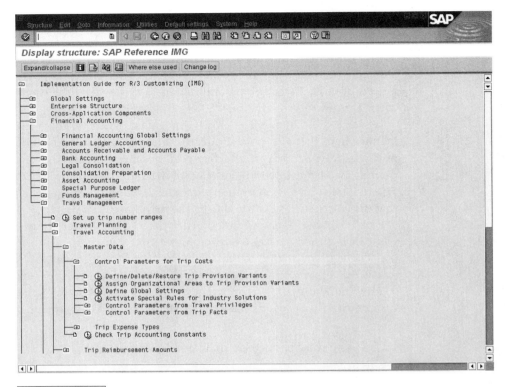

FIGURE 15.1 Master records of Travel Management in SAP R/3 (© SAP AG)

The maximum income-tax-free amounts for travel expenses, meals and accommodation must be stored in Customizing under Travel Countries and Regions. Travel countries for which identical flat-rate amounts apply can be combined into country groups.

15.2.3 Reimbursement Group Trip Expenses/Vehicle Classes

Trip Expenses Reimbursement Group can be used to store company-specific reimbursement rates for trip expense settlement, independent of the employee. These can, in turn, be divided into vehicle types (e.g. car, motorcycle).

Maintaining the period parameters for the distance accumulation controls the graduation of the flat rates payable according to the distance (usually in kilometres) driven per period.

15.2.4 Trip Expense Types for individual receipts

Individual receipts for trip costs are entered in the application menu when you record the trip cost in the Trip Expense Types item. Before you can enter this data, a four-digit alphanumeric number with a period of validity must be recorded for each Expense Type in the Customizing function. The end date of validity cannot be changed later on; this is why we recommend that you enter 31.12.9999.

You can also set default values for the highest rates in the Trip Expense Types in Customizing. If these values are exceeded when you input data, you can specify that the R/3 System issues a warning or error message.

15.2.5 Trip Reimbursement Amounts

The legal daily or flat rates for travel expenses, accommodation and meals are managed here (*see* Figure 15.2). Reductions to the daily or flat rates due to free services (meals etc.) are also defined here in accordance with local income-tax guidelines. Please refer to section 15.1, which has already covered the calculation and extent of the amounts in great detail.

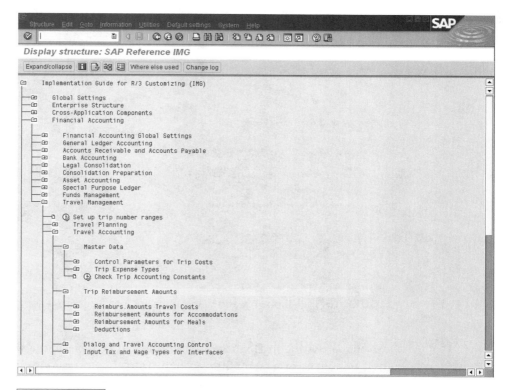

FIGURE 15.2   Trip Reimbursement Amounts in Customizing (© SAP AG)

15.2.6 Input Tax and Wage Types for Interfaces

In this part of the Customizing function, you must set a Wage Type for the tax-free share of the reimbursed amount for each Trip Expense Type so that you can record individual receipts (*see* Figure 15.3). You need to do this so that the Expense Type (a term used in Travel Management) can be transferred via the assigned Wage Type (a term used in Personnel calculations) into the Human Resources Management module of the SAP R/3 System.

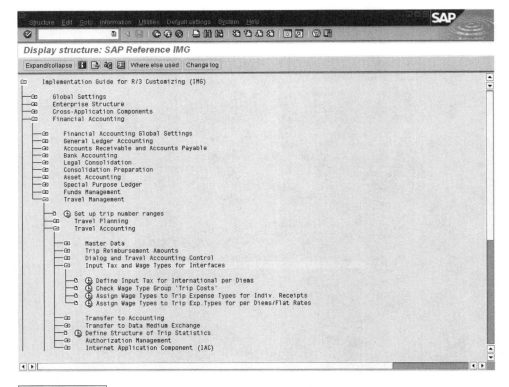

| FIGURE 15.3 | Input Tax and Wage Types for Interfaces (© SAP AG) |

So that a posting in Financial Accounting can take place, the wage type is transferred by means of a 'symbolic' account into the corresponding General Ledger account, with the relevant Input Tax Indicator. This takes place at the point in the IMG shown in Figure 15.4.

The standard version of the SAP System already contains the most important Input Tax Indicators with their associated calculation schemes (*see* Chapter 8).

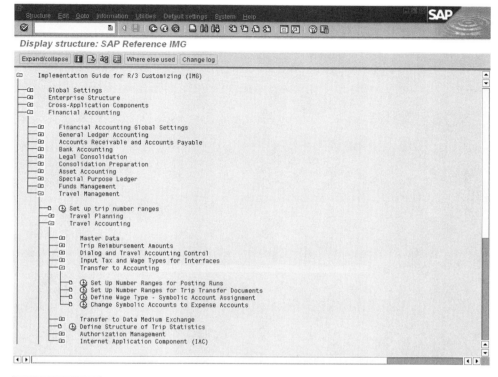

FIGURE 15.4   Transfer to Financial Accounting (© SAP AG)

Glossary

Abbreviated Fiscal Year is a shortened fiscal year resulting from a shift in the fiscal year cycle.

Account Management Specifying how a general ledger account is to be kept. In the SAP R/3 system, there is the possibility of open items management and individual items display.

Account Receivable Claim for payment of goods delivered or services rendered to the recipient. Accounts receivable must be reported in the balance sheet, subdivided according to certain criteria.

Account Type specifies the area (assets, customers, vendors, general ledger account) to which an account in financial accounting belongs.

Account Update For an account update, the open items of an account are balanced.

Accounting Document always consists of a document header and at least two document items that must balance to zero. The accounting document reflects the original document in the system.

Adjustment Document Posting document that documents changes to master data records, tables, posting documents etc. in the system.

Advice Announcement of a delivery or payment.

Allocation to an Account Specifies the accounts to which a business transaction can be posted.

Asked Price Price at which goods, foreign currency or securities are offered for sale.

Asset Account Account containing the acquisitions and retirements of assets. In the uniform industrial system of accounts, the asset accounts are assigned to the account class zero, one, two, three and four. The balance determined at the end of a fiscal year is carried forward to itself.

Assets are all the tangible and intangible 'objects of value' belonging to a company. They are placed on the asset side (left-hand side) of the balance sheet and are subdivided into fixed assets, current assets and accruals and deferrals.

Assignment of Document Numbers Document numbers are assigned by means of the document type. In the R/3 system, each document type is assigned to a *number range*, from which the system automatically assigns numbers (internal number assignment) or from which the user specifies numbers (external number assignment).

Balance Difference between the debit and credit sides of an account or in the case of a posting.

Balance Account An auxiliary account on which postings are collected on a temporary basis for technical reasons. The account must balance at regular intervals.

Balance accounts are used, for example, in the following cases:

● Time differences between business transactions (incoming goods/incoming invoice balance account)

● Organizational distribution of tasks (bank balance account)

● Unclear business transactions

Balance Carried Forward Carrying forward of a balance into the next fiscal year.

Balance Check Process in the SAP system in which a document can only be posted if the debit amount equals the credit amount.

Balance Sheet In the balance sheet, the value of balances of the asset accounts are set against one another at a fixed point in time. The assets are shown on the asset side and the capital of a company is shown on the liability side.

Balancing Manual or computerized procedure whereby open items of an account are marked in the system as balanced. Balancing can take place following an incoming or outgoing payment.

Bank Master Data All the information about a bank that is needed to ensure smooth business. This includes, for example, the name and address of the bank. In the SAP R/3 system, this information is stored at a central point.

Bill of Exchange Bills of exchange are frequently used to settle debts arising from trading transactions in particular. The economic significance of a bill of exchange lies in the fact that it is an instrument for granting and securing a short-term loan on the one hand, and a means of payment on the other.

A bill of exchange is a security that represents a promise to pay on the part of the drawee. A distinction is made between promissory notes that the debtor (= buyer) draws up and drawn bills of exchange that are drawn by the creditor (= vendor).

Book Value is the value at which the assets and debts are reported in the balance sheet.

Business Area is an organizational unit of financial accounting; it is intended to categorize areas of responsibility.

Cash Discount Discount for payments if these are effected within a certain period.

Cash Discount Base Amount Part of the invoice amount for which a cash discount can be claimed. It usually comprises the value of goods without additional costs.

Chart of Accounts Directory of accounting in which all the general ledger accounts of a company are kept. The accounts are used to record values for proper accounting.

Chart of Accounts Directory lists all the charts of accounts that can be used within a client in the SAP R/3 system.

Company A company corresponds to the smallest organizational unit for which accounting requires an individual financial statement. A company can comprise one or more company codes.

Company Code represents the smallest organizational unit of external accounting. It is a legally independent unit that draws up balance sheets.

Company Currency is the currency of a company code in which the ledgers are kept; it is usually the local currency.

Conto pro Diverse (CpD) Account Account that is used in the system for customers with whom business is done only once, or very rarely, and for whom no separate master data record is to be created. The CpD account must be defined using a special master data record in the system.

Contraction of the Balance Sheet (or asset-liability reduction) In the case of contraction of the balance sheet, the reduction of one or more asset items is placed against the reduction of one or more liability items by the same amount.

Conversion Date The date on which an amount is converted into another currency.

Corporation Tax Income tax for joint stock companies, public and private legal entities.

Costs Period-based, regular operating expenditures in a company.

Credit reduces the amount of the accounts receivable or accounts payable.

Credit Control Area Organizational unit in the SAP R/3 system that controls the credit limits specified for customers. This is possible across one or more company codes.

Current Assets comprise the assets which (in contrast to the fixed assets) are only linked to the company for a relatively short period and are intended for the turnover process or have resulted from it. The current assets include e.g. raw materials, trading goods and accounts receivable as well as bank balances and cash on hand.

Customer Someone against whom the company has a claim for payment for services performed or goods delivered.

Customer Master Data Record Data record in the system that contains all the information on the customer that is required for handling the business transactions. For example, the address, agreed terms of payment and bank details are stored in the master data record.

Demand Rate Demand rate of goods, foreign exchange or a security.

Depreciation serves to record the operational reduction in value and the distribution of the purchase and manufacturing costs to the useful life of fixed assets. A distinction is made between ordinary and extraordinary depreciation.

- Ordinary depreciation distributes the purchase and/or manufacturing costs to the forecast useful life of the assets.
- Extraordinary depreciation takes place when unexpected reductions in the value of assets occur.

Depreciation Method determines the rules to be used as the basis for distribution of the purchasing and/or manufacturing costs to the forecast useful life of the asset. The question as to the choice of depreciation method therefore only arises in the case of ordinary depreciation. The two most important methods are

- Linear Depreciation
- Declining-balance Depreciation

Discount is the difference in amount between the repayment amount (nominal value) of a loan or a security and its value when issued. The discount can be interpreted as additional interest to be paid in addition to the nominal interest as remuneration for the provision of capital. Discount is also referred to as loan discount.

Discounting is the sale of a receivable bill to a bank prior to maturity. Here, there is a deduction (discount) for the period between the date of sale of the bill and its date of maturity. The seller receives payment of the amount of the bill from the purchasing bank, less the deduction (discount). From an economic point of view, discounting is a deduction of interest by the bank, imposed on the seller of the bill for the premature payment.

Document The documents are the basis of accounting: 'No posting without a document'. A document is the comprehensible verification of the relation between the external and internal accountable transactions of a company. A distinction is made between original documents and computerized documents.

- Original documents include incoming invoices, bank statements and carbon copies of outgoing invoices.
- Computerized documents include, among other things, accounting, sam-ple and permanent posting documents.

Document Currency Currency in which a document is posted in the system.

Document Date Creation date of an original document.

Document Header Part of a document that contains general information regarding the document, for example the document number and document date.

Document Number Code that clearly identifies every document in a company code within a fiscal year.

Document Principle All postings are always stored in the form of documents.

Document Recording Input of a document in the system. This can take place either manually or automatically.

Document Type is an important control element in the SAP R/3 system. It allows distinctions to be made between the business transactions to be posted. The document type regulates the book entries of the account types.

Doubtful Claims Accounts receivable for which there is no guarantee that they will be settled are transferred to the asset account 'Doubtful Claims'. Signs that an account receivable has become a doubtful claim are, for example, that the customer is the subject of composition or bankruptcy proceedings or a cheque from a customer that is not covered.

Down Payment Down payments are advance payments from customers to vendors before the service is performed (or goods delivered).

Down Payment Request Request to make a down payment at a certain point in time. In the SAP R/3 system, these are saved separately and can be taken into consideration in the dunning area (see below) and in automatic payment transactions.

Dunning Area Organizational unit of dunning within a company code. A dunning area is required if the dunning is performed independently by several organizational units within a company code, for example by divisions or sales organizations.

Dunning Block By assigning a dunning block reason, individual accounts and items can be blocked against dunning. The dunning block can be entered in the master data record of the customers or in the document item.

Dunning Block Reason Cause or reason that must be specified so that a dunning block can be implemented.

Dunning Procedure A procedure defined in customizing for the intervals and form of letters reminding customers of payment or vendors of delivery.

Earnings Company income within an accounting period.

Electronic Commerce Electronic trade on the internet.

Exchange Rate is the relation between two currencies. The rate is used to convert one currency into another.

Exchange Rate Difference Amount of difference resulting from foreign currency conversion at different exchange rates.

Expenditure Expenses of a company within a period. In the profit and loss account, the expenditure is balanced against the earnings, which determines the total income of the company.

Expense Expenses are the monetary countervalue of all the goods and services acquired in the period. If goods and services are paid for in cash, this leads to an out-payment, i.e. to an actual outflow of funds. If the acquisition is financed by credit in the short term, medium term or long term, a liability is posted.

Extension of the Balance Sheet (or an asset-liability increase) In the case of an extension of the balance sheet, a business transaction increases one or more items both on the asset side and the liability side of the balance sheet. This increase can be income-creating or have a neutral effect on income.

Final Accounts All the tasks involved in the

- Daily Financial Statement
- Monthly Financial Statement
- Annual Accounts

Fiscal Year The fiscal year is usually 12 months. For this period, the company must draw up its physical inventory and balance sheet. The fiscal year is not necessarily identical to the calendar year.

Fixed Assets are all the assets that are intended to serve the company on a permanent basis. Fixed assets are meant to be used in the company and are not intended for sale. The fixed assets appear on the asset side of the balance sheet. They are composed of intangible assets, as well as tangible assets and investments. The fixed assets include real estate, buildings or the car fleet of a company.

Functional Area Operational expenditures are classified using functional areas such as Administration, Sales, Marketing, Production or Research and Development.

General Ledger Account An account in general ledger accounting.

General Ledger Account Master Record Data record in the system that contains information on a general ledger account and controls the book entries and administration of the account.

General Value Adjustment See Value Adjustment.

Generally Accepted Accounting Principles are fundamental principles that apply to accounting and drawing up the annual accounts. They lay down the basic requirements for accounting in such a way that a qualified third party can obtain a sufficiently reliable insight into the asset, financial and earnings situation of the company within a reasonable period of time. The Generally Accepted Accounting Principles must be observed by all business entities in the continuous accounting, as well as in drawing up the inventory and annual accounts.

Group A group is a number of legally independent companies with a single management; it is obliged to draw up consolidated accounts.

Hard Currency Country-specific second currency that is used in countries with high inflation.

Index Currency Index currencies are used in countries with high inflation for external reporting.

Individual Items Display Display of documents and their document items for an account. In order to enable individual items display for an account, they must be defined in the master data record.

Individual Value Adjustment Adjustment of an asset that appears in the accounts at too high a value or accounts receivable where payment might not be paid. See also Value Adjustment.

Initial Tax This must be invoiced to customers based on the net value of goods, and paid to the tax authorities.

Inpayment is the actual incoming flow of money in the company. In contrast to the earnings, an inpayment takes place when the customer pays for delivered goods.

Interest is the term used to describe the cost for provision of capital for a certain period. As a rule, the interest rate is specified as an annual percentage. The amount of interest is based on the interest rate, the period of the loan, the amount of the loan, as well as the form of interest calculation. From the company point of view, invoiced interest is expenditure; interest received for the provision of money is earnings.

Interest on Arrears Interest to be paid to creditors if payment is not effected on time.

Inventory is the list of stock that records all the assets and debts of a company according to type, quantity and value on a set day. It only includes secure debts to third parties (accounts payable) and thus contains no insecure debts or own obligations (provisions).

Item Interest Automatic calculation of interest for the period between the due date and payment of an open item.

Ledger is based on any elements of the allocation to accounts block. The task of the ledger is to record totals for the purpose of operational management. Examples of this are the special-purpose ledgers.

Ledger/General Ledger Accounting The ledger is used to draw up the balance sheet and meet the other legal requirements.

Liabilities Debts of a company for which the amount and the due date are known (liabilities to banks, vendors etc.).

Loan Discount See Discount

Manufacturing Costs are the value measure for self-created assets. Manufacturing costs are expenditures incurred through the usage of commodities and services for the manufacture of an asset, its extension, or for an improvement going far beyond its original condition.

Mean Exchange Rate Exchange rate resulting from the arithmetical mean money or bond exchange rate.

Method of Payment shows the method used to effect payments, for example cheque, bank credit transfer or bill of exchange.

Monitory Item A special item in the system that is intended to indicate an event but does not change any account balances. Certain monitory items can be processed by the payment or dunning program.

Net Method Here, cost or stock postings at the time of the invoice posting are reduced automatically by the anticipated cash discount. This is used particularly within the framework of asset accounting to post the precise acquisition value minus the cash discount to asset accounts.

Number Range Assignment of numbers to documents, materials, customers, etc. The system assigns numbers automatically (internal number assignment) or the numbers are assigned by the user (external number assignment).

Open Item Management In the case of open item management, the items of the account must be balanced by other items so that the balance is zero and the account can thus be closed.

Opening Capital Balance is the amount that is transferred from the opening account to the account when the account is opened. Opening capital balances can only exist for asset accounts, whereas profit accounts do not have an opening capital balance.

Original Document Original document for a posting.

Payment Block Code that blocks an account or individual items for payment.

Payment on Account A payment that is not based on a specific direct business transaction. It is thus distinguished from a down payment and installment paid to a vendor.

Permanent Posting If postings recur periodically, for example subscriptions, rent or leasing installments, a permanent posting document for these transactions can be created; this automatically performs the periodical posting in the system when triggered.

Permanent Posting Document is the basis for periodical permanent postings.

Physical Inventory is the process of stocktaking. In addition to the physical inventory by counting, measuring, weighing and estimating to record all the assets belonging to a company without omissions, the book inventory contains separate records of the stock of assets and debts in the form of posting documents. The total of the results of the physical inventory is the inventory.

Plant Plants are production facilities represented in the system.

Posting Block Identification of an account blocked for posting. The block of an account can take place centrally for all company codes or locally for one company code.

Posting Key is a two-digit numerical key that controls the recording of document items. It determines, among other things, the recording input screen and controls the posting of debit and credit.

Posting Period corresponds to a period within a fiscal year, for example a month in which transaction figures can be carried forward.

Posting, Automatic Posting that is created automatically by the system by reporting a separate document item:

- Initial and prior tax posting
- Posting of exchange rate differences
- Posting of cash discount expenses and earnings

Posting, Cross-Company Code In the case of a cross-company code posting, several company codes are involved in the posting. The SAP R/3 system creates a document for each company code involved.

Posting, Statistical Posting of a special purpose ledger transaction where the counter-posting takes place automatically on a specified balance account.

Prepaid Amounts and Deferred Income Adjustment items whose purpose is to allocate payment figures to periods in order to assure calculation of profit appropriate to the period. The difference between the two is as follows:

- Prepaid amounts are expenses paid for prior to the set day of the accounts for which the actual expenditure is only incurred after the set day (example: payment of the rent for January in December).

- Deferred income represents revenues received prior to the set day of the accounts for which the actual earnings are only received after the set day.

Prior Tax Tax that is invoiced to the customer. The deductible prior tax proportion can be reclaimed from the tax authorities.

Profit Account These accounts are separated into expenditure and profit accounts; they record the expenditures and revenues of an accounting period. The balance between all the expenditure and earnings produces the profit for the period.

Profit and Loss Account (P & L) In the profit and loss account, the expenditures and earnings of a company are set against one another to determine the overall result.

Promissory or Negotiable Note If the drawee of a bill of exchange is obliged to pay the sum of the bill, this is a promissory or negotiable note.

Reason for Payment Block Cause or reason for not settling open items.

Receivable Bill A drawn bill of exchange. The drawee corresponds to the payee.

Reconciliation Account Reconciliation accounts group the value items from the accounts of the individual subledgers in general ledger accounting. They thus connect the subledgers with the general ledger accounting.

Report When a report is started, the data from the database table is read and evaluated. The result can be displayed, printed or downloaded. The SAP standard reports can be supplemented by customer-specific reports.

Report Form In the case of a layout in report form, each of the items is grouped and arranged below one another. Subtotals and balances are also formed. The report form is always used for drawing up the profit and loss account of a company.

Request for a Bill of Exchange Request to a customer to settle debts by means of a bill of exchange. A request for a bill of exchange is posted in the SAP R/3 system as a monitory item.

Request for Statement of Account is used by the company and its business partners to check the correctness of the company account.

Revenue is an increase in the monetary assets, consisting of payments and accounts receivable, minus accounts payable. The revenue is in effect an increase in the monetary assets. This does not necessarily imply an actual incoming flow of liquid funds (= inpayment).

Sales Tax Code specifies within a client one or more company codes that form an entity for tax on sales/purchases.

Special Period Special posting period that can be used subsequent to the last posting period for final account work that still has to be performed. In the SAP R/3 system, up to 4 special periods are possible.

Special Purpose Ledger Transaction Transactions in accounts receivable and accounts payable that are shown separately in the ledger and subledger. These include, among others, the following transactions:

- Down Payments
- Bank Guarantees
- Bills of Exchange

Statement of Account With a statement of account, you ask your business partner to check and confirm each individual amount on your account.

Subledgers explain business transactions for customers, vendors and assets. The accounts of the subledgers are linked by reconciliation accounts with the ledger.

SWIFT Code (Society for Worldwide Interbank Financial Telecommunication) This is an internationally applicable identification code for banks. It enables identification of a bank without specifying the address and bank code. In the SAP R/3 system, it is of particular significance for automatic payment transactions.

Tax Code is a two-digit code that regulates the calculation and reporting of tax on sales/purchases.

Tax on Sales/Purchases Generic term for prior tax and initial tax.

Terms of Payment Specification of the periods and permitted deductions for due remuneration.

Transfer In the case of a transfer, the amounts already posted are posted from one account to another. This is required especially within the framework of preparatory postings for the annual accounts.

Useful Life is the period in which a fixed asset can be used in the company. The useful life specifies the period over which the depreciable fixed assets are subject to ordinary depreciation.

Validation Check procedure in the SAP R/3 system that checks entered values and value combinations. The check is based on a Boolean statement defined by the user.

Value Adjustment A value adjustment is an adjustment item that takes account of individual (= individual value adjustment) or general (= general value adjustment) risks and reductions in value of asset items in the balance sheet without directly altering the reported value of the balance sheet item. The value adjustment, which can be openly offset from the balance-sheet value or represents a liability adjustment item, is also termed indirect depreciation. Indirect depreciation on assets is not permitted for joint stock companies, which means that reductions in value can only be taken into account here by means of direct depreciation.

Vendor A supplier of the company for which there are accounts payable for services rendered.

Vendor Master Data Record Data record in the system that contains all the information on the customer that is required for handling the business transactions. For example, the address, agreed terms of payment, and bank details are stored in the master data record.

Vendor Net Method Here, cost or stock postings at the time of the invoice posting are reduced automatically by the anticipated cash discount. This is used particularly within the framework of asset accounting to post the precise acquisition value, minus the cash discount, to asset accounts.

Index

Note: Figures and tables are shown in **bold** type.